D1091165

STUDIES IN HISTORY, ECONOMICS AND
PUBLIC LAW

Edited by the
FACULTY OF POLITICAL SCIENCE
OF COLUMBIA UNIVERSITY

NUMBER 445

EMILE DURKHEIM AND HIS SOCIOLOGY

BY

HARRY ALPERT

EMILE DURKHEIM AND
HIS SOCIOLOGY

BY

HARRY ALPERT, Ph. D.

NEW YORK / RUSSELL & RUSSELL

COPYRIGHT © 1939 BY
COLUMBIA UNIVERSITY PRESS
COPYRIGHT RENEWED, 1967, BY HARRY ALPERT
REISSUED, 1961, BY RUSSELL & RUSSELL
A DIVISION OF ATHENEUM PUBLISHERS, INC.
BY ARRANGEMENT WITH HARRY ALPERT
L. C. CATALOG CARD NO: 61-13089
ISBN: 0-8462-0107-0
PRINTED IN THE UNITED STATES OF AMERICA

ACKNOWLEDGMENTS

To the Institute of International Education for a Franco-American Exchange Fellowship which made possible a sojourn in France;

To Columbia University for a University Fellowship in Sociology under which this study was completed;

To Professor Bonnafous of the University of Bordeaux, Professors MacIver, Abel, Lundberg, Lynd, Chaddock, Casey, von Schelting, Benedict and the late Professor Tenney of Columbia University for guidance and training;

To Professor R. M. MacIver, Professor G. A. Lundberg, and Mr. V. D. Sewny for having read and for having generously commented upon the manuscript;

To the Examining Committee of the Faculty of Political Science of Columbia University which accepted this study as a doctoral dissertation for valuable suggestions and penetrating criticisms;

To Professor T. Abel for having graciously assumed some of the editorial responsibilities;

To Anitra F. Alpert for more than usual forbearance as a wife while this work was being prepared.

5

ABBREVIATIONS

A A	American Anthropologist.
A F L B	Annales de la Faculté des Lettres de Bordeaux.
A J S	American Journal of Sociology.
A P D S J	Archives de Philosophie du Droit et de Sociologie Juridique.
A S	Année Sociologique.
An S	Annales Sociologiques.
A S R	American Sociological Review.
B S F P	Bulletin de la Société Française de Philosophie.
D S	Le Devenir Social.
E S S	Encyclopedia of the Social Sciences.
G E	Grande Encyclopédie.
J P	Journal de Psychologie.
K V S	Kölner Vierteljahrshefte für Soziologie.
M F	Mercure de France.
P S Q	Political Science Quarterly.
R B	Revue Bleue.
R E P	Revue d'Economie Politique.
R I E	Revue internationale de l'Enseignement.
R I S	Revue internationale de Sociologie.
Ri It S	Rivista Italiana di Sociologia.
R M M	Revue de Métaphysique et de Morale.
R N S	Revue Néo-scolastique.
R P	Revue Philosophique.
R Pe	Revue Pédagogique.
Ri P	Rivista Pedagogica.
R S	La Riforma Sociale.
R S H	Revue de Synthèse Historique.
R T A	Revue Turque d'Anthropologie.
R U	Revue Universitaire.
S F	Social Forces.
S P	Sociological Papers.
S R	Sociological Review.
So R	Social Research.
S S R	Sociology and Social Research.

" Si vous voulez mûrir votre
pensée, attachez-vous à l'étude
scrupuleuse d'un grand
maitre; démontez un
système dans ses rouages
les plus secrets."

Emile Durkheim

TABLE OF CONTENTS

INTRODUCTION

THIS study is offered as a contribution to the history of social theory.

The major emphasis in Part I is biographical. No complete biography of Emile Durkheim has yet appeared in any language. This is an unfortunate gap in our knowledge, for to understand a doctrine, one must at least know its history; and the personality of its author, his life, experience, and influences are an essential part of that history. The brief biography here presented does not purport to fill this gap; it is too meager to be able to do that. Moreover, it is based exclusively on published materials, gathered from many sources, whereas we know that the most valuable data for a biography of Durkheim are still unpublished. Part I, therefore, is presented only as a temporary stop-gap. Its purpose is merely to summarize and interpret whatever biographical data are at present available. It is to be hoped that a more thorough and more searching biography will soon supersede it.

Part II discusses only a few of the problems raised by Durkheim's conception of the nature, scope, and method of sociology. Our main effort here is to indicate the advantages of Durkheim's broad view of sociology as a positive science of social behavior, as a rejuvenating method of social investigation, and as a solid foundation for an integral social philosophy. Sociology must don overalls and dig deeply for the fact-stuff that is its life-blood. But it must also, without trepidation, soar into the higher regions of rational thought whence alone come proper synthesis and integration.

The most controversial and vexing problem raised by the Durkheimian conception of sociology seems to be the connection between the theory of *conscience collective* and *représentations collectives* as exposed by Durkheim and the traditional dogmas of group and social minds. Our essential thesis on this point is that while Durkheim used — most unfortunately and quite unnecessarily, it is true—the language of the social realists, he was not of them. He was, in fact, explicitly opposed to a " group-mind " interpretation of his position.

Part III briefly discusses Durkheim's views of the nature of society as unity, regulation, and expression and presents some of the specific investigations into social integration, legal evolution, ceremony and ritual, and personality on which the Durkheimian conceptions rest.

As an army marches on its belly, so a science progresses on its mistakes. Its errors are the very pabulum on which it feeds. Constant self-criticism, persistent self-evaluation are the price of its advance. It is therefore incumbent upon it not to seek the new, the novel and the startling as much as to reexamine and rethink the old. Discovery and invention, sociologists well know, are but the reinterpretation, reevaluation, and recasting of materials already given.

This philosophy of science has guided us in our study of Emile Durkheim and his sociology. What is Durkheimian is surely not to be identified with what is right. But equally as surely there is in Durkheim's life and in his works much that may be termed, to pursue our metaphor, food for thought. " My ideas," Durkheim did not hesitate to remind his readers, " are destined to be modified and reformulated in the future." Nor can it be otherwise. For science begins neither with clear and exact ideas nor with precise instruments. " It begins rather with hazy ideas and inexact measurements but greater accuracy is introduced and indeed made possible by the ideal of a scientific system," Professor Morris R. Cohen has remarked.

However, revision and correction are predicated on fair understanding. If this study has contributed to such an understanding, if it has convinced the reader of the necessity of avoiding oversimplification and erroneous standardized clichés and stereotypes concerning Durkheimian sociology, it has succeeded in its purpose. The minds of great men are too complex and their thoughts are too subtle to be expressed adequately in summary formulae.

PART I

EMILE DURKHEIM: FRENCHMAN, TEACHER, SOCIOLOGIST

1. RABBINICAL BACKGROUND AND EARLY SCHOOLING

EMILE DURKHEIM was born at Epinal (Vosges) in the ancient province of Lorraine on the 15th of April, 1858. His birth occurred about a year after the death of Auguste Comte whose work he was to perpetuate and reanimate.

The future exponent of an ingenious sociological theory of religion was the direct descendant of a long line of rabbinical scholars, and, in keeping with the family tradition, prepared himself for the rabbinate. He studied Hebrew—not systematically we are told — and acquired a familiarity with the Old Testament and with Talmudic and Hebraic lore. Whether or not these rabbinical studies were only a passing fancy, as some have said, we cannot be sure. It is certain, however, that young Durkheim decided to renounce his religious ambitions at quite an early date. This decision was in part due to the influence exercised on the lad by a Catholic instructress. In spite of this renunciation—one is almost tempted to say because of it— these early biblical studies were not wasted. Durkheim later turned them into sociological profit, for he was skilled in utilizing and synthesizing every bit of knowledge he acquired. Thus, references to the Bible abound not only in his works on religion, but also in his analyses of primitive law and social organization. One need only note, for example, the numerous biblical references in *De la Division du travail social*.

The author of *Les Formes élémentaires de la vie religieuse* never forgot his rabbinical background. He was fully conscious of his own predominantly ethical and religious preoccupations and frequently had occasion to recall to his colleagues of the *Année Sociologique* that he was, after all, the son of a Rabbi.

Durkheim received his first formal education in his native city, at the Collège d'Epinal, where he established quite a brilliant record. He "skipped" several grades, as Americans would say, and won prizes and contests without difficulty. Davy's invaluable book on Durkheim includes a picture of the young lad taken while he was at the *collège*.[1] The photograph is not very clear, but in it we perceive the bright youngster as he rests his left arm on the shoulder of a comrade. His high forehead is surrounded by very thick hair which is especially bushy at the sides. The facial features reveal an almost feminine delicacy and sensitivity; a keen intelligence is unmistakably manifested in the boy's visage. The delicate hand we see seems, as it droops from the wrist, to end in unusually long fingers. This sensitiveness of feature and mien remained with Durkheim throughout his life.

While at the *collège* and no doubt because of his remarkable success there, Emile resolved to train himself for the profession of teaching. He therefore went to Paris where he continued his studies at the *Lycée Louis-le-Grand*. Here he prepared himself for admission to the *Ecole Normale Supérieure*, entrance into which is determined by a nation-wide competitive examination. The period of "*cagne*," as this preparation for the *Ecole Normale* examination is called, was not a particularly happy one for the young philosopher. He was not at all receptive to the type of instruction to which he was subjected and could not see the value of a good deal of the required work. Consequently, he had to wait three years before the *Ecole* finally opened its doors to him.

2. Ecole Normale Supérieure: The Revolt Against Dilettantism

This was in 1879. Lanson, S. Reinach and Lévy-Bruhl had just been graduated. Bergson, Jaurès and Belot had entered the year before. Rauh and Maurice Blondel were to be ad-

1 Davy, G., *Emile Durkheim* (Paris: Vald. Rasmussen), p. 33.

mitted two years later. Pierre Janet and Goblot entered along with Durkheim. It is not exaggeration, therefore, to say that a veritable philosophical renaissance was germinating at the *Ecole Normale*. The establishment of the Third Republic, less than ten years previously, had become a sort of signal for France's intellectual awakening. The clarion call of Freedom had been sounded and some of the great minds of the country, like Renouvier, feeling themselves liberated from the to them throttling and repressive Napoleonic régime of the Second Empire [2] could now pursue their labors with revitalized energies.

Although Durkheim was only twenty-one when he entered the *Ecole Normale*, he was already possessed of a mature appearance and a ripe mind. His age was about the average for his class, yet he looked somewhat older than his comrades. In the Davy volume, referred to above, there is a photograph of the class of '79.[3] Exactly when it was taken we do not know. Presumably it is a graduation picture, in which case it would date from around 1882. The photograph reveals Durkheim as a very serious and intense young person. His almost solemn bearing contrasts sharply with the relaxed and even jovial spirit of some of his classmates. His hair has thinned. His face appears to be longer, for it is now partly hidden by an abundant and bushy beard which is clipped more closely

2 *Cf.* Valeur, R., who in *Democratic Governments in Europe*, ed. by Buell, R. L. (N. Y.: Nelson and Sons, 1935), states that " The Second Empire, in spite of all its dynastic pretense, was nothing but a personal dictatorship supported by the army" (p. 263) and who speaks of the monarchists and republicans alike keeping " a bitter memory of the eighteen years of arbitrary dictatorship 'of Napoleon III " (*ibid.*, p. 283).

See also Maurain, J., who in the conclusion of his more than 900 page study of *La Politique ecclésiastique du second empire de 1852 à 1869* (Paris: Alcan, 1930), states that the government of the Second Empire permitted the church alone to remain free " in an oppressed society " (p. 941). The oppression of the working class by the government of Napoleon III is noted by Professor Georges Weill in his *Histoire du mouvement social en France (1852-1910)*, (2nd ed.; Paris: Alcan, 1911), p. 46.

3 Davy, *op. cit.*, p. 57.

on the sides than on the chin, and by a dark, thick, overgrown moustache. One cannot mistake that serious demeanor which caused Durkheim's classmates to bestow upon him, with an irony that they could little appreciate, the nickname of " The Metaphysician." His maturity was, as Holleaux put it, " precocious," [4] and his physical appearance changed but very little from this time on.

The *Ecole Normale* was a great disappointment to the critical young man. He nevertheless always remained sentimentally attached to it and emphasized its dominant role in forging in France an intellectual and moral unity such as is found in few other countries.[5] The kind of faults that Durkheim found with the School are truly indicative of certain basic attitudes in his thinking. He condemned especially the ultra-literary, and hence too unscientific nature of the instruction and had a great contempt for the dilettantism, superficiality, and mysticism which it tended to encourage. In fact, it would be no distortion to view Durkheim's entire sociological career as an intransigent and relentless battle fought on two major fronts: against the dark, unfathomable forces of mysticism and despair, on the one hand, and against the unsubstantial ethereal forces of the dilettantic cult of superficiality on the other. These he combated with the clarifying—enlightening, to use the Anglo-Saxon equivalent — methods of science and with the productive, fecund techniques of collective, cooperative activity. Sociology, he repeatedly asserted, can survive as a vital discipline only if it fulfills two necessary conditions of existence: it must shed its literary glamour and assume the more drab garbs of science and it must cease to be an impressive, but essentially vain, solo act and become a more work-a-day, but a more creative, cooperative enterprise.

Durkheim felt that there was too great an emphasis on idle rhetoric. Thinking was evaluated in terms of its literary rather

4 Quoted by Davy, R M M, XXVI (1919), 184.

5 Durkheim, E., R S, III (1895), 691. See bibliography (Appendix A), item 95e.

than its rigorous quality. Words were employed preciously rather than meaningfully. In short, pure humanism, in its worst form, was rampant. In this essentially literary training, Durkheim later saw one of the basic reasons for the backwardness of the science of society. How, indeed, could there possibly be such a science when the intellectual milieu encouraged a purely humanistic, i. e. non-scientific approach to the problems of social life?

Durkheim has himself described, in far from laudatory terms, the type of philosophical training prevalent in his student days.[6] The young students of philosophy, he tells us, set out to do something distinctive, that is, something startling and " original." The rare, the new, the latest " *nouveauté* " were their prime values. And above all, one had to be individual, have a " personal " system. " To think as your neighbor was the thing to be avoided at all costs." The emphasis was on a brilliant tongue, on a striking talent. The budding philosophers of the period were led " to seek above all, not exactitude in analysis and rigor in proof, i. e. the qualities which make the scientist and the philosopher, but I-know-not-what literary talent of a particularly bastard kind, which consists in combining ideas the way the artist combines images and forms: in order to charm the taste, not to satisfy reason, to arouse esthetic impressions, not to express things." [7] Scientific thinking was thus relegated to an insignificant and inferior position. The dilettante, in short, was the order of the day.

Let us grant that Durkheim's picture represents an exaggeration of the actual state of affairs. It is nonetheless significant as a revelation of his state of mind. He was completely horrified by this dilettantism. He saw in it, to use Professor Bouglé's picturesque language, "the most dangerous of manias, the true sin against the mind." He always fought against it. We need solid reasoners, not delicate minds, he urged. That

6 R P, XXXIX (1895), esp. pp. 129-135. See bibliography, item 95b.
7 *Ibid.*, p. 129.

Durkheim felt very strongly on this subject is evidenced by the fact that his doctoral dissertation centered around it. *De la Division*, in fact, might just as well have been entitled *"Contre le dilettantisme."* For as a contribution to the science of ethics, it essentially aimed to prove the moral worthlessness of the dilettante and of those who are " too enamoured of an exclusively general culture." [8] This is, of course, a negative statement of the thesis. More positively, it attempted to demonstrate that specialization in modern societies is a moral duty.

Also, many years later, in a discussion of proposed changes in the *agrégation de philosophie*, Durkheim, in submitting his recommendations, insisted on the very same principle. He argued that the examination should above all be made less superficial. He condemned the practice of questioning candidates *de omni re scibili* on the ground that success on such an examination is determined " neither by knowledge, nor by firmness and solidarity of thought; for a solid and firm mind cannot improvise solutions to a question upon which it hasn't had the opportunity to meditate. . . ." [9]

Superficiality, however, was not the only element in dilettantism that irked him. He bitterly condemned its intellectual anarchy as well. The dilettante philosopher, being concerned with erecting his private, individual system of thought, was so set on the elaboration of his own views that he lost sight of the fact that he was, after all, cooperating with others in a collective enterprise. Thus, instead of having a unified group of minds working towards a common end, we had only isolated individuals, smug and complacent in their pretended independence. As long as such a condition prevailed, philosophy, Durkheim thought, could only lead to sterility. " If one compares the subjects of the theses passed before the Faculty of Paris these past years," he wrote, " one will see that it is impossible

8 *De la Division.* See item 93b of bibliography. Our page references are to the sixth edition. P. 397. *Cf.* pp. 5, 298-299, 398, footnote 1.

9 R I E, LVII (1909), 159-161. See bibliography, item 09b.

to discern in them a common tendency. Each philosopher works apart, as if he were alone in the world and as if philosophy were an art." [10] With each systematizer going his own way, anarchy alone could result. To the vanquishing of this superficial and anarchic dilettantism, the future founder of the *Année Sociologique* was destined to devote a great deal of his energy.

Because of this belligerent attitude towards the humanities and literature, Durkheim did not have an easy time of it at the *Ecole Normale*. He had difficulty especially with Latin and literature, and regarded a good deal of the material he had to learn as sheer poppycock. It is not surprising, therefore, that he had almost as much difficulty in getting out of, as in getting into, the School. When the 1882 rank-list of successful *agrégation* candidates appeared, the name of Emile Durkheim was only one from the bottom.

3. Ecole Normale Supérieure: Friends, Professors, Intellectual Influences

It should not be assumed from what we have said of Durkheim's attitude towards the School, that the *Ecole Normale* did not exercise an influence over him. On the contrary, it had a profound effect on the formation of his personality and intellectual orientation. The friends he made, the professors under whom he studied, and the authors he read, all played a significant role in molding the young man who was to become the most eminent sociologist of his country and generation.

Durkheim did not make many friends, but to the few he had, he manifested a devotion, loyalty, and attachment that were profoundly rooted. He who regarded friendship as a sacred trust suffered the great misfortune of seeing his dearest friends prematurely snatched away from life. There was his classmate Hommay, his most intimate companion at the *Ecole Normale*, who was killed accidentally only a few years after

10 Durkheim, E., item 87a, p. 437.

their graduation. There was Jaurès, the great Socialist leader, whom Durkheim had veered away from " the political formalism and the hollow philosophy of the radicals " [11] and who was so brutally assassinated at the outset of the World War. And, we may add, going beyond the *Ecole Normale* days, there was Hamelin, Durkheim's brilliant colleague at Bordeaux, who was drowned in an effort to save the life of others. The untimely death of these three friends caused the inwardly sensitive and kindly Durkheim no end of grief. He was a living example of that " attachment to others " which he made one of the essential features of his ethical system.

There were other friendships acquired at the School, those with Lucien Picard and Holleaux, for example. To the latter one is greatly indebted for our knowledge of Durkheim as a *normalien*.[12]

Although the budding sociologist did not unbosom himself readily, he was by no means introverted. On the contrary, he liked social life, and would frequently mingle with groups of people, especially on festive occasions. This gave him the opportunity to imbibe what he called " the spirit of the collectivity." It also sharpened in him that special " sense of the social " which Davy regards as a necessary requisite for sociological thinking.[13] It made him sensitive to social currents, social feelings and social exhilaration, concepts that were to become basic in his system of sociology. He also enjoyed serious discussion groups and delighted in the exercise of vigorous dialectics. But he was disgusted by the sophisticated and shallow sarcasm of many of his fellow *normaliens*. "Absolutely simple," Holleaux wrote of him, " he hated all affectations. Profoundly serious, he hated flightiness."

Of the professors at the *Ecole Normale*, there were only a few to whom the eager Durkheim was attracted. Two of them

11 Mauss, M., in Introduction to item 28a, p. viii.

12 His recollections are reported by Davy, R M M , XXVI (1919).

13 Davy, G., R M M , XXVII (1920), 88 and in *Traité de Psychologie* of G. Dumas, vol. ii, p. 766.

he particularly admired: Fustel de Coulanges, the great historian who became director of the School in 1880, and Emile Boutroux, the equally eminent philosopher from whom much of present-day French philosophy stems. These two teachers were real sources of inspiration to him. The author of *La Cité Antique* was an advocate of the introduction into history of rigorous critical and scientific methods. His insistence on the use of critically sifted factual evidence and his penetrating keenness of intellect appealed to the young Durkheim and won him over. The teacher-historian and the pupil-sociologist, however, never came to agree as to the relations between their respective fields.[14] To the memory of Fustel de Coulanges, Durkheim dedicated his Latin thesis on Montesquieu.[15]

The influence of Boutroux was more direct and more significant. That he suggested the topic of the dissertation on Montesquieu is incidental. Of greater import is the fact that the distinguished author of the brilliant thesis on the contingency of the laws of nature indelibly impressed upon Durkheim the necessity of constantly subjecting to relentless critical analysis the problems pertaining to the nature, scope, and methods of science. How well the pupil learned his master's teachings in this regard we shall make evident in Part II of this study.

Many of the fundamental tenets of Durkheimian sociology are, indeed, directly traceable to Boutroux. It was from him that the founder of the "French school of sociology" learned, among other things, the inadequacy and fallaciousness of the simplistic doctrine of atomism, the principle of the creative synthesis, or emergentism, as it is better known in America, the nature *sui generis* of the life of the mind, and the postulate that each science must explain its phenomena in terms of its own specific principles. A synthesis cannot be explained by its

14 On this point see Durkheim's preface to volume I of *L'Année Sociologique*, pp. ii-iii.

15 Item 92a.

elements, Boutroux taught, for the multiplicity of the elements does not explain their unity. Consequently, each realm of reality has a " newness " which makes it impossible to deduce the more complex from the more simple. The vital aspect of biological phenomena must therefore be explained biologically, not in terms of the physical and chemical. Likewise, the psychical aspects of the mind can have only a psychical explanation.[16] One needs only to extend this view to arrive at the Durkheimian principle that social facts must be explained socially. Durkheim himself acknowledged his indebtedness to Boutroux's doctrine of the autonomy of the respective sciences. " Very much imbued with this idea," he wrote, in explanation of the origin of his views, " I applied it to sociology." [17] The author of *Les Règles de la méthode sociologique* never lost the critical alertness to methodological problems that he acquired from Boutroux. His gratitude for the guidance given by this master was expressed in the dedication of *De la Division: "A mon cher maître M. Emile Boutroux: Hommage respectueux et reconnaissant."*

No less influential than these friends and teachers in shaping Durkheim's intellectual orientation were some of the authors whose works he studied while at the *Ecole Normale*. Of these we should like to single out three as of special significance: Renouvier, Kant and Comte. But in turning from the influence of friends and teachers to that of authors read, we place ourselves on less solid ground. When, for instance, did Durkheim first read Comte? Was it at the *Ecole Normale* or afterwards? And if the latter, how soon afterwards? We cannot answer these questions with certainty. But we may legitimately infer that the influence of Comte was felt by Durkheim only after his acquaintance with Boutroux and only after an examination of the writings of the French Neo-Kantian, Renouvier.

---

16 *Cf.* Boutroux, E., *De la Contingence des lois de la nature*, (8th ed.; Paris: Alcan, 1915), esp. chap. 1. The first edition dates from 1874.

17 See item 07b, p. 613; *cf. Les Règles de la méthode*, eighth edition, pp. vii-viii and item 98b. All references to the *Règles* are to this eighth edition.

In the same letter in which he explained that he learned the principle of the autonomy of the sciences from his *Ecole Normale* teacher, Boutroux, and that he merely extended this principle to the social realm, Durkheim also wrote: " I was confirmed in this method by the reading of Comte." It is clear from this that, at least on this score, the influence of Boutroux was primary, while that of Comte was, to follow Durkheim's own expression, only confirmatory. In any case, the implication is obvious that Comte was read only after Boutroux had been, so to speak, digested. And after Renouvier, too, had been well masticated. That the influence of the neo-criticist definitely preceded that of the positivist we can affirm on the authority of Durkheim himself.[18]

Thus, the influence of Comte on Durkheim, while no doubt present, as the latter has often acknowledged,[19] was not really as crucial as is sometimes supposed. Between the two most outstanding French sociologists there was an affinity rather than a master-disciple relationship. Nor should it be forgotten that Durkheim objected to being called a positivist and explicitly rejected Comtist metaphysics and the Comtist conception of sociology. Of course, once having decided on a sociological career—and it is doubtful whether Comte exercised any influence on this decision—it was imperative that Durkheim familiarize himself with the positivist's writings; for it is requisite for every scientist to know the work of his predecessors. And if *De la Division*, for instance, treats of problems and presents theses not unlike those found in Comte [20] this is to be explained by an affinity of goal and interests between the writers and by the fact that every science has certain root questions which are inevitably reexamined generation after generation.[21] Therefore, we are inclined to believe that

18 A S, XII, p. 326.
19 *Cf.* B S F P, item 14b, p. 35.
20 *Cf. De la Division*, p. 244, footnote 1.
21 *Cf.* Durkheim, item 11d, p. vii, and 09d, p. 756.

in spite of many appearances to the contrary, it is not to Comte as much as to Boutroux and Renouvier that Durkheim is closely related.

The French neo-criticist's writings were subjected to a very thorough analysis by the latter. " The first time I saw Durkheim in private," M. Maublanc relates, " he said to me, ' If you wish to mature your thought, give yourself over to the meticulous study of a great master; take a system apart, laying bare its innermost secrets. It is what I have done, and my educator was Renouvier.' " [22]

Although he never held an academic or public teaching position, Renouvier was one of the most influential philosophers of nineteenth century France. Durkheim was subjected to his influence at an early date and many are the points on which there is a marked resemblance between the neo-Kantian and the sociologist. From Renouvier, for instance, Durkheim might well have acquired his contempt for philosophical shams and his detestation of the " brilliant " littérateur and dilettante. From him, too, he could have learned the facileness and shallowness of eclecticism. *"Il faut choisir"*—one must choose— is a phrase, for example, that recurs time and again in Durkheim. In criticizing Tönnies' concept of *Gesellschaft*, the French sociologist wrote, " To conciliate in this manner the theory of Aristotle and that of Bentham is simply to place contraries in juxtaposition. One must choose . . ." Likewise, he objected to the eclectic conciliatory positions of Fouillée, Kant, and Rousseau.[23] Other basic Renouvierist themes that Durkheim came to make his own are the beliefs that ethical and moral considerations occupy a central position in philosophical thought, that there is need for a science of ethics, that philosophy should serve as a guide to social action, that it should, specifically, contribute to the reconstitution of the moral unity of the Third Republic, that a fundamental, if not

22 Maublanc, R., *Europe*, XXII (1930), 299.

23 89b, p. 421; 95e, p. 692; 98c, p. 9.

the fundamental moral concept of modern society is the dignity of the human personality. Durkheim adopted these views, but placed them in a sociological, rather than, as Renouvier would have it, in a neo-Kantian framework. Thus, the former could conceive of a science of ethics only as a branch of positive, empirical sociology, whereas the latter made it a neo-criticistic, and hence a purely deductive, *a priori* science. Likewise, Renouvier hoped to make neo-criticism the philosophy of the Third Republic, whereas Durkheim insisted that only a positive and social science of moral phenomena could serve as a reliable guide to social action, etc. The latter's indebtedness to the neo-Kantian, as well as to Boutroux, for having impressed upon him the postulate that a whole is qualitatively different from the sum of its parts has been explicitly acknowledged.[24]

One cannot study Renouvier without an intimate acquaintance with Kant, whose " apostolic successor " he endeavored to be. Durkheim knew the German philosopher well, and always remained wary of him. We include Kant among the formative influences to which the French social theorist was subjected not so much on account of the positive effect of his ideas on the Frenchman as because he forced the latter to take a critical position with regard to him. Kant's frequent neglect of the social aspect of reality and his constant confusion of the imperative with the declarative mode impressed upon Durkheim the need of giving the moral question a different type of orientation. Professor Bouglé has referred to the *mot:* Durkheimism is Kantism revised and complemented by Comtism. The formula is too facile to be unqualifiedly exact. It nevertheless aptly indicates that Durkheim's moral preoccupations were focal, and that a starting point in the evolution of his own system of ethics was his realization of the inadequacies of the Kantian solution. It is interesting to note the amount of space that Durkheim intended to give over to a

24 13a 4, p. 326.

critique of Kant in his unfinished *magnum opus* on *La Morale.*[25] At one time, however, he wrote that "of all the philosophies which Germany has produced, Kantism is the one which, if wisely interpreted, can best be reconciled with the exigencies of science."[26]

Renouvier and Kant, and later Comte, were, then, among the outstanding thinkers who, in addition to friends and teachers, directed, in part, the intellectual orientation of the *normalien* Emile Durkheim. We may note in passing that the influence of Renouvier was later reenforced at the University of Bordeaux through the friendship that developed between Durkheim and Hamelin, Renouvier's most eminent disciple. This time, however, the emphasis was less on ethical questions than on the problems of representations and the categories of the understanding. Durkheim's concern with these matters culminated in the sociological theory of knowledge briefly sketched in the Introduction to *Les Formes élémentaires de la vie religieuse.*

4. Towards a Science of Society

The resultant of all these somewhat diversified influences was a definitive decision made by Durkheim just about the time of his graduation from the *Ecole Normale Supérieure,* that is, around 1882, to consecrate his energies to the scientific study of social phenomena. From this moment on, the course of his life was definitely set: he was to be a sociologist.

Durkheim, it seems, arrived at this significant decision on several grounds. These may be subsumed under two major rubrics: (a) his dissatisfaction with the state of the philosophical disciplines, (b) his desire to contribute to the moral consolidation of the Third Republic. We have already mentioned his critique of contemporary philosophy: its purely dialectic, literary and non-scientific character, and its snobbish aloofness from social reality. We may turn, therefore, to the second consideration.

25 See below and item 20a.   26 87a, p. 330.

All human beings are products of time, place and circumstance. Philosophers and scientists are not exceptions. They, too, must be viewed as active creatures moving within a specifically definable milieu. Durkheim, for instance, can be understood only as an actor in a human drama the program notes of which read: Place—France; Time—The Early Days of the Third Republic. His entire career, in fact, is inextricably interwoven with the trials and tribulations, the struggles and misfortunes, the triumphs and achievements of a nation in the process of its own remaking. A people had determined to rule itself and was faced with the task of firmly establishing itself socially and morally. Its ideal goal was Democracy, and hence it busied itself with the reconstruction and creation of democratic institutions. It soon came to realize, however, that democracy demanded a national moral unity on a secular basis. The church and religion were regarded as pillars of the old régime. If the powers of the old order were to be permanently crushed, then secularism had to be the price of democracy. This secular democracy was to be achieved and maintained by a lay system of popular education, a free, universal, compulsory, non-religious, state school system. Obviously, such an endeavor involved developing new bases for national solidarity. Some thinkers turned hopefully to science and its methods for guidance in this enterprise and believed that both the foundation and the superstructure of the new morality required by secular democracy could be solidly constructed by following the articulations of scientifically acquired knowledge. Many leading Republicans did not for a moment question such positivistic theses as that a social order can maintain itself only if it is founded on the nature of things, that it is therefore necessary to know first what that nature is, and that the only valid guide to objective knowledge is science. Democracy, secularism, and positive science were, in short, the Republic's ideals.[27]

27 This represents, of course, only one side of the story. France in the early days of the Third Republic was sharply divided on the issues of

In this task of socially and morally reconstituting a nation, *his* nation, which had just thrown off the yoke of the Empire but which, at the same time, suffered an ignominious and humiliating defeat at the hands of the enemy, Emile Durkheim was anxious to play a role. He had a mission. Now, combine the discontent with philosophy with the desire to serve the Republic, add a belief in the efficacy of scientific procedure, and one is almost inevitably led to the realization of both the necessity for, and the important function of, a science of social phenomena. Suppose that we start first with the notion that philosophy should become scientific in method and spirit. This means not only that it should treat its problems in accordance with the procedures of the positive sciences, but also that it should make itself consistent with whatever findings are arrived at by these sciences. It should, in other words, have its roots in, and should always remain in conformity with, scientific knowledge. Apply this principle specifically to those branches of philosophy which deal with the phenomena of social, ethical,

church and state, secularism, the clergy, and lay education as well as on the question of the republican form of government. If there were those who espoused the republican and secular causes and placed their faith in positive science, there were others, in considerable number, who reaffirmed their attachment to religion and espoused the causes of the church. Thus while some French intellectuals welcomed the fall of the Empire as a liberation, others saw in the events of 1870-71 a need for greater affirmation of their belief and faith in God and church. Still a third group turned to religion but at the same time remained critical of the church and the clergy. On this last group see Sabatier, P., *L'Orientation religieuse de la France actuelle* (2nd ed., Paris: Colin, 1912). On the movement for secular education see Ferry, J., *Discours et Opinions de Jules Ferry* (published by P. Robiquet; Paris: Colin, volumes 3 and 4, 1895, 1896) ; and Bouglé, C., *Un Moraliste laïque: Ferdinand Buisson* (*Pages choisies précédées d'une introduction*), (Paris: Alcan, 1933). On the clerical question see Faguet, E., *L'Anti-cléricalisme* (Paris: Société Française d'Imprimerie et de Librairie) and Maurain, *op. cit.* For a general history of the period see Seignobos, C., *Le Déclin de l'Empire et l'Etablissement de la 3ᵉ République* and his *L'Evolution de la 3ᵉ République*, being respectively volumes 7 and 8 of *Histoire de France Contemporaine*, edited by Lavisse, E. (Paris: Hachette, 1921), and for a history of the social and labor movements of the period, see Weill, G., *op. cit.*

moral and religious life, and the implication is obvious: these phenomena, too, must be made the subject of scientific investigations. Or suppose that we begin with the desire consciously and rationally to direct social action and reform. If we postulate that there is no other reliable guide to action than knowledge, and that the only valid kind of knowledge is that which is scientifically attained, it follows that before we can manipulate social realities, we must first have scientific data concerning their nature and behavior; in other words, a science of social facts. Thus, whether we start from the one or the other line of interest, the conclusion is the same: a positive science of sociology is necessary and desirable.

Durkheim conceived this science as having three major functions: (1) the objective and theoretical pursuit of the truth regarding the laws and the facts of social life; (2) the reexamination, reevaluation, and recasting of the principles and theories of philosophy so that they may be made consistent with the data and findings of the new science; (3) the establishment of a basis for the guidance of social action and practice. Each phase of this three-fold task received its due consideration from him; to all of them he contributed amply and suggestively. Because he thought of the three goals as necessarily interrelated and intertwined, there is scarcely a study of his that ignores any one of them.[28] Durkheim, then, set out to establish a science of sociology that was to transform philosophy and guide political conduct. One cannot help being impressed by the daring ambitiousness of the enterprise; one can only marvel at the extent, however limited, to which it attained fruition.

28 The emphases, of course, are different. The practical consequences of *De la Division* were fully developed only in the preface to the second edition. In *Les Formes élémentaires*, practical considerations are very incidental whereas philosophical import looms large. A good balance between sociological analysis, philosophical significance and practical consequences is seen in *Le Suicide*.

5. APPRENTICESHIP AND DÉBUT

The young *agrégé* had to forge his own way. Upon graduation from the *Ecole Normale*, he became a professor of philosophy and was assigned, for periods of varying length, to the *Lycées* of Sens, Saint-Quentin, and Troyes. He taught in the *Lycées* from 1882 to 1887, except for the school year 1885-86 for which he obtained a leave of absence that was devoted to further study. These were the years not only of apprenticeship but also of sociological début.

Among Durkheim's many accomplishments, one cannot neglect his ability as an administrator. In that capacity he was aided considerably by his having taught in the *lycées*. In his later activities as a member of examining juries, of university councils, of committees to choose subjects for contests, prizes, and examinations, and in his investigations into recommendations for changes in the teaching of philosophy, his personal experiences as a *lycée* instructor served him well.

It must have been during these early years of his teaching career that Durkheim underwent the influence of Spencer, Schäffle, and Espinas. They affected the young sociologist profoundly; so much so, in fact, that it took him more than a decade to liberate himself from the yoke of their biological orientation. True, they were not " pure " organicists in the manner of Lilienfeld,[29] yet their approach to the study of society was essentially biological in nature. Durkheim hesitatingly but freely took over their organicistic views. His early sociology was, consequently, very Spencerian in spirit. He was a severe critic of the English philosopher, it is true, but he quite often met Spencer on the latter's own biological ground.[30] A good deal of *De la Division du travail social* could very well have been written by an organicist. Such concepts as " social

29 Durkheim, 85a, p. 85; 85c, p. 627; 88a, p. 34.

30 *Cf. De la Division*, pp. 204-205 for just one example. In 1885 Durkheim wrote, " For it is quite certain that the social world plunges by its roots into the world of life: Espinas and Perrier have demonstrated it." 85c, p. 634.

body," " social organ," " social brain," " social protoplasm,"
" the cerebro-spinal system of the social organism," and " the
visceral life of society " etc. are frequently utilized in the
volume.[31] Evidence from biology is even used not merely to
illustrate but to verify certain of the sociological principles
established.[32] And is not the struggle for existence given an
eminent role in the causal explanation of the development of
the division of labor?[33] We are far from maintaining that
Durkheim can be called, even in the earliest stages of his development, an organicist; it is impossible, however, to mistake
the decidedly biological tinge of his first works. His contemporaries had no difficulty in recognizing it. Worms, himself
an organicist, quickly perceived the essentially Spencerian tone
of Durkheim's doctoral thesis.[34] Lapie, who later became a
collaborator on the *Année Sociologique*, strongly objected to
Durkheim's definition of socialism (which appeared in the
same year as *De la Division*) precisely because of its biologism.[35] Sorel, too, sensed a certain organicism in Durkheim.[36]
There can be no doubt that the latter fell victim to the widespread epidemic of Spencerianism that raged at the end of the
nineteenth century. Though the attack may have been mild, it
took considerable time for the patient to rid himself of its
effects. Spencer, indeed, enjoyed a great vogue in France.
His works were made available in translations and the pages
of French periodicals such as the *Revue Philosophique* were

31 *Cf.* pp. 50, 72, 122, 149, 184, 195, 198, 260, 319, etc.

32 Pp. 202, 328-329 etc. Note also the numerous references to the biologists
Perrier and Bordier.

33 Pp. 248 ff. *Cf. Règles*, p. 114. For our interpretation of Durkheim's
causal analysis, see Part II, below.

34 In R I S, I (1893), 359-361. More recently, the similarity between
Spencer and Durkheim has been pointed out by Rumney. Rumney, J., *Herbert
Spencer's Sociology* (London: Williams and Norgate, 1934). *Cf.* p. 87 where
Rumney speaks of "the profound influence Spencer exercised over Durkheim."

35 Lapie, P., "La Définition du socialisme," R M M, II (1894), 199-204.
See item 93c.

36 Sorel, G., "Les Théories de M. Durkheim," D S, I (1895), p. 170.

open to him. His *Principles of Psychology* were translated by no less eminent figures than Ribot and Espinas.

It was from the latter that Durkheim acquired the concept of a collective consciousness. He also learned from him the importance of studying particular social types instead of philosophizing on society in general. Because *Des Sociétés Animales* so clearly formulated the nature *sui generis* of society and because it studied social facts solely for the purpose of establishing scientific principles and not in order to demonstrate the symmetry of some grand philosophical system, Durkheim considered it the " chapter one of sociology." [37]

The young sociologist made his professional début in 1885 as a collaborator on Ribot's *Revue Philosophique* to which he contributed keen analyses of recent sociological literature. He immediately gave evidence of sharp critical acumen, an ability to summarize long volumes succinctly and clearly, and a facility with foreign languages, especially German and English. These were qualities which he later put to good advantage on the *Année Sociologique*. His first published article was a review of volume one of Schäffle's *Bau und Leben des Sozialen Körpers*. In this review, we find him expressing many ideas to which he afterwards gave more systematic formulation. The notions that " society is not a simple collection of individuals," but has " its own life, consciousness, interests, and destiny," that " one must return to Comte's conception: social science, studying a new world, must have a new method," that " from the fact that nature does not proceed by leaps and bounds it does not follow that all things are similar and can be studied in accordance with the same procedures," that " evolution is not a monotonous repetition; continuity is not identity," that the stuff of society consists of "ideas and sentiments " and hence is psychical in nature, that " as a last resource against individualism there remains what Schäffle calls the sense of solidarity, *Gemeinsinn* " are all emphasized.

37 88a, p. 38.

However, on at least two of the opinions here expressed, Durkheim later came to change his mind.

With reference to Schäffle's use of biological metaphors and analogies, he rather impatiently queried, " Is it not time to throw them away and face facts squarely? " But not many years afterwards, he wrote that the biological analogy, while dangerous, was nevertheless fertile and valuable,[38] and in *De la Division* we are told that biological language, although metaphorical, is nonetheless convenient.[39] It would perhaps be more accurate, on the whole, to characterize Durkheim's first attitude towards the method of analogy as ambivalent and wavering. However, it must be emphasized that by the time of the founding of the *Année Sociologique*, his break with the organicist tradition was rather complete.

The second point on which Durkheim later reversed his position was, as he himself put it, " Schaeffle's robust faith in reason and the future of humanity." " We are beginning to feel that all is not clear and that reason does not cure all ills. We have reasoned so much!", the reviewer objected. Yet he too was soon to avow explicitly his " faith in reason " and in the " enlightened consciousness of which science is only the highest form." [40] Without entering into the controversy whether or not Durkheim was an anti-intellectualist, we may note that whatever may have been his later views, a definite anti-intellectualistic strain recurs frequently and unmistakably not only in the analysis of Schäffle but also in the other critical reviews that soon followed.[41]

38 88a, p. 35. *Cf.* also 87c, p. 279, and 85c, p. 634.

39 P. 198.

40 *Règles*, p. viii, *Le Suicide*, Nouvelle édition, p. 162.

41 See R P for years 1885 and 1886, notably XXII, pp. 65-69. On the controversy just referred to, see Parodi, D., *La Philosophie contemporaine en France* (2nd ed.; Paris: Alcan, 1920), chap. V and the same author in Supplement to Janet, P. et Séailles, G., *et al, Histoire de la philosophie: les Problemès et les Ecoles*, entitled " La Période contemporaine " (Paris: Delagrave, 1929), chap. XII for one point of view and Davy, G., R M M, XXVII (1920), 71-72, 75-76 for the other.

For within the two years 1885 and 1886, Fouillée, Gumplowicz, Spencer, Régnard, Coste and DeGreef were likewise passed through Durkheim's refined critical mill. The reviewer showed that he had an alert mind of his own and the courage to use it. Through this contact with the *Revue* he was afforded the opportunity not only to sharpen his critical tools but also to make an impression on the thinking public of France.

Durkheim's relationship with the founder of the *Revue* also had intellectual consequences. Ribot's insistence on the use of experimental procedures in psychology, his critique of the prevalent type of psychological analysis, and his emphasis on the social as well as the physiological influence on psychical life made a deep impression on the maturing social scientist. In fact, many of the objections which Durkheim levied against psychology are found all prepared, so to speak, in Ribot's study of the contemporary conditions of that science in England.[42] Was it not Ribot who very early emphasized that if psychology, as he expressed it in his posthumous preface to Dumas' *Traité*, starts with biology, it has its ultimate efflorescence in sociology?[43] To the father of contemporary French psychology we can trace at least two major notions of Durkheimian sociology: (a) the significance of the non-conscious aspects of human activity and (b) the principle that a study of the pathological throws light on the nature of the normal. On the first of these ideas Durkheim based his attack on " finalistic " theories of social behavior and on the second he attempted to erect a positive science of social pathology.[44] Nor should it be forgotten that the sociologist, in urging the need for methodical, scientific experimentation, had in Ribot an eminent model to follow.

42 Ribot, Th., *La Psychologie anglaise contemporaine* (Paris: Alcan, 1870).

43 Dumas, G., *Traité de Psychologie* (Paris: Alcan, 1923), vol. i, p. viii.

44 *Règles*, Chaps. V and III. *Cf.* Durkheim's review of Ribot's *La Logique des sentiments*, A S, IV, pp. 156-158.

It was just about this time, i. e. around 1886, that Durkheim's doctoral dissertation began to take on definite shape. He had first posed the problem rather abstractly as the relation of individualism to socialism. In 1883 he made it more concrete, changing his subject to the relations between the individual and society. A first plan was drawn up in 1884. It soon became evident to Durkheim that the problem was essentially a sociological one and that its solution could be stated only in terms of the yet barely existent science of social life. By 1886, when the first draft of the thesis was ready, the essentials of the theory of solidarity and social evolution were already formulated.[45]

Always self-critical, Durkheim knew that there were certain lacunae in his training. He therefore took a leave of absence in 1885-86. Thus liberated from his teaching duties, he was able to devote himself to further study. To this end, he went to Paris where he spent the first half of the year. While at the capital city, Durkheim received valuable guidance from Lucien Herr who was then completing his course at the *Ecole Normale*. Herr was the kind, popular, and erudite socialist who in 1888 became the *Ecole Normale's* permanent librarian. Herr, however, was not merely the School's " guardian of the books;" he was, in a sense, the student's father confessor, and their unofficial but capable " vocational councillor." It was only after discussions with him that many a hesitant and undecided *normalien* determined his professional career. The librarian was also instrumental in directing students to important and revelatory bibliographical sources. It was he who directed Durkheim's attention to Frazer's articles on totemism and thus evoked in the young sociologist the interest in the phenomena of primitive religion that was to have its ultimate flowering in the monumental study of *Les Formes élémentaires.*[46]

45 Mauss, M., in 28a, p. v. *Cf.* 93b, pp. xliii-xliv.

46 Mauss, M., " Notice sur Lucien Herr," A S, n. s., II (1927), 9. On Herr, see Andler, Ch., *Vie de Lucien Herr* (Paris: Rieder, 1932).

Durkheim spent the second half of his year of leave in Germany. He had had an important conversation with Louis Liard who at the time was *Directeur de l'Enseignement supérieur*. Liard was an ardent believer in the necessity of a scientific study of social life. Only the "universal methods of science," he felt, could provide the basis for the moral reconstruction of the Third Republic. He discussed with Durkheim various problems pertaining to the teaching of philosophy and the development of the social sciences. As a result of this discussion with Liard, the sociologist decided to go to the land of Kant and Hegel.[47]

Durkheim's stay in Germany was devoted to two main purposes: (1) to investigate the methods and the contents of the instruction in philosophy offered in the German universities; (2) to study the state of the social sciences in that country, in particular, the science of ethics. On each of these two subjects he wrote rather lengthy and thorough reports which were published shortly after his return to France.[48]

His researches took him to several universities but he stayed longest at Berlin and Leipzig. His most protracted sojourn was in the latter city, to which he had been attracted by the international reputation of Wundt. The founder of the first psycho-physical laboratory deeply impressed Durkheim whose admiration he readily won. His instruction " is a model of clarity and even of elegance " and " in doctrine as in method " he is " circumspect and moderate," the young Frenchman wrote of the German philosopher. As for the Psychological Laboratory itself, Durkheim's enthusiasm was almost without bounds. In his report, he described the experiments that were in progress during his stay at Leipzig and noted how " precise and restricted " in nature were the problems undertaken. " Nothing," he added, " is more capable of awakening in young minds the love of scientific exactitude, of breaking them

47 On Liard, see Lavisse, E., " Louis Liard," R I E, LXXII (1918), 81-99.
48 87a, 87c.

of the habit of vague generalizations and metaphysical specu-
lations." [49]

The now fifty-year-old survey of philosophical instruction
in Germany contains many shrewd observations and wise
recommendations that even today merit serious consideration.
Americans should be particularly interested in it since our own
university system is largely modeled on the German one. But
aside from its value as an administrative document, the report
deserves attention as a contribution to sociology. Among other
things, it outlines the fundamental principles of an independent
positive science of moral facts which is to be integrated in the
system of the social sciences along with the study of economic,
juridical, religious and other social phenomena. The report is
also significant because it explicitly assigns to philosophy and
to the moral and social sciences a political, aye, even national
purpose. It is on this point that the study concludes; and
Durkheim's eloquence is here equal to his patriotism. " M.
Lavisse," he writes, " has told us how history can and ought
to render service to national education. Philosophy should
dedicate itself to the same task, which it has too frequently
neglected; and it is particularly in France that this duty is incumbent upon it. We are—to our misfortune perhaps—thirsty
for logic. We wish above all to know the *raison d'être* of
national sentiments and patriotic faith; whether they are
founded in the nature of things or whether, as is maintained—
openly or not—by so many doctrinaire persons, they are only
prejudices and survivals of barbarism. Now these problems
belong to psychology. It is necessary, in order to answer them,
to teach students the nature of sympathy and sociability, and
to make them see completely their reality and their advantages.
It is necessary to explain to them that our personality is for
the greater part made up of borrowings and that taken out of
the physical and social environment which envelops him, man
is only an abstraction. It is necessary, finally, to show them

49 87a, p. 433.

that sympathy is exercised only in the midst of groups that are unequally extensive but always confined and closed, and to indicate the place of the fatherland among these groups. To the teacher of philosophy also belongs the task of awakening in the minds that are confided to his care the idea of what a law is, of making them understand that psychical and social phenomena, like other things, are facts subject to laws that the human will cannot upset simply by willing, and that consequently revolutions, in the true sense of the word, are things as impossible as miracles." [50] Philosophy, then, through the psychological and moral sciences, is to provide the *rationale* for social and national sentiments that historical consciousness alone cannot supply. To achieve this end, it is necessary for these sciences, once they have been developed as systematic disciplines, to become the subject of general instruction. In a democracy it cannot be otherwise. "In truth, is it not astounding that we make such little effort to enlighten opinion when it is the sovereign power among us?" [51] The above passage clearly reveals Durkheim's orientation with respect to the problems of the Third Republic, it makes manifest his moral and political preoccupations.

These are even more forcefully brought out in the second study he conducted while in Germany. In it, he surveyed for the French philosophical public the then not too well known developments taking place on the other side of the Rhine in the direction of a positive science of ethics. The movement towards a special science of moral phenomena received its impetus, Durkheim reported, not so much from professional moralists as from economists and jurists. In fact, " it is from political economy that the whole movement received its impetus." Consequently, we are first introduced to the efforts of the *Kathedersozialisten* such as Wagner and Schmoller to effectuate an intimate rapprochement between political economy

50 87a, pp. 439-440.
51 *Ibid.*, p. 440.

and ethics. The work of Schäffle is next considered. Then follows an analysis of the theories of Jhering who is taken as representative of the tendency among jurists to study law as a societal expression and to view it in relation to other social and moral phenomena. Wundt, of course, receives the most extended treatment since it is in his *Ethik* that the whole movement was given its most precise formulation. Before concluding Durkheim reviews, in addition, the abundantly detailed work of Hermann Post.[52]

Although he deplored the extreme generalness of the problems studied by most of these German writers, Durkheim nevertheless heartily endorsed their efforts; but not without being severely critical of specific aspects of their theories. The economists, for example, placed too great confidence in the efficacy of regulating social affairs by legislative action; Jhering was too "finalistic", while Wundt, forgetting that there are as many systems of ethics as there are social types, was too monistic. Post, on the other hand, was too indiscriminate in his use of data, substituting "imperfect enumeration" for methodical comparison.[53] But in spite of these weaknesses, Durkheim thought their enterprises praiseworthy. He approved of their insistence on treating moral facts as empirical data *sui generis*. He agreed with their view that moral duty was social in nature and origin and applauded their desire to have ethics take its place as an independent positive discipline alongside of the other social sciences.

The German writers served to vindicate Durkheim in his decision to devote himself to the scientific study of moral life. By their works, they gave confirmation to his conviction that such a discipline was not only necessary but also feasible and fruitful. The science of ethics, he realized from his German experience, did not have to be created *ab ovo;* its conception was already a thing of the past. Rather, this science was now

---

52 There is also a brief mention of Lorenz von Stein, 87c, pp. 278-279.
53 *Ibid.*, pp. 45, 47, 52, 142, 283.

at the stage of parturition and needed only careful midwifery
to be kept alive. The infant, it may be noted, was not long in
becoming a favorite child and indeed always remained one.
" Of all the branches of sociology," Durkheim announced
shortly after his return from Germany, "the science of ethics
is the one which attracts us by preference and which will command our attention first of all." [54]

With the publication, in 1887, of these two surveys of German philosophical instruction and of the contributions to the
positive science of ethics made in Germany, Durkheim's reputation as an outstanding sociologist was established. Thus, at
the age of twenty-nine he was already recognized as a mature
and serious social thinker. He had behind him several years
of experience as a *lycée* teacher of philosophy, a fruitful sojourn in Germany, and a not inconsiderable literature which
included the studies just mentioned and the critical analyses
that appeared in the *Revue Philosophique*. In addition, the
manuscript of a significant doctoral dissertation was assuming
definite form. The foundations of Durkheimian sociology were
already laid.

1887 also witnessed the beginning of Durkheim's inspir-
ing, thirty-year-long university career. In that year, at the
instigation of Liard, a course in social science was created
for him at the Faculty of Letters of the University of Bordeaux. This was the first time that a French university had
ever officially opened its doors to this rather suspect subject.
The event was not without significance.

From the appearance of Comte's *Cours de philosophie positive* right up to the closing years of the nineteenth century,
sociology was generally regarded in French university circles
as *scientia non grata*. The traditional moralists and university
philosophers had the greatest contempt for the upstart science
of social phenomena. They looked upon it not as a proper
philosophical discipline, but rather as an amiable pastime to

54 88a, p. 45.

be dabbled in by mathematicians, doctors, engineers, and physicists. Thus when Alfred Espinas, in the course of his defense of his doctoral dissertation *"Des Sociétés Animales"* before a committee of the Faculty of Letters of Paris in 1877, insisted on the worth and dignity of the science of society, his point of view caused a veritable furor among his examiners. Caro and Paul Janet were especially hostile. The latter even ordered Espinas' historical introduction suppressed because the author refused to delete from it the name of Comte.[55] A decade later, however, this hostility towards sociology had somewhat abated. Moreover, some of the young men who had embarked on their university careers in the wake of the treaty of Frankfort and who believed in the importance of the positive study of social phenomena as a means of achieving the moral unity of the Third Republic were now in administrative positions which permitted them to translate their views into action. It is only in relation to the early struggles of the Third Republic that the positive recognition of sociology as a respectable university discipline takes on significance.

Durkheim's appointment to the University of Bordeaux as a *Chargé de cours* imposed upon him the duties of teaching not only sociology, but pedagogy as well. These two subjects he always taught jointly.[56] His colleagues in the Department of Philosophy at Bordeaux—it was to this department that the course in social science was assigned — were Espinas whose dissertation battle, which we have just mentioned, had helped pave the way for the introduction of sociology into the universities, and Hamelin, the brilliant Renouvierist. The former was ever a source of inspiration to Durkheim; the latter became a bosom friend.[57]

55 *Cf.* Espinas, A., "Etre ou ne pas être: ou du postulat de la sociologie," R P, LI (1901), 449 ff.

56 On Durkheim's pedagogical work see Fauconnet, P., "L'Oeuvre pédagogique de Durkheim" in Durkheim, 22a, pp. 1-33. This study also appeared in English in A J S, XXVIII (1923), 529-553. *Cf.* 38a.

57 For the similarity of views between Durkheim and Espinas see the latter's article referred to above.

Durkheim's professional career was now definitely fixed. The remaining thirty years of his life were spent in complete devotion to his duties and functions as a sociologist and university professor. Contemporary man, however, is a member of a multiplicity of social groups and therefore has many attachments and loyalties other than his occupational ones. Thus, we should not ignore the fact that Durkheim, despite his ardent absorption in his professional activities, seldom neglected his obligations and tasks either as a *père de famille* or as a Frenchman, or in any of his other social roles.

Durkheim the sociologist, Durkheim the Frenchman, and Durkheim the professor were but a single personality, and the fact of this unity explains the interrelatedness of the activities of the three. How Durkheim as a social person enacted each of these three social roles from the year of his university appointment to the outbreak of the World War we shall now consider.[58]

6. Sociologist

The main facts of Durkheim's sociological preoccupations are too well known to need elaborate treatment. A brief review of them should suffice. When Durkheim assumed his teaching duties at the University of Bordeaux, he in no way interrupted the steady flow of his scientific articles. In 1888, for example, there appeared, in addition to the opening lectures of two of his courses, a study which endeavored to clear up certain mis-

58 We omit Durkheim's family life because our knowledge concerning it is extremely meager. Durkheim married at about the time of his appointment to Bordeaux. To his indefatiguable wife, Louise Dreyfus Durkheim, who did not long survive him, sociologists are indebted for having made possible the publication of several important manuscripts. It was her anonymous assistance in correcting proofs, preparing notes, etc. that insured the prompt appearance each year of the *Année Sociologique*. She relieved her husband of many domestic burdens and supervised the education of the children Marie and André. This enabled him to concentrate more fully on his professional work. Of Durkheim's devotion to his son we shall have more to say later on. *Cf.* Mauss, M., " Notice sur Louise Dreyfus Durkheim," A S, n. s., vol. II, pp. 8-9.

conceptions regarding Schäffle's economic views and also a contribution to moral statistics, *Suicide et Natalité,* which was a foretaste of the masterly volume on suicide that was published nine years later. Next followed more critical reviews, including an extremely interesting one of Tönnies' *Gemeinschaft und Gesellschaft.* In 1893, Durkheim defended his doctoral theses "*De la division du travail social: Etude sur l'organization des sociétés supérieures*" and "*Quid Secundatus politicae scientiae instituendae contulerit*" before the Faculty of Letters of Paris.

The thesis jury included Paul Janet, Brochard, Marion, Boutroux, Séailles, and Waddington. When discussion of the Latin essay on Montesquieu came up, Janet reprimanded Durkheim for scorning the works of earlier writers. How could anyone knowing Aristotle regard Montesquieu as the founder of Political Science, the examiner queried. (Janet returned to a pet peeve of his and reminded the candidate that Aristotle was as scientific as Comte.) And what about Spinoza and Hobbes, Brochard interposed. In reply to these objections, Durkheim made precise the difference between the views of Montesquieu and those of the earlier writers.[59] Muhlfeld, whose account of the dissertation defense we are following, notes at this point, " I am too often obliged to describe the candidate as browbeaten by the superiority of his jury not to be happy for once, as compensation, to speak of a thesis defense in which the candidate constantly held the upper hand. M. Durkheim is not only a scientist of great value, he is the surest and most delightful of orators." " He will be a master," Muhlfeld adds prophetically.[60]

In the discussion that followed Durkheim's résumé of his major thesis, Marion ingeniously objected that since the work purported to be scientific, it should have left aside the question

59 *Cf.* 88a, pp. 24-28. Such favorite expressions of Durkheim as " the necessity of things," " founded in the nature of things " are clearly Montesquieuan.

60 Muhlfeld, L., R U, I (1893), 440-443.

of ethics. (Durkheim had offered his study as "above all, an effort to treat the facts of moral life according to the method of the positive sciences.") [61] Janet took up this objection and accused Durkheim of mistaking function and duty. Waddington pursued the same line of criticism, bitterly asking questions about duty, and impatiently remarking that "we are in the lower regions of ethics." The candidate answered each of his examiners with full confidence. Nor did he lack the courage to point out, whenever necessary, that the matter brought up by the examiner was irrelevant. Everyone was centering the discussion not so much on the thesis itself as on the relation of Durkheim's book to the consecrated formal systems of ethics. Finally, Boutroux, to whom the thesis was dedicated and who had to swallow hard in accepting what Professor Bouglé has aptly called "this demonstration of deterministic tenor in which one felt reborn something of the spirit of Taine", broke away from this insistence on the ethical aspects of the volume, and posed a question about the concept of scientific method that the candidate had employed. Many more objections followed, but the defendant came off with flying colors. Throughout the session he showed a keen presence of mind, and a simple and sincere eloquence. He made no attempt, however, to hide a certain impatience with the proceedings.

In 1893, there also appeared Durkheim's famous definition of socialism which he later incorporated, in modified form, in his course on the history of socialist doctrines. The following year the articles on *The Rules of Sociological Method* were published. They appeared in book form in 1895. Two years afterwards *Le Suicide* was presented to a public obviously fascinated by what was going on in the mind of the professor from Bordeaux. In the preface to the volume Durkheim was able to write that sociology, practically unknown ten years previously, was now "in fashion." In the meantime, the pro-

61 *De la Division*, p. xxxvii.

digiously active sociologist began to organize the *Année Sociologique.*

As a reviewer for the *Revue Philosophique,* Durkheim soon perceived the necessity of keeping the sociological public in touch with the copious works that were being published each year. This was evidently an impossible task for any one person to undertake. True, an *"année sociologique"* made its appearance in the *Revue de Métaphysique et de morale* in 1895, but the single reviewer could pay attention only to an infinitesimal fraction of the yearly sociological output.[62] With the increasing interest in things sociological, the time seemed ripe for an independent, collective, annual periodical that would systematically and methodically review the state of the social sciences.

Aside from its invaluable services in classifying and analyzing the literature of sociology, the *Année*, as Durkheim conceived it, had other functions to fulfill. For one thing, it was to serve to bring all the social sciences closer together. The special social disciplines were remaining too aloof from one another to their mutual disadvantage, Durkheim felt. To effect a rapprochement among them and by this rapprochement to alter and redirect their methods and organization, to prove that all social science is essentially one, such was the program of the *Année*.[63] Furthermore, it aimed to cultivate the taste for specialized social investigation and thereby to usher in the " era of specialization." Sociology, in Durkheim's opinion, had too long limited itself to general questions such as the nature of society, the nature of the family, the course of social evolution, etc. Before questions of this kind can be adequately answered, however, a good deal of preliminary spade work

---

62 *Cf.* the "années sociologiques" of the R M M, III (1895), 308-339; IV (1896), 338-361; and V (1897), 489-519 with any volume of Durkheim's *Année.* See the analysis of volume V below.

63 A S, prefaces to vols. I and II. For Durkheim's conception of sociology as the corpus of the social sciences, see 03c, pp. 465 ff.; 09e, esp. pp. 276-278; 00c, pp. 127-148. These articles are the best expression of the view of sociology underlying the *Année.*

must be undertaken. Data must be collected, facts must be substantiated, particular societies and specific institutions must be analyzed. To this endeavor too the *Année* dedicated itself. Thus to the motto: unity of the social sciences was added the slogan: specificity of research. It may be noted that the *Année's* first article, Durkheim's essay on the prohibition of incest, was a specialized study of a specific institution, and that practically all the succeeding *mémoires* were of the same nature.

Durkheim had still a third intention in founding the *Année*. Science is essentially a cumulative body of systematic knowledge and necessarily involves cooperative action on the part of many persons. It is therefore a collective, not a personal enterprise. Its ideals of objectivity and impersonalness are admirably fostered by a team of workers performing specialized tasks in a common endeavor. Consequently, if the science of sociology is to be objective and impersonal, it must be cooperative and collective. Thus far, Durkheim thought, it has been too personal, too dependent on the individuality of the particular writer. The *Année*, he hoped, would by precept and example encourage group- and team-work in sociological investigation.

From its very inception, the *Année Sociologique* was eminently successful. Its reviews were cogent critiques and its original articles were masterly contributions to the science it served. A perusal of the titles of these *mémoires* will reveal their significance.[64] As to the reviews, we can best indicate their scope by reproducing the analysis of volume V (1900-01) of the *Année* that Victor Branford published about thirty years ago.[65]

64 For a list see Gehlke, C. E., *Emile Durkheim's Contributions to Sociological Theory* (Columbia University, New York, 1915), pp. 124-125.

65 It first appeared in S P, I, p. 13, and was reprinted in S R, X, p. 78. Branford's paper on the origin and use of the word sociology which the analysis first accompanied was republished in the A J S, IX (1903), 145-162, but the analytical table was unfortunately omitted.

TABLE I

ANALYSIS OF THE SOCIOLOGICAL LITERATURE

(In Books and in Periodicals Summarized in the " Année Sociologique " for 1902. Volume V, 1900-01.)

	Number of Publications in						
	France	Italy	U.S.A.	Germany	England	Other Countries	Total
I. General Sociology	26	10	8	6	5	1	56
1. Objects and methods of sociology	9	5	2	2	–	–	18
2. Social philosophy—General theory	7	2	4	2	–	1	16
3. Mentality of groups ..	5	2	–	–	–	–	7
4. Civilization in general and types of civilization	1	1	1	1	2	–	6
5. Collective Ethology ..	2	–	–	–	2	–	4
6. The Social milieu and the race	2	–	1	1	1	–	5
II. Religious Sociology ...	29	5	12	75	29	11	161
1. General conceptions of methodology	4	1	1	2	–	–	8
2. Elementary forms of religious life	1	1	5	18	11	5	41
3. Magic	1	–	1	5	–	3	10
4. Beliefs and Practices concerning the dead ..	4	–	1	4	2	1	12
5. Ritual	4	1	2	9	5	1	22
6. Religious representations	12	1	1	27	8	1	50
7. Religious society	1	1	1	6	1	–	10
8. General studies of the great religions	2	–	–	4	2	–	8
III. Juridical and Moral Sociology	45	15	5	34	7	10	114
1. General considerations	10	4	–	–	2	–	16
2. Social organization in general	2	–	1	5	2	–	10
3. Political organization .	5	2	1	1	–	4	13
4. Domestic organization	11	2	–	14	2	–	29
5. Law of property	2	1	–	1	–	1	5
6. Law of contract	4	–	1	–	–	1	6
7. Criminal Law	7	1	–	8	–	4	20
8. Procedure	1	3	–	1	1	–	6
9. Miscellaneous	3	2	–	4	–	–	9

TABLE I (*Continued*)

	France	Italy	U.S.A.	Germany	England	Other Countries	Total
Number of Publications in							
IV. Criminal Sociology and Moral Statistics	12	9	1	5	3	5	35
1. Statistics of domestic life	2	–	–	2	–	–	4
2. General criminality in the different countries	1	2	1	1	–	1	6
3. Factors of g e n e r a l criminality	4	3	–	1	–	2	10
4. Special forms of criminality and immorality	2	2	–	1	2	1	8
5. Crime-making mileux. Societies of Malefactors and their customs	2	2	–	–	–	1	5
6. Functioning of the repressive system	1	–	–	–	1	–	2
V. Economic Sociology ...	21	4	5	35	5	3	73
1. Methodology—general problems	1	1	1	2	3	–	8
2. Economic systems ...	2	–	1	–	1	–	4
3. Regimes of production	–	2	1	6	–	2	11
4. Forms of production .	1	–	–	7	–	–	8
5. Elements of distribution	1	–	1	1	–	–	3
6. Economic classes	2	–	–	2	–	–	4
7. Professional associations	1	–	–	1	–	1	3
8. Special e c o n o m i e s (agrarian, commercial, colonial)	4	–	–	8	1	–	13
9. Social legislation	4	1	–	4	–	–	9
10. Miscellaneous	5	–	1	4	–	–	10
VI. Social Morphology ...	7	1	1	6	2	4	21
1. Geographic base of society	1	–	1	–	1	–	3
2. Population in general	3	–	–	3	1	2	9
3. Urban and rural groupings	3	1	–	3	–	2	9
VII. Miscellaneous	6	4	–	4	1	2	17
1. Aesthetic Sociology ..	2	2	–	2	1	1	8
2. Technology	2	1	–	–	–	1	4
3. Language	1	–	–	1	–	–	2
4. War	1	1	–	1	–	–	3
Grand Totals	146	48	30	165	52	36	477

To make clearer the concept of sociology that underlay the *Année*, we may supplement this analysis with the following formulation, by Durkheim, of the field and scope of the science.[66]

TABLE II

The following table represents schematically the principal divisions of sociology:

I. Social Morphology.
   1. Study of the geographical base of peoples in its relation to social organization.
   2. Study of population; its volume, density, the way it is disposed over the soil.

II. Social Physiology.
   1. Religious sociology.
   2. Moral sociology.
   3. Juridical sociology.
   4. Economic sociology.
   5. Linguistic sociology.
   6. Esthetic sociology.

III. General Sociology.

The first volume of the *Année* was published in 1898. It contained 563 pages and was the joint product of 13 collaborators.[67] In the same year the *Revue de Métaphysique et de morale* printed Durkheim's brilliant philosophical declaration of sociological independence: the essay on *Individual Representations and Collective Representations*. This article contains a scathing critique of the atomistic reductionist approach to the phenomena of consciousness, especially as manifested in the theories of psycho-physiological parallelism and epiphenomenalism. From this demonstration of the inadequacy of

66 ope, p. 278.

67 This should be compared with the 1012 pages and 34 collaborators of the first volume of the new series (1923-24).

this type of explanation—and his analysis here is very remin-
iscent of Bergson's *Matter and Memory* [68]—Durkheim argues
that the psychical realm constitutes an autonomous domain
whose phenomena are realities *sui generis*. He then proceeds
to establish, by analogy, the equal autonomy of the realm of
social phenomena and collective representations. This latter
domain he qualifies as hyperpsychical to emphasize the fact
that the phenomena it includes are psychical in nature and yet
are not altogether the same as, and hence are not explicable
in terms of, the facts of the psychology of the individual.
Thus, on the basis of the principle of creative synthesis, i. e.
emergentism, he justifies the independence of psychology with
respect to physiology and of sociology with regard to the
former. Independence, it must be understood, does not mean
" complete divorce from " but merely " not reducible to."
Durkheim carefully insists on the physiological basis of psychical facts and on the individual basis of social phenomena.
These bases, which he calls *substrata,* cannot serve as *sufficient*
causal explanations, although it is necessary to recognize that
they are, as Durkheim frequently reiterates, necessary conditions.[69]

The essay made quite a sensation. It achieved a widespread
notoriety and brought all sorts of calumnies upon its author.
Durkheim modestly intended the article to be a contribution to
the justification of " psychological naturalism." For his pains
he found himself accused of scholasticism and mysticism on the
one hand and of realism and substantialism on the other. He
embodied a reply to his critics in the preface to the second
edition of *Les Règles* which appeared in 1901.

From the time of the publication of the first volume of the
Année, right up to the beginning of the World War, sixteen
years later, Durkheim's published sociological writings fol-

68 First published in 1896. *Cf.* Blondel, Ch., *Introduction à la psychologie
collective* (Paris: Colin, 1928), p. 44.

69 *Cf.* 24a, pp. 32-33, 39; *Règles,* preface to second edition; 97e, p. 648.
For a discussion of these principles see Part II.

lowed four main lines. To use the *Année's* terminology, we may call these major fields general sociology, juridical and moral sociology, religious sociology, and the sociological conditions of thought.

Durkheim continued, of course, to give systematic and precise formulation to his views on the nature of sociology, the relation of the social sciences to one another, and on questions of methodology. In 1900 there was published in Italian a paper on sociology and its scientific realm, the first part of which was devoted to a critique of Simmel's formalistic conception of the science. Three years later, an article on sociology and the social sciences, written in collaboration with Professor Fauconnet, was printed in the *Revue Philosophique*. It appeared shortly afterwards in an abridged English translation in the *Sociological Papers*. The same subject was treated later in briefer form and along with historical and methodological considerations, in the chapter contributed by Durkheim in 1909 to the volume *De la Méthode dans les sciences*. In the meantime, the reviews and notes in the *Année* were hammering home the same points.

He likewise pursued further the field of sociology which first attracted him and with which his earliest studies were concerned: juridical sociology and the science of moral phenomena. Under this rubric fall the study of the division of labor, the analysis of the social rates of suicide, and the researches into the sociology of the family. Durkheim explicitly stated in 1900 that he had limited his researches—except for necessary excursions into bordering domains—to the study of juridical and moral rules either in their development and genesis by means of history and comparative ethnography, or in their functioning by means of statistics.[70] Indeed, from the very inception of the *Année*, the greatest number of his reviews appeared in the sections on " juridical and moral sociology " and " criminal sociology and moral statistics." In this

70 oob, p. 648.

field, the *Année* published in 1901 his " Two Laws of Penal Evolution." Five years afterwards, he read before the French Society of Philosophy a paper on the " Determination of the Moral Fact." It turned out to be the finest expression of his ethical views to appear in his lifetime, for, unfortunately, his systematic works on Ethics and on the Family were destined to remain in fragmentary form at the time of his death. Durkheim, we must add, took an active part in the many discussions of ethical questions which took place at the meetings of the philosophical society. Thus, his contributions to juridical and moral sociology were more considerable than his published works in the field reveal.

The eminent French sociologist not only continued the two main lines of activity just mentioned, but also undertook to blaze two new trails. One led to the introduction into the sociological fold of the phenomena of religious life, the other facilitated the road towards a sociology of thought and knowledge.

A few years prior to the organization of the *Année Sociologique*, Durkheim began to devote himself to a systematic sociological analysis of religion. Under the influence of Robertson Smith and the English school of anthropologists of religion, he came to understand the crucial role that religious phenomena play in social life. In 1897, in a review of a study of the materialistic conception of history, he wrote, " Sociologists and historians tend more and more to agree on this common affirmation : that religion is the most primitive of all social phenomena. It is out of it that there have come, by successive transformations, all the other manifestations of collective activity, law, morality, art, science, political forms, etc. In the beginning, all is religious." [71] Similar views were already included in *Le Suicide* published that same year.[72] With the closing of the century Durkheim became more and more en-

71 97e, p. 650.

72 Pp. 352-53, 380-81. These pages virtually announce the theses of *Les Formes élémentaires*.

grossed in the phenomena of religion. In 1899, his preliminary definition of religious facts was published in the *Année*. Three years later, the essay on totemism appeared, to be followed shortly thereafter by an analysis of the matrimonial class system of Australia. The materials for a projected study of religion were assuming precise form. By 1909 this work was in its last stages. In that year its Introduction and what became chapters 2 and 3 were made available as articles in the *Revue de Métaphysique et de Morale* and in the *Revue Philosophique*. The large volume itself was published in 1912 under the title: *Les Formes élémentaires de la vie religieuse: Le système totémique en Australie*. The novelty of the thesis it presented gave rise to a lively discussion. The year after the book appeared, Durkheim attempted to brush away certain misunderstandings and to reaffirm his fundamental propositions by explaining the volume's basic principles in a paper, presented to the French Society of Philosophy, on the " Religious Problem and the Duality of Human Nature." The theme of this paper reappeared in 1914 in an article in *Scientia*. These studies of religion, ranging over a period of twenty years contain some of the most brilliant of Durkheim's analyses.

Closely connected with the theory of religious thought and behavior are the sociological analyses of knowledge and of the categories of the understanding. In fact, all these related theories were regarded simply as special aspects of a more general and more embracing sociological theory of thought. *Les Formes élémentaires*, it should not be forgotten, was originally entitled the " Elementary Forms of Thought and of Religious Life " and has as one of its essential theses the identity of religious thought and of social thought and consequently the social character of thought in general. At the very outset of his sociological career, Durkheim became convinced that ideas and thoughts, the ideational conceptions and theories of men were reflections of a specific type of social structure, and that consequently it was in the social organization of a given people that one was to find the explicative factors of that people's modes of viewing and conceiving things. Ideas, he felt, cannot arise anywhere, anyhow, at any time. They appear at their appointed hour, so to speak, that is, when the conditions necessary for their appearance are given.[73] Thus, he stated in the preface to the first edition of *De la Division* that "if the ancient Romans did not have the broad conception of humanity that we have today, it is not because of an error due to the narrowness of their understanding but because such ideas were incompatible with the nature of the Roman social organization (*cité*)."[74] And in 1897 he wrote that "religious conceptions are the products of the social milieu" and that "socialism expresses a state of society."[75] Previously, with reference to the revolutionary principles of 1789, he had remarked that the authority of these principles came "not from their accord with reality, but from their conformity with national aspirations."[76] But it was only after he had gone deeply into his religious researches that he perceived a means of systematically demonstrating the social origins not only of our ideas and thoughts, but of the very categories and concepts of our thinking. The essay of 1903 on "Some Primitive Forms of Classification" written with Professor Mauss as a "Contribution to the Study of Collective Representations" was an initial formulation. The Introduction to *Les Formes élémentaires* which, as we have mentioned, first appeared in 1909, was the Declaration of Principles of the sociological theory of knowledge, and, along with other sections of the volume, outlined specific analyses of such concepts as space, time, genus, force, totality, personality, and causality.[77] And shortly before the publication of the volume itself, Durkheim offered a sociological explanation of the origin of values and ideals in a paper read before

73 97e, p. 649; 86a, pp. 67-69.

74 P. xxxviii.

75 97a, p. 245; *cf.* also pp. 228-230, 244; 97d, p. 205.

76 90a, pp. 450-451.

77 *Les Formes élémentaires*, second edition, esp. pp. 1-28, 200-222, 268-292, 518-528, 609-638.

the Fourth International Congress of Philosophy at Bologna.[78] As these analyses followed one another, it became clear that a veritable rehabilitation of the study of the philosophical problems of knowledge was under way. But here too inexorable death struck inopportunely, and the ingenious and far-reaching work thus begun by Durkheim remained unfinished.[79]

We have endeavored to review briefly (and by no means exhaustively) the scope and content of Durkheim's contributions to sociological theory from 1887 to 1914. But this eminent French social scientist, it should not be forgotten, assigned to sociology a practical as well as a theoretical end. " Our researches," he wrote in his dissertation, " would not merit an hour of effort " if they had only a speculative interest. And elsewhere he remarked that science, deprived of all " practical efficacy ", would lose much of its *raison d'être*.[80] Thus, a consideration of Durkheim's contribution to social action and practice is a necessary complement to our review of his theoretical works.

7. CITIZEN

Durkheim always endeavored to use the beacon of sociological knowledge to cast light upon practical questions. He was not averse to bringing to the immediate social and political problems of his day the full force of his scientific and philosophical learning. Nor did he in whom the sense of moral duty was so strong ever shrink from his responsibilities and obligations as a citizen. Indeed, he participated actively in the multitudinous discussions of vital social matters. From the science of sociology he drew " practical consequences " on such im-

---

78 11b. For an account of the impression Durkheim made on his audience, see R M M , XXIV (1917), 749.

79 We should not like to neglect mentioning the influence of Hamelin on Durkheim's theory of knowledge. The eminent Renouvierist is, indeed, mentioned in the Introduction of *Les Formes élémentaires* (pp. 13, 15). Moreover, it should be noted that Durkheim adopted Hamelin's view that reason is essentially the categories of thought.

80 *Division*, p. xxxix; *Règles*, p. 60.

portant issues as the reorganization of the educational system, the training of statesmen and functionaries, pedagogy, religion, secularism, separation of church and state, divorce, marriage, occupational groupings, suicide, regulation of economic life, family structure, justice, crime and punishment, sex education, morality, social equality, political reform, pacificism, etc. There was hardly a social problem of the day for which Durkheim did not offer constructive suggestions. Here we can mention but a few of the ways in which he linked social theory to social engineering, or, as he called it, the art of social living.

From his analysis of the nature of the social bond in contemporary society, he developed a series of recommendations for the re-creation of occupational groups as the basis for a new social integration. This suggestion to strengthen social ties on a functional basis was first made in *Le Suicide* but was given its most systematic formulation in the preface to the second edition of *De la Division* (1902). However, it was implicit in the latter volume from the beginning.[81] Durkheim's doctoral dissertation also contains many other practical proposals. It emphasizes, of course, the significance of specialization in modern society, and hence the need to train people to assume a special function. Its analysis of the anomic condition of economic life leads to recommendations for the regulation and coordination of production, consumption, distribution, and the relations between employer and employee.[82] Economic functions, Durkheim urges, must pass from "the diffuse state in which they are to an organized state." [83] Furthermore, *"The Division of Labor in Society"* pleads for the establishment of justice and social equality through the abolition of

---

81 *Le Suicide*, esp. pp. 434-442. *De la Division*, pp. i-xxxvi; *cf.* pp. 157-167. For a good discussion of this particular recommendation for social reorganization, see Barnes, H. E., " Durkheim's Contribution to the Reconstruction of Political Theory," P S Q, XXXV (1920), 236-254. Also 37a.

82 *De la Division*, Bk. III, Chap. I.

83 93c, p. 510; *cf.* p. 512.

inheritance and hereditary class positions, and through the lifting of the barriers to free vertical social mobility.[84] To each according to his ability, Durkheim insists, so that class and status differentiation may rest not on special privilege but on organico-psychical capacity. He perceives, too, the need for social action to mitigate the injustices arising from the fact that social inequality renders free and spontaneous contracts impossible. And the temporary and unstable character of relations based on the use of physical force and constraint leads him to urge the establishment of moral understandings as the basis of national and international relationships.[85]

From his views on the nature of society and of social solidarity, Durkheim also derived a considerable number of educational and pedagogical principles. These were well brought out in the articles on *Education* and *Pedagogy* that he contributed to Buisson's *Nouveau Dictionnaire de pédagogie et d'instruction primaire*, and in the published lectures of his courses on the science of education, the history of secondary instruction in France, and moral education.[86] His view of the process of education as a "methodical socialization of the young generation" and his definition of education as "the action exercised by the adult generations on those which are not yet ripe for social life" and his insistence that the aim of education is to "create and develop in the child a certain number of physical, intellectual, and moral states which both the political society as a whole and the special milieu for which he is particularly destined demand of him" have remained justly famous.[87]

Durkheim was particularly fond of his researches on the family, and regarded the familial group as one of the most important of social institutions. He was alarmed at the trend

84 *De la Division*, Book III, Chap. II. A whole socialistic philosophy is summed up in these pages.

85 *Ibid.*; *cf.* also p. 89.

86 22a, 25a, 38a.

87 22a, p. 49.

towards facile domestic dissolution. Thus, in *Le Suicide*, he recommended a tightening of divorce regulations, urging, at the same time, an increased participation of women in social life. And when, almost a decade later, there was widespread discussion in favor of establishing divorce by mutual consent, Durkheim commandeered the statistical data of the suicide study to demonstrate the undesirable consequences of the proposal.[88]

In 1898, with the storm of the Dreyfus case bursting all around, Durkheim, who had become an energetic warrior for justice in the affair, mustered his theory of the social origins of moral values in general and of the belief in the sanctity of the human personality in particular, to inveigh against the confused views of many intellectuals.[89] He always contributed his opinion freely to the numerous investigations of the attitudes of outstanding personalities on a variety of questions ranging from war and militarism and the introduction of sociology into the secondary schools to secular ethics, religious dissolution, and separation of church and state. Moreover, whenever practical issues such as pacifism and patriotism, social equality, and sex education were discussed at the French Society of Philosophy, Durkheim did not fail to enter into the proceedings and enliven them by pertinent questions and wise observations and comments.[90]

Thus, the theoretical social scientist unravelling the intricacies of the matrimonial system of Australian tribes, or ratiocinating on the origins of the prohibition of incest and the alert citizen pondering over the immediate practical questions of social reconstruction were but two complementary aspects

88 *Le Suicide*, pp. 442-444; 06d.

89 98c. We regret not having more information about Durkheim's part in the Dreyfus case. He was among the unsung heroes of that dramatic struggle for justice and civil liberty. He exerted himself unstintingly for the liberal cause. See Kayser, J., *The Dreyfus Affair* (tr. Bickley; N. Y.: Covici, Friede, 1931), p. 183 where Durkheim's name appears among the volunteers in the "Army of Justice."

90 99b, 99c, 05b, 07c, 05e, 08a1, 10b, 11a.

of the same personality. The one necessarily supplemented the other, and, as Durkheim himself has declared, the most remote and most abstract of theoretical researches nevertheless had for him a most contemporaneous bearing.[91] This, as we shall see, was made strikingly evident with the outbreak of the World War.

8. Teacher

This eminent sociologist and devoted citizen was also an outstanding teacher. Perhaps the most fortunate circumstance in Durkheim's life was his appointment to a university position as a sociologist. This permitted him to coordinate his scientific studies with his teaching duties. He was thus spared the inconvenience of having his sociological activities interfered with by his professional tasks. For this he was ever grateful.

The externals of Durkheim's professorial career may be stated briefly. Nine years after his appointment to Bordeaux, that is, in 1896, a full professorship in social science, the first one in France, was created for him at the same university. In this " *chaire magistrale* " he continued his sociological and pedagogical work for six years more. In 1902 he was called to the University of Paris as a *chargé de cours* to substitute for Buisson who had asked to be relieved of his teaching duties to take his place in the Chamber of Deputies. Buisson occupied the chair of the Science of Education at Paris and in this chair Durkheim succeeded him in 1906. Although nominally a Professor of the Science of Education and obliged to teach courses in that field, the sociologist was nevertheless permitted to give instruction in the subject of his predilection as well. The incongruity of this situation, which required this renowned social theorist to give courses in the subject for which he was eminent from a somewhat strange chair and only by stretching a point, was mitigated in 1913 when, by a special decree of July 12th of that year, Durkheim's chair was officially changed to " Science of Education *and Sociology*." This constituted

91 12a, p. 2.

a real triumph; it was the first time that the barbaric cognomen which Comte had bestowed upon the science of society was used in the official title of a French university chair. At Bordeaux Durkheim's professorship was technically in " Social Science." He taught at Paris up to the very moment of the illness which led to his death. Thus, his university career of three decades was approximately evenly divided between Bordeaux and Paris.

Durkheim was one of those rare spirits who are endowed both with outstanding ability for scientific research and with the exacting qualities requisite for good teaching. His success at Bordeaux was immediate. Not only did the number attending his courses increase rapidly, but he attracted to sociology some of the most capable students of the university. His lectures were diligently prepared and throughout his stay at Bordeaux were written down in entirety. His manner of presenting his subject, the cogency of his demonstrations, and the eloquence of his delivery made it difficult for his listeners to escape being convinced, and, so to speak, enchanted. Of Durkheim's forcefulness one of his students has written, " Those who wished to escape his influence had to flee from his courses; on those who attended he imposed, willy-nilly, his mastery." This observation is seconded by the tribute paid to Durkheim by the late Xavier Léon in a passage the eloquence of which is hard to translate: " Ce qui explique son action, ce n'est point seulement la force dominatrice de sa pensée philosophique, la richesse des champs de travail que la nouveauté de sa méthode découvrait à la curiosité et à l'activité de ses disciples; c'était cette figure et ce corps d'ascète, la lueur étincelante de ce regard profondément enfoui dans l'orbite, le métal et l'accent de cette voix où s'exhalait une foi ardente qui, chez cet héritier des prophètes, brûlait de forger et de forcer les convictions de ses auditeurs." [92] Durkheim, so it seems from the opinion of his students, adopted in practice the suggestion he himself made in his report on the universities of Germany; that in delivering one's lectures "the care for form, the art of composition, a moderate animation are very well reconciled with the best interests of science." What he wrote of Wundt in the same report applied equally well to him: "A model of clarity and even of elegance." His students felt that they had before them one of the great heroes of human thought, "the equivalent of an Aristotle, of a Descartes, of a Spinoza or of a Kant," one of them has said.[93]

But it was hardly the sparkling eloquence of his delivery that made Durkheim a great teacher. Rather, it was the profundity and the scope of the contents of his courses and the power of his reasoning. Durkheim's courses, in fact, are the best evidence we have of his sociological interests and developments. They, much better than his published works—for publication depends upon so many contingencies—reveal what his scientific preoccupations were at a given time, in what direction his researches were heading and what his sociological orientation was at any particular period of his life. We therefore present in schematic form a *representative* list of the courses taught by Durkheim both at Bordeaux and at Paris.[94]

93 Maublanc, R., *Europe*, XXII (1930), 298.

94 The table that follows may not be absolutely accurate. We have had to compile it from indirect sources such as (1) Newsnotes in the periodicals R I E and R I S; (2) the feature "La Philosophie dans les Universités" which used to appear in the supplements of the R M M; (3) Prefaces by Mauss and Fauconnet to the posthumous works of Durkheim; (4) Mauss, M., "In memoriam: L'oeuvre inédite de Durkheim et de ses collaborateurs," A S, n. s., I (1923-24), 7-29. We had a sort of check of internal consistency when we came across the partial list of Durkheim's Bordeaux courses published in R I S, XXIII (1915), 468-469. This list tallied exactly with the one we had drawn up independently of it. We are less sure of the Paris courses. Those we have assigned to 1914-15 may well have been given in 1915-16 (see 37a). The course listed as the Social Philosophy of Comte and / or St. Simon is referred to by one source as the Social Philosophy of Comte, and by another as the Social Philosophy of St. Simon. For obvious reasons, we have stressed the sociology, rather than the pedagogy courses. The table, it must be emphasized, is representative, *not complete.*

TABLE III

A Representative List of Courses Offered by Emile Durkheim—
1887–1916

School year	Where taught	Topic of course	Nature of contents
1887-88	Bordeaux	Social Solidarity	Cf. *De la Division*
1888-89	Bordeaux	Sociology of the Family	See Davy, G., *Sociologues d'hier et d'aujourd'hui*, pp. 103-157
1889-90	Bordeaux	Suicide	See *Le Suicide*
1890-91	Bordeaux	Physiology of Law and Ethics	Cf. *De la Division*. See course for 1896-97.
1891-92	Bordeaux	The Family	See Davy, *loc. cit.* and item 21a
1892-93	Bordeaux	Criminal Sociology Pedagogy in 19th Century Psychology Applied to Education	See 38a
1893-94	Bordeaux	Criminal Sociology (cont.)	Theory of Sanctions. Cf. Fauconnet, P., *La Responsabilité*
1894-95	Bordeaux	Religion	See item 99a
1895-96	Bordeaux	History of Socialist Doctrines in France	See item 28a
1896-97	Bordeaux	General Physics of Ethics and Law	Part 1. Objective: 1. Classification of moral and judicial rules. 2. Explanation of the most important moral rules: principal penal sanctions, constitutive rules of the domestic order, of the contractual order. Part II. Subjective moral obligation as it is experienced by the subject; responsibility; moral consciousness, merit, etc.
1897-98	Bordeaux	Continuation of above course	Domestic ethics and law; occupational ethics and law

TABLE III (*Continued*)

School year	Where taught	Topic of course	Nature of contents
1898-99	Bordeaux	Continuation of above course	End of part I (objective aspect): Civic ethics. Rights and duties independent of any specific social grouping (respect for person, for property, contractual ethics and law); and part II: Subjective ethics; responsibility, moral consciousness, individual moral ideal
1899-1900	Bordeaux	Punishment and Responsibility	See 01a1; cf. Fauconnet, *op. cit.*
1900-01	Bordeaux	The Social Organization of Primitive (Australian) Societies	See 02a1, 05a1, 12a
1901-02	Bordeaux	History of Sociological Doctrines	
1902-03	Paris	Moral Education	See 25a. (This course was frequently repeated.)
1903-04	Paris	Pedagogy at the beginning of 19th century	
1904-05	Paris	History of Secondary Instruction in France	See 22a. (This course was frequently repeated.)
		Ethics	See 37a. Cf. Bordeaux course 1897-1900
1905-06	Paris	Formation and Development Secondary Instruction in France	See 38a
		Intellectual Education in the Primary School	See Fauconnet in 22a and AJS, XXVIII (1923), 545-549
1906-07	Paris	Religion: Its Origins	See 12a
1907-08	Paris	Evolution of Marriage and the Family	See Davy, *op. cit.*
1908-09	Paris	Ethics	See course of 1896-97
		History of Pedagogic Doctrines	See 18b, 19a, 38a

TABLE III (*Continued*)

School year	Where taught	Topic of course	Nature of contents
1909-10	Paris	Ethics (continued) The Great Pedagogic Doctrines from the 18th Century on	38a
1910-11	Paris	Ethics (continued)	Law of property, contractual ethics, individual ethics
1911-12	Paris	Moral Education in the School	Cf. course of 1902-03
1912-13	(Durkheim on leave from the Sorbonne)		
1913-14	Paris	Pragmatism and Sociology	The significance of sociology for philosophy, the social origins of the concept of truth
1914-15	Paris	Theoretical and Civic Ethics	See 20a, and 37a
1915-16	Paris	Social Philosophy of Comte and/or St. Simon Great Pedagogical Doctrines of 18th and 19th Centuries.	Cf. 28a

The table speaks for itself. Most of the courses have been the subject of printed volumes which were either prepared for publication by Durkheim himself or were published posthumously in lecture form. A number of them, however—and not the least significant—have not as yet been made available to the sociological public. These include the ones on Ethics, which Durkheim intended to incorporate into a *magnum opus* that he hoped would be his crowning achievement, those on the Sociology of the Family which was one of his favorite studies, those on Intellectual Education, on the History of Pedagogical Doctrines, on the History of Secondary Instruction in France, and the one in which he most fully developed the philosophical implications of sociology, Pragmatism and Sociology. Professor Mauss holds out the hope that we may yet see some of these courses in print.   (Note, indeed, item 38a.)

We should like to single out, as of special significance in Durkheim's sociological development, the courses on Religion, Ethics, and Pragmatism. The one on religion (1894-95) had a most decisive influence on him. " It was only in 1895," he wrote in reply to a critic, " that I had a clear understanding of the capital role played by religion in social life. It was in that year that, for the first time, I found the means of approaching the study of religion sociologically. It was a revelation to me. The course of 1895 marks a line of demarcation in the development of my thought; so much so, that all my previous researches had to be taken up again with renewed efforts in order to be placed in harmony with these new views." This change of orientation was attributed by Durkheim " to the studies of religious history I had just undertaken, and notably to the reading of the works of Robertson Smith and his school." [95]

It is important in this connection to note that the change of emphasis on Durkheim's part came rather early in his career, that is, just shortly after the appearance of *De la Division* and prior to the publication of *Le Suicide*.

As for the lectures on Ethics which contained the very soul of Durkheim, we can best indicate their nature by reproducing the titles of those which were destined, in whole or in part, or in summary form, to be included in his *Morale:* [96]

> Object of the Course: Traditional Conception of Ethics.
> Critique of Traditional Ethics.
> Critique of the Conception which makes Ethics Something
>   completely Subjective.
> Critique of the Theory of Tarde.
> The Question and the Kantian Solution.
> Critique of the Kantian Ethics.
> Value Judgment and Ideal (Sociological Idealism).

95 07b, p. 613. *Cf.* Introductory note to Bibliography, below.
96 The list is given by Mauss, item 20a, p. 80. See also 37a.

The Individual Moral Consciousness and Objective Ethics (Ethics and Moral Consciousness).

Objective and Subjective Point of View. (Sentiment of Justice, Idea of Justice).

Relation of Public Ethics and Individual Ethics (autonomy and the Kantian Solution).

Collective Type and Average Type.

Unity of the Two Elements (Ideal and Duty).

How Can We Attach Ourselves to Society?

Opening Lecture of Course on Domestic Ethics.

Divorce.

Three Zones of Kinship.

Property: The Kantian Theory.

Consensual Contract and Sanctions.

What a monumental study these titles promise! They lay bare the full extent of the irreparable loss brought about by Durkheim's death.

This loss is the more emphasized by the failure to retrieve any publishable material from the course Pragmatism and Sociology. A philosopher by initial training, Durkheim had hoped that the science of sociology, in its fullest maturity, would become an indispensable tool for philosophical ratiocination, and would open up many an unexpected vista to the surveyors of philosophical horizons. At the very beginning, however, the science, in order to be firmly grounded, had to be freed from metaphysical biases. Our sociological method, Durkheim wrote in concluding Les Règles, " is independent of all philosophy." But after fifteen years of sociological effort, with the era of specialization definitely launched, with the Année an established institution, it seemed feasible to drop the haughty attitude of isolation, and even of hostility, and to enter into more friendly relations with philosophy.[97] The

97 Cf. Davy who speaks of Durkheim as having passed from "an attitude of war to one of armed peace with regard to adverse doctrines." Davy, G., Emile Durkheim, p. 44.

bridges could now be let down from the sociological castle and the deep moats that had been dug around it could now be re-filled. Sociology, Durkheim announced in 1903, will return with accumulated interest to philosophy what it has borrowed from it and will create a common body of doctrines which will become the subject-matter of a renewed and rejuvenated social philosophy that will be positive and progressive.[98] Our specific, scientific, sociological knowledge of man, he felt, must necessarily be organized and synthesized if it is to be rationally utilizable. It must, in other words, lead quite inevitably to a synthetic philosophy of man, human nature, and society. Durkheim thus conceived of a sociological philosophy as one of the end-products of social investigation. This philosophy is generally referred to today as *sociologism*. It may be defined as the effort to crown the special, objective, and comparative studies to which social scientists consecrate themselves with an explicative theory of human nature in its various aspects.[99]

In Durkheim's conception, then, sociology is to be both a positive, rigorous special science, and a philosophical system. To this view, ever implicit in his works, he gave precise formulation in 1909 in the conclusion of the article on " Religious Sociology and Theory of Knowledge." [100] Here Durkheim explains that because he has endeavored methodically to liberate sociology from any philosophical tutelage that might prevent it from becoming constituted as a positive science, he has been accused of being systematically hostile towards philosophy. Such an attitude, he protests, is not his, and surely it is hardly sociological. " For the sociologist must posit as axiomatic

98 03c, pp. 496-497.

99 *Cf.* Bouglé, C., in 24a, p. viii.

100 09d. This essay was written, as we have already said, as the Introduction to *Les Formes élémentaires.* However, when the volume appeared, the last section of the article, the one in which Durkheim explained his views on the relation of sociology both to psychology and to philosophy, was not reproduced. See 09d, pp. 754-758.

that questions which have held an important place in history can never be superannuated; they can be transformed, they cannot perish. Therefore, it is inadmissible that metaphysical questions—even the most audacious of them—which have disturbed philosophers can ever fall into neglect. But it is equally certain that they are required to be recast anew. Now, precisely, *we believe that sociology, more than any other science, can contribute to this recasting.*" [101]

Durkheim justifies assigning this role to sociology on the ground that it fulfills the requirement of being " a science which, while being sufficiently restricted to be able to be grasped by one and the same mind, occupies, nevertheless, a position central enough to be able to furnish the basis for a unitary, and hence philosophical, speculation." Since sociology permits the philosopher to perceive the unity of things, it is, of all the disciplines, the most useful of propaedeutics. [102]

More precisely, Durkheim goes on to show, sociology and philosophy are linked through the theory of the categories of the understanding. If these categories cannot be adequately accounted for by interrogating the individual mind, but really have the social origin attributed to them, then " it is necessary, if one wishes to philosophize on things and not on words, to begin by facing them squarely, as one faces unknown realities whose nature, causes and functions it is necessary to determine before seeking to integrate them into a philosophical system." Consequently, numerous specific researches which fall within the jurisdiction of sociology need to be undertaken. This science is thus " destined to furnish philosophy with the bases which are indispensable to it and which it at present lacks. One may even say that sociological reflection is required to be continued, out of its own material and by its natural development, in the form of philosophical reflection; and everything permits us to presume that, approached from this angle,

101 *Ibid.*, p. 756, italics ours. *Cf.* 11d, p. vii.
102 09d, pp. 756-757.

the problems treated by the philosopher will reveal more than one unexpected aspect." [103]

These propositions Durkheim developed more fully in his lectures on Pragmatism. Since the course endeavored to explain the principles of the "Anglo-American" doctrine and to evaluate them in the light of the philosophical position which, in Durkheim's opinion, our sociological knowledge demands of us, it was necessary for the lecturer to formulate explicitly the tenets and postulates of this sociological philosophy. This Durkheim did. Among other things, he outlined a sociological explanation of the concept of truth, by means of which he attempted to bridge the gap between mythological constructs and the exigencies of science.[104] A considerable portion of the lectures was devoted, among others, to Dewey, for whom the French theorist had great admiration.[105] This course was the philosophical crowning of Durkheim's life work. In it, this "metaphysician who clipped his own wings," as Maublanc says, for once let himself go and fully indulged his taste for systematic construction. Organizing the scattered data in his works, he revealed clearly the bases of his system.[106]

The materials here presented can give but a meager picture of Durkheim's significant position as a university professor. They should suffice, however, as an indication that France's eminent sociologist and distinguished citizen also exercised a great influence in the classroom and lecture hall.

103 *Ibid.*, p. 758.

104 See Lenoir, R., M F, CXXVII (1918), 588-589.

105 On Dewey and Durkheim, *cf.* Jyan, Choy, *Etude comparative sur les doctrines pédagogiques de Durkheim et de Dewey* (Lyon: Bose frères et Riou, 1926). Jyan opposes the "psycho-pedagogical" position of Dewey to the "socio-pedagogical" one of Durkheim.

106 Maublanc, *loc. cit.*, p. 298. Durkheim's most pertinent contributions to sociologism are 12a, 06b, 11b, 14a, 13b.

9. Pro patria Mori

Our method of taking Durkheim the man and abstracting for purposes of exposition the sociologist, the citizen, and the professor becomes unnecessary once we arrive at the outbreak of the World War. For with the declaration of war, Durkheim the sociologist, and Durkheim the professor begin to occupy a rather insignificant place alongside of Durkheim the Frenchman. True, he found time in 1915 to write a brief review of French Sociology for the San Francisco Exposition and he continued to give his lectures at the Sorbonne until illness overtook him in 1916, but his heart and soul were with his country and her perils, and to her he devoted all his energies, and even, indirectly, gave his life.

However, it was as a teacher and a sociologist that he could serve his country best, and in these two capacities he gave himself over to patriotic and propaganda work. As a teacher, he energetically participated in the activities of moral encouragement, or "moral refreshment," as he termed it. By oral as well as by written word—for he well appreciated the power of oratory and was himself an admirable speaker—he endeavored to teach the nation the necessity and the virtue of "patience, effort, and confidence." As a sociologist, he interpreted the contemporary events for the people, endeavoring to be ever scrupulous to apply the rigorous methods of scientific analysis, and to support assertions with facts and documents.

He was responsible for, and became secretary of, the Committee for the Publication of Studies and Documents on the War. Lavisse was the Committee's president, and among its members were such illustrious personages as Charles Andler, Bédier, Bergson, Boutroux, Lanson and Seignobos. The principal object of the studies published by this Committee was "to depict Germany as the war has revealed her to us." [107] One of the first pamphlets issued was written by Durkheim in collaboration with Professor Denis and fixed upon Germany

---

107 Durkheim, 15c, English translation, p. 3.

the blame for wanting the war. " Like all historical events, the present war depends in some measure," these authors wrote, " on causes of a profound and remote nature. . . . But whatever may be the importance of these impersonal causes (demographic, economic, ethnic, etc.), they cannot act by themselves; they can only produce their effect through the will of man. When war breaks out it is because some State wishes for war and that State must bear the responsibility." [108] Though we cannot today accept Durkheim's assertion that he has given us " a complete and objective account of events," — he himself acknowledged the unavailability of many diplomatic documents—nevertheless we must admire the ingenious and convincing manner in which he developed his case. Davy is certainly right in comparing the " subtle ingeniousness " of this brief with that of the study in which Durkheim unravelled " the inextricable complications of Australian marriage systems." [109]

In the same series Durkheim also published a study of German mentality which purported to explain the morbid and pathological character of " the mental and moral system " which is summed up in the famous slogan: *Deutschland Über Alles*. The author bases his description of this mentality chiefly on the writings of Treitschke whom he regards as a " preeminently representative personality.." Durkheim's conclusion is that " we are clearly in the presence of a case of social pathology." [110] In the course of his analysis, he makes a number of revealing comments on the nature of the state and of its relations to society. These remarks indicate a new orientation on his part with respect to political problems. In fact, we learn from Professor Mauss that Durkheim's ideas on the

108 15b, English translation, p. 3. For a discussion of the theory of social causation here implied see Part II.

109 Davy, R M M, XXVI (1919), p. 190.

110 15c, English translation, pp. 4, 5, 46. One is struck with the similarity in many pages between the views of Treitschke and those of Pareto. *Cf. ibid.*, esp. pp. 18-26.

State had evolved and that he had modified certain portions
of his political theory as a result of his study of the Treitschke
doctrines.[111] The sovereignty which we ordinarily attribute to
the state, we find Durkheim writing in this pamphlet on German mentality, is always merely relative. "We well know
that in fact the State depends upon a multitude of moral forces
which, though they may not have a form and organization
absolutely juridical, are nonetheless real and effective. It depends upon treaties it has signed, upon moral principles which
its duty is to see respected, principles which it must therefore
itself respect. It depends upon the goodwill of its subjects and
the goodwill of foreign nationalities, which it is obliged to
take into consideration." He gives even more succinct formulation to this notion. "There is something which is generally
accepted as superior to the State: this is morality. Morality
is no doubt merely a matter of ideas; but these ideas are forces
which move and dominate men. If it (the state) is under their
authority, its sovereignty has limits which it is not within its
competence to transgress at will." On the relation of the State
to the people, that is to the general body of its citizens, Durkheim has this to say: "In a democratic society, the People
and the State are merely two aspects of a single reality. The
State is the people awakened to a consciousness of itself, of
its needs and its aspirations — a more complete and definite
consciousness." Society, he goes on to show, exists prior to
the state. The latter, in fact, presupposes the former. Thus, he
defines a nationality as "a group of human beings who for
ethnical, or perhaps merely for historical reasons, desire to
live under the same laws, and to form a single state, large or
small as it may be." [112]

Aside from the political doctrines therein expressed, this
study has significance also as a contribution to the sociology
of thought. For Durkheim, in an all too brief passage offers
an explanation of the origin and ideology of Pan-Germanism.

111 Mauss, M., A S, n s., I, p. 9.
112 15c, English translation, pp. 7, 18, 27, 30, 40.

Germany, he states, created this myth which represents it as "the highest terrestrial incarnation of divine power" in order to explain to itself "the ebullition of energy of which she was conscious." The myth, then, is only the expression of a spiritual state which is its cause and which may be defined as: "a morbid hypertrophy of the will, a kind of will-mania." [113] We see, then, that although his war pamphlets were primarily propagandistic in purpose, Durkheim offers in them many suggestive ideas for social theory.

The publication of these studies was only one of the many tasks he created for himself. He undertook also to publish a series of "Letters to All Frenchmen" with the purpose of keeping up the nation's morale in the face of the disastrous defeats on the Eastern Front in the summer of 1915. Here, too, he was secretary of the Committee on Publication. He contributed several of the letters and in the first one created the motto: *Patience, Effort, Confidence* which became the slogan of the entire series. Other contributors were Lavisse, General Malleterre, Denis, Meillet, Cazamian, and Admiral Degouy. The preface to the letters is not signed, but we may suspect Durkheim's influence in its insistence that recourse be had to "facts, figures, and documents."

There was no restraining Durkheim in the performance of his duties to his country. As a member of the Council of the University of Paris, he conceived and undertook to organize a cooperative volume which aimed to explain and make familiar to the many foreigners in France, and particularly to Americans, the university life of Paris. He himself wrote several of the chapters in the book which appeared only after his death.[114] In addition, he served on a considerable number of committees and councils, ranging from one in the Ministry of the Interior to societies on Franco-American Fraternity, Uni-

113 *Ibid.*, pp. 43-44.
114 18a.

versity Rapprochement, For the Jews in Neutral Countries, and the Republican League of Alsace-Lorraine.[115]

During all this time, and in the midst of these truly hectic and feverish activities, Durkheim had to bear an additional worry—the safety of his son, André. André Durkheim who was fighting on the Eastern Front had already been wounded once. The father was deeply troubled. Then, just before Christmas, 1915, word came of the son's death in a Bulgarian hospital. He had been wounded again while commanding a section of the extreme rear guard during the retreat from Serbia. The death of André was a crushing blow from which Durkheim never recovered. It is no exaggeration to say that it hastened his own end. André was more than a son to him. He was his pupil, one of the brightest among them, and one of his most promising disciples as well. André Durkheim had begun to study linguistics under the late Professor Meillet, and was destined to become the " purely sociological linguist " that the *Année* so sorely needed. The father tried to keep his overpowering grief private. He practically never spoke of his son's death, and his friends were forbidden to mention it in his presence. He mourned silently and stoically, but his sorrow gnawed away his strength.

He tried to keep up his indefatigable services for his nation. Meetings had to be attended, discussions had to be resolved, and above all the morale of the nation had to be strengthened and rejuvenated. Patience, Effort, Confidence. To Durkheim, these were not mere words, they were a living reality. *He* lived them. But in December, 1916, sickness overcame him. He had had his first attack on leaving one of the numerous meetings where important questions about the war were being discussed and where he never failed to give of himself as much as he could.

He knew this was the end. He began to rearrange his papers and manuscripts so as to facilitate their publication. In the

115 See the list given by Davy, *loc. cit.*, p. 193.

summer of 1917, at Fontainebleau, where he was staying, he summoned all his energies in a final and supreme effort to write down the opening paragraphs of his never-to-be-completed work on Ethics.[116] A few months later, on November 15th, he passed away at the age of fifty-nine and a half, and with most of his work still ahead of him.

10. Exegi Monumentum

But as if to indicate that physical death is no barrier to the activities of the spirit, his name continued to appear over articles and books. The notes on Rousseau which he had designated for Xavier Léon were published in 1918 and 1919 in the *Revue de Métaphysique et de Morale*. The *Revue Philosophique* printed not only the " Introduction to Ethics " to which reference has just been made, but also the closing lecture of his course on the family. His lectures on the "History of Socialism " also made their appearance. Four significant posthumous volumes have been published. Two are collections of articles that have previously appeared in periodicals, one is Durkheim's course on Moral Education, and the fourth is the series of lectures on Socialism. One anxiously awaits additions to this list of posthumous studies from Durkheim's pen. Only this year (1937) the *Revue de Métaphysique et de Morale* has begun publication of Durkheim's lectures on " La Morale professionelle " while the *Revue d'Histoire politique et constitutionelle* has printed a French translation of his Latin thesis on Montesquieu.[117]

And so, his spirit moves forward. The torch has been passed on; it continues to be carried high. The French Institute of Sociology, the *Année Sociologique*, now the *Annales Sociologiques,* and the ever-growing number of volumes in the collection of the *Année* attest to this. One need only glance at Professor Bouglé's balance sheet to be convinced of it.[118]

116 20a.

117 To this list of posthumous works must be added the two volumes of *Pedagogical Evolution in France* (38a).

118 Bouglé, C., *Bilan de la sociologie française contemporaine* (Paris: Alcan, 1935).

Such was the life of Emile Durkheim who by the force of his own powers hewed out a new discipline and gave it form and shape. He made thereby an indelible place for himself in the history not only of sociology, but of all human thought.

Social science has found it necessary to correct him on several scores, and will no doubt have to continue to do so in the future, but it can never be too grateful for the impetus he gave it, the new horizons he revealed to it, and the unexplored regions he charted for it. Emile Durkheim lives as a vital and integral part of the heritage of contemporary sociology.

PART II

DURKHEIM'S CONCEPTION OF THE NATURE, METHOD, AND SCOPE OF SOCIOLOGY

I. INTRODUCTION

EMILE DURKHEIM'S place of eminence among the great sociologists of the pre-war generation is hardly disputed. In America, as elsewhere, his significance in the history of sociology is firmly established. We may not have gone so far (as an English periodical did shortly after his death) as to acclaim him the greatest sociologist in the world since Spencer's passing away, but we too have been lavish in recognizing his greatness. It is therefore surprising to find that some of his most fertile ideas have taken but little hold in this country. His conception of the scope of sociology, for example, has been, for the most part, politely ignored.[1] On this account, and because, as Durkheim taught, the root questions of a science need to be subjected to constant analysis, it will not be amiss to reexamine this French social theorist's conception of the nature, scope, and method of the science to which he contributed a wealth of fertile ideas and suggestive researches. Such a reexamination will help to determine to what extent contemporary sociology may well profit from an excursion among the principles, thoughts, and ideas of France's distinguished social scientist.

We shall be concerned here chiefly with the manner in which Durkheim conceived of sociology as a theoretical discipline, rather than with his views of it as a guide to social action and as a philosophical system. In Durkheim's conception, sociology, as a systematic body of theoretical principles, is a nat-

1 We may mention, however, the recently founded *Journal of Social Philosophy* which, in Durkheimian spirit, is devoted to a synthesis of the social sciences.

ural, objective, specific yet synthetic, collective, independent and unitary science of social facts. Each of these terms requires explanation. Although we are going to discuss them one by one, we shall endeavor not to lose sight of their essential interrelationship.

2. A Natural Science: Causes, Functions, Becauses

Viewing sociology as a natural science implies accepting the following principles:

(1) Social facts are in nature, i. e. have distinctive empirical properties and form real systems.

(2) They are linked by necessary general relations deriving from their very nature; they are, in other words, subject to the same principle of determinism that has been so fruitfully postulated by all the sciences.

(3) We can therefore uncover invariant relations, i. e. laws, which express the necessary bonds between social phenomena, or between social facts and other forces which act upon them.

(4) Moreover, we can establish between certain of these phenomena relations of causation and of interdependence.

(5) And, in discovering the nature of social phenomena, the laws of their behavior, and the patterns of their development and changes, we must use the methods of accurate observation, logical validation, and systematic generalization that are characteristic of the scientific approach.

To accept these principles is to admit that sociology is a natural science. However, such acceptance in no way commits one to any particular philosophy of social reality other than the philosophy of science that is implied in these very principles. Whether social life is essentially psychical or material, whether or not it refers to an inner realm of experience, whether we can or cannot understand its operations without reference to human volition and valuation are important questions but as such do not enter into the problem of whether or not social phenomena are natural, i. e. belong to a determinate and determined realm of nature. Rather, these questions have reference to what that nature is, which is quite a different matter. Hence, the controversy over whether sociology is a " natural " or a " social " science, as it has been waged in America, is irrelevant to the notion of naturalness as we have just defined it. For the protagonists on neither side have, as far as we know, denied, in this sense, the naturalness of social data. In fact, such a denial would necessarily involve denying altogether a science of sociology, for whoever refers to science must refer to a realm of natural data which that science investigates. That social phenomena are necessary, determinate, and natural is, then, the very first of the first principles of a science of society.

When Durkheim enunciated this proposition almost a half-century ago, it evoked furious opposition in many quarters. A defeated France, smarting under the humiliating treaty of Frankfort seemed to remember little the glorious tradition of Montesquieu and Condorcet, of St. Simon and Auguste Comte. Part of the nation, its eyes fixed towards *Sacré Coeur* and divine intervention,[2] had small patience with those who like Taine proclaimed that vice and virtue were as natural products as sugar and vitriol.[3] It scorned an Espinas who attempted to demonstrate that society, human and animal, was a natural reality amenable to scientific investigation. Today the debates of forty years ago seem rather futile, for we are inclined to accept the naturalness of social life as self-evident. Of course, the acceptance of this postulate does not by any means settle the fundamental problems of methodology which social science faces; it merely gives rise to these questions.

2 See Sabatier, P., *L'Orientation religieuse de la France actuelle* (2nd ed., Paris: Colin), esp. pp. 46-52. Sabatier even speaks of certain months in 1871 during which " the vast majority of Frenchmen were instinctively drawn back to the Church of their birth " (pp. 48-49).

3 Taine never meant—it was only his critics who invented the meaning—that one must study vice and virtue as chemical entities, which is pure nonsense.

One of the methodological consequences that Durkheim derived from the principle of the naturalness of social life is summed up in his famous, but not altogether unambiguous rule to consider social facts as things.[4] This rule, like the dictum of Taine mentioned above, has been subjected to numerous interpretations completely unauthorized by its author and frequently in direct contradiction to his intended meaning. To treat social facts as things, Durkheim explained in the preface to the second edition of *Les Règles*,[5] means simply to adopt a certain frame of mind in undertaking to study them. It implies assuming that social data are unknowns, that is, that we do not know anything about them with any certainty prior to our investigations. It requires us to be on guard against our prenotions, prejudices, and preconceptions.[6] It means that we are to distrust our personal past experience, to become wary of consulting our own consciousnesses for real knowledge and of accepting that knowledge as verified truth merely because we have found it in our consciousness. The rule, in sum, only urges us to adopt an attitude of mature skepticism with regard to what we think we already know about social facts on the basis of our own sentiments, feelings, thoughts and rationalizations, and to accept as a matter of principle, and as a working hypothesis, the proposition that the phenomena we are studying have properties which we do not yet know, which we cannot possibly suspect, and which all our introspection and ratiocination cannot uncover in advance.

Thus interpreted—and Durkheim himself is the interpreter—the rule is, as its promulgator admitted, only a truism. To Durkheim it implied, however, a complete break with the type of sociologizing which was prevalent up to the last decade of

4 *Règles*, Chap. II. For discussion of Durkheim's use of the word *chose* see below.

5 Pp. xi-xiv; *cf.* 09e, p. 284.

6 We cannot, as Durkheim proposes, make complete *tabula rasa* of them and discard them completely. *Règles*, p. 40; 09e, p. 284. We can only try to become conscious of them and, as much as possible, to discount them.

the nineteenth century. This was an *a priori* mode of analysis of social life characterized by the arbitrary creation of concepts whose validity and reality were scarcely doubted, and about which deductions were made on the basis of an *ad hoc* conception of the laws of human nature. Now, Durkheim refused to accept any notion of " man as he had to be " in order that a particular metaphysical or philosophical doctrine might be vindicated. By his rule he required consulting the data of history and ethnology for a theory of human conduct which would describe man as he really is. The rule also demanded that our scientifically established concepts (which as concepts are necessarily abstractions) should be made precise and definite and follow the articulations of reality, instead of being ideas which arouse in us " only confused notions, and indistinct mixtures of vague impressions, prejudices and passions." [7]

The principle of the naturalness of social facts, which Durkheim adopted " not as a rational necessity but only as an empirical postulate, product of a legitimate induction " [8] also raises a number of questions concerning the nature of cause. For the postulate of determinism implies a principle of causation and hence requires the working out of a scheme of causal analysis.

Durkheim took the principle of causality for granted.[9] To him there could be no science which did not attempt to establish causal relations. Today, however, the concept of cause has fallen somewhat into disrepute. A number of physicists and astonomers turned philosophers have driven it from the laboratories of the physical sciences. Some writers have claimed that we cannot go beyond establishing correlations. A Vilfredo Pareto has urged that we give up the notion of causality entirely and instead search for functional interdependence. Others, assuming that causal relations can be only physical, have hast-

7 *Règles*, p. 29.
8 *Ibid.*, p. 173.
9 *Ibid.*, pp. 51, 53, 74, 157, 173.

ened to exclude them from sociology lest they contaminate and vitiate the ideational and valuational character of the social facts. Still others, confusing the *cause* of a social phenomenon, that is, the necessary and efficient conditions which have brought it about, with its *because*, that is, the effective motivations of the individuals involved, have argued that only " becauses " should be considered as the sufficient causes of human behavior. In the face of these variant doctrines, it will be helpful to reconsider the Durkheimian position on the matter of causation.

Durkheim's doctrine of causality may be summed up in the following propositions:

(1) Sociology cannot dispense with the principle of causality, which, though it is only a postulate, has nevertheless proved itself a workable one.[10]

(2) The complexity of sociological data requires us frequently to establish not a simple cause and effect relation, but an intricate causational situation.

(3) In social causational situations, we must include among the causal factors, the axiological significances attributed to things by human beings. By axiological significances we mean the ideals and values of human beings which, in a given situation, give direction to their behavior. However, axiological significances do not exist in a void. They too are effects of causes and must be related to these latter.

The first of these principles does not need elaborate discussion. The history of sociology, with its cumulative evidence of social uniformities, has amassed overwhelming empirical arguments in its favor. As for the second and third, we can best clarify them by describing a concrete example of their application. The illustration we have chosen is the causal explanation that Durkheim has offered for the progressive preponderance of the role of the division of labor in the course of social

10 *Cf.* Znaniecki, F., *The Method of Sociology* (New York: Farrar and Rinehart, 1934), p. 303.

evolution.[11] It should be emphasized that we are concerned here only with the *schema* of analysis and not with the accuracy of the particular explanation given.

It is generally assumed that Durkheim's causal theory of the division of labor is a somewhat mechanical one.[12] The responsibility for this interpretation rests upon Durkheim himself. He deliberately set out to give his theory as mechanistic a tone as possible. He hoped thereby to strengthen his case in his effort to demonstrate the possibility of approaching social and moral phenomena in the manner of the positive sciences. However, even though he explicitly stated that his theory is "*mécanique*" and that the causal sequences follow one another "mechanically"—"*tout se passe mécaniquement*", he reiterated,—it can nevertheless be demonstrated that, in Durkheim's usage, the term "mechanical" only expresses (misleadingly, of course) the notion of *necessary sequence within a given axiological system* and that it in no way excludes reference to human will and valuation. Indeed, did not Durkheim write that "a mechanistic conception of society does not exclude the ideal"?[13] Thus, we may accept Merton's statement that Durkheim sought to determine "those mechanically induced laws which under given conditions obtain with ineluctable necessity,"[14] but only with the proviso that the phrase "under given conditions" be changed to read "under given axiological conditions," and that the word "mechanistically" be substituted for "mechanically." For the point we are making, to put the matter another way, is that Durkheim's view of social causation, while mechanistic, i. e. deterministic, is not on that account mechanical, i. e. physical. Our later discussion of *Le Suicide* will reaffirm this distinction which, we may note here, is implicit in Durkheim's belief in sociological laws, i. e.

11 *De la Division,* Book II.

12 *Cf.* Merton, R., "Durkheim's Division of Labor in Society," A J S, XL (1934), 319-328.

13 *De la Division,* p. 331. *Cf.* the above quotation from *Who Wanted War?*

14 Merton, *op. cit.,* p. 319.

laws (mechanistic view) that are *socially sui generis* (non-mechanical). It is therefore more accurate to translate " *méca-nique*," wherever it is used by Durkheim to refer to social causation, as mechanistic, not as mechanical. It is for this reason that we have placed the latter term in quotation marks in this paragraph.

After having established in Book I of his dissertation that the course of social evolution reveals a change from the type of society which is significantly held together by bonds of similitude to a type wherein the essential social tie is created on a functional basis, Durkheim goes on, in Book II, to inquire into the causes and conditions of this historical change. The terms " causes and conditions " are Durkheim's, and their use in the plural indicates immediately that we are dealing with a complex causational situation.

Our first step in causal analysis is to define specifically what it is we are trying to explain. We must make clear with what aspect of our problem we are concerned, for it is impossible to treat a phenomenon in all its empirical manifestations and ramifications. Causal analysis is conceptual analysis and conceptual analysis, being rational, necessarily involves selection. Hence, what is selected, and how it is selected must be made explicit. In the particular case under consideration, Durkheim declares that his intention is to deal with the division of labor as a general fact; that is, he will investigate not the specific ways in which the phenomenon has developed in any particular time and place but rather its general development in the course of history.

We start, then, by defining our causal problem. This precept seems too obvious to need explicit formulation. Yet the failure to observe it has led to serious methodological impasses, as, for example, the dilemma of the " plurality of causes " which proved such a stumbling-block to John Stuart Mill, the " fallacy of misplaced concreteness " described by Whitehead, and the question of the theoretical significance of the " exception " which has been recently broached by Znaniecki.

The next step is to subject existing causal explanations to a critical review. This critical analysis is to be made on both rational and empirical grounds. It may be shown either that a theory rests on logical and rational difficulties such as illogical reasoning, incorrect assumptions, or untenable consequences or that it does not conform, and cannot be made to conform, with the actual data on hand. Durkheim, for instance, takes up the view which explains division of labor as caused by the desire of man to increase his happiness. He first examines its assumed axioms, which he finds untenable. Then, he proceeds to inquire whether, as a matter of fact, there *is* a positive correlation between increased happiness and increased division of labor. The evidence, he endeavors to show, tends to support the contrary view that if any correlation exists at all, it is more negative than positive. Thus, in the light of both rational and empirical considerations, this theory is eliminated.

One recognizes here a characteristic feature of Durkheim's style, what we may call the *argumentum per eliminationem*. We find it in all his major works. In *Le Suicide*, Book I is devoted to eliminating psychopathic, psychological, biological, and cosmic theories of suicide, and in *Les Formes élémentaires*, the second and third chapters purport to reveal the inadequacies of the theories of animism and naturism. The method of elimination is a mode of argumentation which has decided stylistic advantages, but at the same time is fraught with logical dangers. Durkheim's masterful use of it is in large part responsible, we feel, for the purely esthetic enjoyment one derives from a reading of his works. The argument by elimination has the advantage of being psychologically appealing and convincing. It clears away the debris of the older views and at the same time lays down the foundation for the new structure. The latter basks in the glory indirectly cast upon it by the ignominious destruction of the previously established theories. As these crumble, the new view impresses itself more firmly in our minds. But, if it plays the role of being psychologically seductive, the *argumentum per eliminationem* is not on that account any less logically dangerous, and must be tested to see whether it can stand up on the logical thin ice on which it rests. The argument is based on two implied premises. The first is that the theories eliminated include *all* the possible explanations *save one*. However, it is extremely rare that a study is so exhaustive that all possible alternatives are examined. This objection is surely applicable to the case we are discussing. Durkheim critically reviews only two alternative theories, the happiness explanation just mentioned, and the theory that explains division of labor in terms of a desire for new experiences which arises from the need to salvage already existing pleasures from the corrosive effects of repeated satisfactions and indulgences. Durkheim in general tends to be rather high-handed in his readiness to dismiss alternative views.[15]

The second implied premise of the argument by elimination is that the factors treated as possible causes are mutually exclusive. It is assumed that the causes must, for instance, be *either* cosmic *or* psychological, *or* biological, *or* social. However, eliminating the first three does not warrant an unqualified acceptance of the last. For, in addition to trying to treat each factor separately, as if it were sufficient unto itself, we must endeavor to consider them in their interrelations, since there always remains the possibility that the causal factor is not any one of the alternatives taken singly, but several of them in interdependence and interaction. In other words, the argument: either a, or b, or c, or d; not a, b, c; therefore d is not conclusive, since one must also take cognizance of the possibility: a *and* b *and* c *and* d. Moreover, a, b, c and d may be but different expressions of the same thing and hence not have the independence with respect to one another that is often assumed. Thus, several of Durkheim's disciples have revolted against the master's brute type of analysis and have proposed a soci-

15 One of the most thorough examples of a study which adequately subjects alternative explanations to critical review is the late Professor Simiand's work on *Le Salaire, l'évolution sociale, et la monnaie* (Paris: Alcan, 1932). But this three-volumed opus was the result of more than thirty years of labor.

ology of "total phenomena," that is of social phenomena which are viewed not as being either religious or judicial or economic, but rather as being at the same time religious *and* judicial *and* economic, *and* moral, *and* magical *and* legal, etc.[16]

Having defined our problem and having eliminated prior causal theories, we are in a position to procede to the more positive part of our task. We begin with the process we are trying to explain, in this case, with the fact that the regular development of functional social structures, and consequently of the division of labor, is directly related to the breaking up of the segmentary types of social structures.[17] This direct and regular relationship between the two phenomena permits us to assume that there *may* be a causal connection between them. We use this assumption as a starting point and as a working hypothesis.

(This is our own statement of position, not Durkheim's. The latter is far more positive. From the fact that the division of labor develops regularly as segmentary structures are effaced, he deduces that either the effacement is the cause of this development or the latter is the cause of the former.[18] Such a deduction, however, is a clear violation of Durkheim's own rule that correlation is not causation. Therefore, we have taken the liberty of modifying his position in the above manner. We have done this on the principle that unless correlations are proved on theoretical grounds to be spurious or purely accidental, as e. g. a correlation between the rate of growth of the membership of a trade union in the United States and the rate of increase in the number of telephone poles in Persia, they may be taken as guide-posts to causation. It may be presumed that by following them through and analyzing them further, we shall be placed on the road to causal nexuses.)

16 *Cf*. Mauss, M., "Le Don," A S, n. s., I, pp. 30-186; Halbwachs, M., *Les Causes du Suicide* (Paris : Alcan, 1930) ; and Bonnafous, M., "La Sociologie et l'étude des phénomenes totaux," R T A, March, 1926, pp. 35-54.

17 For this terminology, see *De la Division*, Book I, chap. VI.

18 *Ibid.*, p. 237.

Thus, we may say that either the division of labor (a) is the cause of the breaking up of segmentary structures (b) or *vice versa*. This does not preclude the possibility of an inter-action between cause and effect. Once a cause has produced an effect the latter may react on the former and become itself, in some respects, the cause of its cause. But this can only be a subsequent development since the effect, before it can become a cause, must first be an effect.

It is possible from the start to eliminate the first of the above alternatives; (a) cannot be the cause of (b) because the first process cannot become operative until the second one has already begun. Therefore, (b) is the cause of (a). (Al-ways on the assumption that our either-or proposition is valid.) But our causal chain is hardly complete. We must find out what actions are involved in, and what consequences are en-tailed by, the breaking up of segmentary structures. We must, in other words, make explicit what in this breaking up process gives rise to the growth of the division of labor. Now this breaking up, we know, implies bringing individuals together and getting them into more intimate contacts with one another. It involves greater interaction among individuals, and this, in turn, means increases in the quantity, intensity, and diversity of social relationships. Durkheim calls the re-sultant of these multiple aspects of social interaction " moral or dynamic density." It is preferable to use the more usual and, surely, less equivocal expression " degree of social inter-action." However, it should be kept in mind that either phrase, when applied to a given society, refers to the number and frequency of the social contacts, to the number of qualitatively different types of social relations, and to the degree of inti-macy of the social relationships which prevail in that society at any given time.

We may now state our causal relationship more precisely: the cause of the development of the division of labor is an increase in the degree of social interaction, or, to use the

Durkheimian expression, of moral density.[19] This is a preliminary and tentative statement of causal connection. It is based on the empirical data adduced by Durkheim in Book I, on rational considerations such as the elimination of alternatives, and on the assumption that the extremely high correlation established between the development of the division of labor and the effacement of segmentary structures must necessarily entail *some* causal nexus. Furthermore, it rests on the belief that one has analyzed the correlated factors sufficiently to be able to know what that causal nexus is.

It is important at this point to interrupt our exposition to call attention to the fact that the particular causal proposition stated in the preceding paragraph is not the one at which Durkheim stops. The latter gives us the following causal law: " The division of labor is directly proportional to the volume and density of societies, and if it progresses in a continuous manner in the course of social development it is because societies become regularly more dense and very generally more voluminous." [20] If we accept this statement at face value, we must conclude that Durkheim's causal explanation of the division of labor is couched, contrary to his own methodological postulate that social facts must be explained socially, in biological, or, more exactly, in demographical terms. It is no wonder, then, that his book has been qualified as Malthusian.

But although these words are the words of Durkheim, their spirit is not his. We have already alluded to the fact that in presenting his doctoral dissertation, he was anxious to make it appear as mechanistic as possible. This, we believe, is why he did not make more explicit the proposition which makes moral density or social interaction the causal factor (and which, in our opinion, more accurately expresses his views)

19 *Ibid.*, p. 238. " The more individuals there are who are sufficiently in contact to be able to act and react on one another, the more the division of labor develops." " The development of the division of labor is directly proportional to the moral or dynamic density of society."

20 *Ibid.*, p. 244; *cf.* p. 330.

and, instead, preferred to establish more material and overt factors as the immediate causes. It can be shown, however, that his exposition and discussion of the causal factors, on the one hand, and his formulation of the causal law, on the other, are not consistent. On his own grounds, his causal law is, to be most generous, misleading.

After establishing the relation between division of labor and moral density, Durkheim goes on to say that a necessary though not sufficient condition for the increase of the latter is an increase in material density, which is defined broadly enough to include not only the number of inhabitants per surface area, but also the development of means of communication and transportation.[21] In addition, the *volume* of the population is brought in as a causal factor. However, Durkheim himself admits that material density and volume are not in and by themselves causal determinants of the division of labor. They are related to the latter phenomenon only through the intermediary of moral density or social interaction. It is only to the extent that they affect this dynamic density that they become causally operative. But this they do not always do. Therefore, they must be regarded as having causal relevance only whenever, and only insofar as, they multiply the social relations between individuals.[22] It is this multiplication which is the immediate cause. We are thus justified in restating Durkheim's law to read: " the division of labor is directly proportional to the degree of social interaction of societies, and if it progresses in a continuous manner in the course of social development it is because societies become regularly characterized by greater social interaction. Now, this increasing social interaction is frequently, though not invariably, the consequence of corresponding increases in the density of population of peoples, in their volume, and in their means of

21 *Règles*, p. 140. This confusion of the factors of population and communication is most unfortunate.

22 *De la Division*, pp. 242-243, p. 266 footnote 4; *Règles*, pp. 139-141, esp. p. 140 footnote 1.

communication and transportation." This restatement not only more accurately expresses Durkheim's view, but, far more than his own formulation, reenforces his claim that he is establishing relations of necessity.

Let us return, after this long aside, to our exposition of the schema of causal analysis. Having developed a tentative causal relationship, we must procede further to determine whether or not this causal connection is real. We can more firmly establish the assumed causal nexus by seeking out its *rationale*. This means that we must try to explain it, find out why it exists and why it is what it is. In other words, we must make the causal connection intelligible and hence understandable. Why, indeed, does an increase in social interaction *necessitate* a growth in the division of labor? Obviously, there are intermediary links in the causal chain that we have not yet determined.

The chief of these links, in Durkheim's opinion, is the increased intensity and severity of the struggle for existence which arise when societies attain a greater degree of social interaction. But why, it may be asked, should this be so? The answer is that it needn't be. However, if it is so, it is because, given certain conditions, it cannot be otherwise.

Let us suppose that we are given: (a) an already existing society whose members, linked together by moral and ideal bonds, participate in the common life of that society and hence are attached to one another by a common system of values; (b) as an integral part of that system of common social values, a value attached to the society itself and to its survival, i. e. a desire that the society exist and persist; (c) the will to survive on the part of each of the members of the society.

Now these three conditions may be termed the axiological orientation of the society and its members, for they pertain to the values attributed to things by individuals. Let us assume that under these given conditions there arises — whether because of population pressure or because of new modes of communication, or on some other account, it doesn't matter—an increased intensity of social interaction. In such a situation, an increased severity of competition must result, because, on the one hand, the conditions of life have become harder by the very fact that there are more persons to be taken care of in the same environment, and because, on the other hand, individuals, on account of their axiological orientation, wish neither to perish (condition c), nor to leave their society (condition a), nor to let the society itself dissolve (condition b). There is only one thing they can do if they do not wish to give up any of these values: they must adjust to the new circumstances created by the increased intensity of social life. Now, so long as the people do not prefer to change their axiological orientation, there is but one way in which this adjustment can be effected: by specialization of function, or, to use the time-honored phrase, the division of labor, since by this means competition is made less severe while at the same time existing values are held intact. Of course, there are many other ways out, such as migration, suicide, civil war, crime, etc., but each of these alternatives involves an axiological redefinition or reorientation; migration a change in condition b, suicide in condition c, civil war in conditions a and c, etc. Specialization, on the other hand, preserves, and even reenforces the very values which we have posited as given conditions.[23] In some such manner, then, we demonstrate the rationale of the causal nexus and thereby establish it more firmly. We uncover the intermediate links in the causal chain and make these links understandable.

Thus, Durkheim's insistence that his theory is mechanistic should not mislead one to suppose that it ignores the ideational and axiological aspects of social life; no more than one should assume that his emphasis on the constraint element of social facts precludes his recognition of their valuational nature. For did he not write that this constraint aspect of social prenomena is due to the prestige with which they are invested? [24]

23 Cf. *Règles*, pp. 114-116; *De la Division*, pp. 259-260, 270.
24 *Règles*, p. xxi.

The schema of causal analysis, up to this point may be presented, in résumé, as follows:

(1) Define the problem to be analyzed.

(2) Subject existing theories to critical review.

(3) Posit a tentative causal nexus on the basis of firmly grounded correlations.

(4) Demonstrate the intelligibility of the causal nexus. Make it understandable by placing it in a given axiological system.

Having terminated the demonstration of the causal nexus and of its rationale, it is helpful to make explicit and examine the consequences of one's explanation, to test their validity, and to compare them with existing views. Such a critical analysis helps to substantiate the rational and empirical considerations which have preceded.[25]

But even this does not complete the causal explanation. Secondary factors still remain to be considered. Our search, we announced at the outset, was for causes *and* conditions. Having determined the former, we may now turn to the latter. These, interchangeably called by Durkheim necessary conditions, permissive factors, or secondary factors, are the limiting conditions which either facilitate, interfere with, or completely impede the development of a given phenomenon. They are the factors that make this development possible, although, of themselves, they are causally impotent. We have said, for instance, that struggle for existence (x) is the cause of specialization (y). However, given x, one does not always get y because there are certain conditions (r, s, t) which impede the action of x on y; r, s, t, then, are permissive or limiting factors. In other words, whenever y is produced it is produced by x; but x does not always produce y; however, given x *and* conditions r, s, t, one always gets y. If x is the cause, r, s, t are the secondary factors.

But why should we call x the cause while refusing to attribuate causal efficacy to r, s, t? It might be argued that x is no different from these other factors, because given r, s, t, we do not get y unless x is present, and likewise, given x we do not get y unless r, s, t are present. On what grounds, then, can one factor be called a cause and the others only conditions? In some contemporary discussions, in fact, the distinction between permissive and efficient conditions (causes) is held to be equivocal. However, we feel that a valid distinction between the two can be made if one has recourse to one of the implications of the concept of cause, namely, the principle of concomitant variations. Let us suppose the following to be true: (a) All y's are preceded by x, r, s, t (conditions and causes); (b) Within the limits set by r, s, t, y varies as x; (c) Within the limits set by x, y does not vary as r, s, t, nor as r, nor as s, nor as t. It follows that we may distinguish the variable x from the other factors, and, all other conditions being equal, and having previously established x on other grounds as a possible causal influence, we may call it the cause, and these other elements the permissive factors. This is not the only justification of the distinction; we present it merely as one possible way in which it can be maintained. Durkheim himself makes no effort explicitly to justify his differentiation between causes and secondary factors. The argumentation here presented is offered on our own responsibility.

Thus, our causal explanation is supplemented by a consideration of secondary factors. Durkheim brings out two. The first consists in a greater independence of individuals relative to the group, the second refers to the organico-psychical bases of individual behavior. The first factor creates the social consent for individual variations, the second makes them biologically and psychologically possible. These limiting conditions are treated in the same manner as the causal factors, and the whole analysis is rounded out by deducing the consequences of the established propositions and causal laws, and subjecting them to critical tests. The schema is thus completed by the following steps:

(5) Establish the operative secondary factors.

(6) Treat each of them in the same manner as one has analyzed the causes.

(7) Derive and critically review the consequences of the established propositions and laws.

Durkheim, then, offers us a mode of causal analysis which, with the reservations we have made, is fairly rigorous and in harmony with the complexities and essential properties of the reality to which it is applied. It recognizes that cause and effect relations are not simple, but involve a multiplicity of variables, and that an explanation of social facts cannot ignore the axiological aspects of social life.

Durkheim returned to the problem of social causation in *Le Suicide*, this time more fully conscious of the difficulties involved. His study of suicide rates remains, forty years after its publication, one of the clearest and surest demonstrations of how quantitative data rationally systematized and analytically treated can contribute to the understanding of social phenomena. The volume is truly seductive in its efforts to vindicate the author's belief in the reality *sui generis* of social facts. From the viewpoint of social causation its major contributions are its differentiation of various modes or levels of causation and its development of a schema of analysis for assigning to these levels their particular roles in the causational conspiracies that produce social situations.

In *Le Suicide*, as in *De La Division*, our first step is to define the problem, i. e. to determine what it is that we are seeking to explain causally. Durkheim's immediate search is not for the reasons which lead any particular individual to commit suicide, but rather for the causes which in a given society explain the more or less constant and definite *social rates of suicide*. A social rate is one that is characteristically distinctive of a given group or of a subdivision within the group. As regards suicide, statistics reveal that social rates exist for groups of varying complexity, size, culture, religion, marital and familial composition, and political organization. Durkheim's specific and, indeed, only concern is with the wherefore of these social rates, their uniformities and constant variations.[26]

This first step of definition prevents us from committing the fallacy of particularism. It is understood from the start that we are not seeking *the* cause of suicide; it is assumed that there is no such single cause. A preliminary examination of the suicide statistics confirms this assumption. The data indicate that we are confronted with a welter of operative factors. We find, for example, that: (1) the rates of suicide are higher in the summer than in the winter; (2) they are higher among people suffering from mental diseases than among the mentally normal population; (3) men have a higher suicide rate than women; (4) in the United States, the suicide rate for whites is higher than that for Negroes, but lower than the rate for Chinese and Japanese; (5) older people have a higher suicide rate than younger people; (6) the suicide rate is higher in urban than in rural areas; (7) soldiers have a higher rate of suicide than the civilian population; (8) Protestants have a higher suicide rate than Catholics; (9) the suicide rate is higher among single, widowed and divorced persons than among the married; and (10) among the latter, it is higher for those who have no children than for those who are parents as well as spouses.

The suicide rates referred to in the above statements are standardized and comparable, and the variations among them must be explained on other than a chance basis.[27] We are in the presence of correlated factors which can guide us in our causal pursuit.

26 *Le Suicide*, pp. 15, 120, 142.

27 All of the above statements appear in Dublin, L. I., and Bunzel, B., *To Be or Not To Be: A Study of Suicide* (N. Y.: Smith and Haas, 1933) ; and all except statements (2) and (4) are found in Durkheim's volume.

Assuming that the variables in the above data are clues to causation, we may proceed to analyze them further. In this analysis, a preliminary task is to classify the various factors on the basis of the level or realm of reality represented by each.[28] We may distinguish (a) the factors belonging to the *social* realm: religion, marital status, family organization, mode of life (whether rural or urban), mode of occupation (whether military or civilian) from (b) those that are as such *non-social;* and among the latter we may further differentiate (b[1]) the physical factors (seasons, temperature), (b[2]) the biological factors (sex, race, age), and (b[3]) the psychological factors (mental disease). This classification is not meant to be complete. It is not necessary for our immediate purpose to mention all the possible factors that affect suicide rates; a representative list should suffice. We omit, for example, purely technological considerations such as the availability and the relative efficiency of various *means* of self-destruction. Durkheim, for instance, relates the case of an incipient suicide epidemic where the wave of self-destruction ended immediately upon the removal of the particular means used by those taking their own life, in this instance, a certain hook.[29]

Now all these factors influence the rate of suicide. Our focal task is to determine *how*. But *how* must not be confused with *how much*. As Professor MacIver says, to understand social causation, " it is not enough to enumerate factors, to set them side by side, to attribute to them different weights as determinants of change. The first and essential thing is to discover the way in which the various factors are *related* to one

28 In this discussion of *Le Suicide* we are not adopting the mode of exposition followed by Durkheim. We believe, however, that there is no significant logical difference between the method of analysis we are here outlining and the one used by the French theorist. We remain critical, of course, of the extravagant and cavalier manner in which Durkheim used the method of elimination. Nor are we sure that his polemic style makes for clarity. We have, therefore, restated his schema of analysis in more positive terms.

29 *Le Suicide*, p. 74.

another, the logical order within which they fall, the respective modes in which they enter into the causal process." [30]

Let us consider the social factors first. We apply to them what may be termed the method of *direct breakdown*, i. e., we analyze them more and more carefully so as to determine what element in, or what aspect of them is, according to the various logical tests and particularly that of concomitant variation, most closely related to the social rate of suicide. What, for instance, is the feature of religion that bears relevance to suicide? What is there in Protestantism and in Catholicism that makes the adherents of the former more susceptible to suicide? Is it the particular character of the respective religious beliefs? Is it what Durkheim termed "the obligatory prudence of minority groups"? Our data do not support these hypotheses. More consistent with our empirical evidence is the view that the differential suicide rates of the religious groups stem from the fact that the Catholic church is *as a social group* more closely knit, more cohesive, and more strongly integrated than the Protestant churches. This hypothesis not only permits us to account for most if not all of the other observable variations in suicide rates according to religious grouping, but also is heuristically valuable in our analysis of the other social factors. Among the latter, too, we find that the relevant feature with regard to suicide is the degree of social integration or cohesion that is represented in each. Marriage, parenthood, and rural life make one less susceptible to suicide because they are socially integrative and hence protect the individual against the sense of social isolation. On the other hand, the higher suicide rate among the military as against the civilian population must be understood as resulting from an excessive social integration among the former.[31] Generalizing, then, we may say that the social rate of suicide varies with the degree of

30 MacIver, R. M., *Society: A Text Book of Sociology* (New York: Farrar and Rinehart, 1937), p. 478.

31 This rather dubious explanation of Durkheim has been rightly challenged. See Halbwachs, M., *Les Causes du Suicide*, pp. 85-89.

integration of the social group, the rate increasing as the degree of integration goes above or below a certain level.

Thus far, however, we have concerned ourselves exclusively with the social realm and have found that on the sociological level there is a causal relationship between social cohesion and variations in the social rates of suicide. But what of the non-social factors? How do they enter into the causal situation? Belonging to a different level, this relationship to *the social rate of suicide* can only be indirect. We must apply to them the method of *indirect breakdown*. This is a procedure which involves analyzing a non-social factor in such a manner as to single out the element or aspect of it which is most closely related to some social phenomenon which bears, in turn, a close relationship to the particular social matter we are studying. We must, in short, make our way from the non-social to the social level.

Consider, for example, the data which reveal a seasonal variation in the suicide rate. Statistics invariably show the rate of suicide to be higher in the summer than in the winter. It's the heat, some geographical determinists have explained. The empirical evidence, however, does not support this contention. But even if it did, the explanation would not be complete. We would still have to trace the *connection* between heat and suicide. Since these phenomena pertain to different levels, we cannot posit a direct nexus between them. Heat does not cause suicide in the same way that it melts ice. The latter process is purely physical; the former, involving a mixing of two levels of causation, requires a search for intermediate links.

But further analysis of the seasonal data indicates that the relevant physical element is not the temperature, but the length of the day. The latter factor influences the rhythm of social life. The longer day makes for more intensive and more active participation in social events, and this in turn affects the individual's sense of isolation. We thus move a considerable distance away from the simple heat-suicide causal formula. We isolate the relevant element in the seasonal factor and relate it to social situations. Having arrived on the sociological level, we can establish the more direct causal nexus.

Durkheim, we feel, did not pay sufficient attention to the analysis of the seasonal variations in social life, hence, his particular explanation needs supplementation, perhaps by a study of a modern community in the manner that Mauss and Beuchat investigated Eskimo society.[32] This comment, however, does not reflect on the adequacy of the schema of analysis we are presenting. It is made in order to indicate the need for pursuing this mode of analysis further.

In like manner we subject the biological factors to indirect breakdowns. The sex differences in the social rates of suicide, for instance, become understandable when we analyze the respective social positions of men and women, their different modes of participation in social and economic life, and the varying cycles of their social activities. Here again, we must move from one level to another. We cannot be content with a simple " sex is the cause of suicide " type of statement. We must show how the factor of sex is socially and culturally defined and how this social and cultural definition influences the suicide rate.

Similarly, we must search for the social intermediates that link the biological phenomenon of race with the social rate of suicide. In many instances an analysis of the social composition of a particular racial group provides helpful clues. Thus, the fact that in the United States the Chinese male population outnumbers by approximately 4 to 1 the Chinese female population, is a significant guide to the understanding of the very high Chinese suicide death rate in this country.[33] In fact, a good deal of the " racial " data on suicide has to be reinterpreted in the light of similar social and cultural conditions. As Klineberg remarks apropos of the failure of statistics to

32 Mauss, M., and Beuchat, H., " Essai sur les variations saisonnières des sociétés eskimos," A S, IX (1906), 39-132.

33 Dublin and Bunzel, *op. cit.*, p. 37.

support McDougall's analysis of racial tendencies to suicide, this racial data should be studied " particularly from the point of view of uncovering some of the cultural factors which may enter. These, rather than race, may make it possible to understand the observed differences." [34] The " rather than " may be unwarranted in the absence of conclusive evidence, but in any case, it is necessary to seek out the cultural and social factors if the racial explanation is to be made at all intelligible.

So, too, with the question of age. How the different age-levels are socially and culturally defined, how age affects the cycle of one's social life, how it determines the mode and the degree of participation in social activities are elements that serve to connect the physiological factor of age to the social rates of suicide. A pure and simple direct causal relationship cannot be imputed; it would have no meaning.

The same procedure of indirect breakdown must be followed with respect to the mental disease factor. Psychiatrists [35] who make suicide exclusively a psychopathological phenomenon either ignore the fact that of the total number of suicides in a given year only a fraction (estimated somewhere between 20 and 50 per cent) are committed by persons known to suffer from mental disease,[36] or they are merely tautological, defining suicide in advance as a mental aberration. As Dr. Dublin, who is favorably disposed towards the psychiatric explanation of suicide, remarks, " it is certainly extreme to assert that all suicides are insane — unless we assume *a priori* that self-destruction is, in itself, a definite indication of psychosis. In short we think there are many cases of suicide among those who should be designated as ' sane '." [37] Moreover, the psychiatric thesis that the cause of suicide is manic-depressive psychosis must be interpreted in the light of the evidence

34 Klineberg, O., *Race Differences* (N. Y.: Harper, 1935), pp. 227-229.

35 See e. g. Delmas, F.-A., *Psychologie pathologique du suicide* (Paris: Alcan, 1932).

36 Dublin and Bunzel, *op. cit.*, chap. 22.

37 *Ibid.*, pp. 307-308.

gathered by Professor Bonnafous in his study of suicide in Constantinople.[38] M. Bonnafous found that among the inmates of institutions for the mentally diseased, the notion of suicide, i. e. the desire and the attempt to take one's own life, varied with the cultural level and the social background of the patient. The frequency with which the desire to commit suicide occurred varied rather regularly with the degree of Europeanization and Westernization characteristic of the group from which the patient came. Manic-depressive psychosis, this material tends to show, is " suicidogenic " in Western society, but " non-suicidogenic " in the non-westernized portions of Mohammedan society. Data of this sort suggest that social and cultural factors must be taken into account to explain the manner in which the incidence of mental disease affects the social rate of suicide.

We see, then, that Durkheim's study of suicide is a pioneering contribution to social causation. Although he himself may not have fully perceived the significance of his analysis of the non-social factors in suicide, this part of his study is important for contemporary sociology in that it illustrates the fecundity of the type of analysis which deliberately attempts to show how these non-social phenomena are related to the social world in which men live.[39]

The establishment of causal nexuses by no means exhausts the kind of significant knowledge we can obtain concerning social facts. It is also revealing to determine the functions of social phenomena; not that they all have functions, but as Radcliffe-Brown has said, they *may* have and hence it is legitimate to seek them out. Durkheim, we believe, was among the first to attempt systematically to apply the concept of function to social reality. What did he mean by it?

38 See Bonnafous, M., " Le Suicide: Thèse Psychiatrique et thèse sociologique," R P, CXV (1933), 456-475.

39 For a detailed review of Durkheim's study, see Halbwachs' *Les Causes du Suicide*.

He developed the idea of function as an alternative to, and as a correction of, the finalistic or teleological mode of sociological analysis.[40] Many sociologists assumed — and still assume — that a social institution is sufficiently explained and accounted for when one has shown its utility, that is, has indicated what needs it satisfies, and how it satisfies them. Thus, Comte explained human progress in terms of a drive for betterment, and Spencer and the Utilitarians in terms of a desire for greater happiness. In America, William Graham Sumner built his sociological system on four fundamental drives, W. I. Thomas his on four wishes and Lester F. Ward erected a sociological structure on numerous desires serving as " social forces ". But desire and will are in themselves causally inefficacious; they become operative only as they are translated into appropriate action. Willing, in fact, has significance only as it is active, and might well be thought of as itself a type of acting. Willing, it has been said, " is simply the self-determined acting of a living thing, its being itself in action." [41] Likewise the perception of the utility of something does not suffice to bring that thing into being; here, too, some kind of action is necessary. Hence, to explain a social phenomenon exclusively in terms of needs or desires is to ignore significant aspects of it, and, as likely as not, to be atomistic in one's approach, that is, to account for the complex by the simple. Moreover such explanations turn out, for the most part, to be mere tautologies.[42] But one should not hastily conclude from the fact that desires, ends, needs, drives, and wishes are not

40 *De la Division*, pp. 11-12; *Règles*, chap. V, esp. pp. 110-120.

41 MacIver, R. M., *Community* (3rd ed.; London: Macmillan, 1928), p. 6.

42 *Cf.* Dollard, J., *Criteria For the Life History* (New Haven: Yale University Press, 1935), pp. 155-171. Dollard in these pages shows, by apt quotations, the rather bewildering manner in which Thomas and Znaniecki interpret a Polish immigrant's behavior in terms of the " wishes." We shall have occasion to return to this problem in another connection. *Cf.* Znaniecki, F., *Social Actions* (N. Y.; Farrar & Rinehart, 1936), p. viii, where Znaniecki admits that the mode of causal explanation used in the *Polish Peasant* was " much too simple."

self-sufficient causal factors in social life, that they must therefore be excluded from all sociological explanation. Such a
conclusion is not only unwarranted, it is false. There remains,
and it is possible to adopt, the alternative position, which is
essentially Durkheim's, that one can reject finalistic interpretations and still make a place for human needs and desires in
sociological explanations.[43] However, these needs and desires
are not immutable; they evolve and change, and must themselves be causally explained.

Thus, Durkheim proposes the methodological rule that in
analyzing a social phenomenon it is necessary to seek out separately the efficient cause which produces it and the function
it fulfills. While the utility of a phenomenon does not explain
its coming into being, since we cannot say that it has come
about merely because it was deliberately willed with a view to
satisfying certain ends, it nevertheless does make intelligible
why the phenomenon persists and maintains itself.[44]

Now the term function, as Durkheim uses it, is explicitly
borrowed from biology.[45] Of the two meanings that it has in
that science, he adopts the one which implies that between a
given physiological process (e. g. respiration) and some general need of the organism (e. g. introduction of gases into
tissues) there exists a relation of correspondence. Translated
into social terms, we may say that the function of a social
institution is the correspondence between the institution and
some general need of the society in which it exists. For instance, to inquire into the function of the division of labor in
a given society means to ask to what need of that society it
corresponds. Thus, in contemporary societies, the function of
the division of labor is to integrate the society and to assure

---

43 *Règles*, pp. 115-116.

44 *Ibid.*, pp. 117, 119.

45 *De la Division*, p. 11; *cf*. Radcliffe-Brown, A. R., " On the Concept of
Function in Social Science," A A, n. s., XXXVII (1935), 394-402. Radcliffe-
Brown follows closely Durkheim's connotation of the concept.

its unity.[46] Durkheim chooses the word function because he feels that other expressions such as aim, end, objective, results, or effects are either inexact or equivocal or do not evoke the idea of correspondence. The term role or function, on the other hand, has the advantage of implying this idea without prejudicing in advance the question of whether the correspondence is or is not intentional and deliberate. To say that the division of labor in modern society has an integrating function does not mean that it was deliberately created in order to have that function.

Even to talk of the " need " of a society is unsatisfactory, for the notion of need lends itself quite easily to the very type of teleological interpretation that Durkheim wishes to avoid. We may, therefore, follow the proposal of Radcliffe-Brown that the concept " necessary conditions of existence " be substituted in its place.[47]

The concept of function is methodologically tenable only if one accept the propositions that there *are* social systems and that they *do* have necessary conditions of existence. This is clearly indicated in the definition of function given by Radcliffe-Brown. Function, this anthropologist writes, is " the contribution which a partial activity makes to the total activity of which it is a part. The function of a particular social usage is the contribution it makes to the total social life as the functioning of the total social system. Such a view implies that a social system (the total social structure of a society together with the totality of social usages in which that structure appears and on which it depends for its continued existence) has a certain kind of unity, which we may speak of as a functional unity. We may define it as a condition in which all parts of the social system work together with a sufficient degree of harmony or internal consistency, i. e. without producing persistent conflicts which can neither be resolved nor regulated." [48]

46 Durkheim, *op. cit.*, p. 26.
47 Radcliffe-Brown, *op. cit.*, p. 394.
48 *Ibid.*, p. 397.

This statement may be taken as corresponding closely to Durkheim's meaning of " function ".

The Durkheimian concepts of cause and function are his methodological elaborations of the postulate of sociological determinism. Thus, he assigns to sociology the tasks of finding out (a) in what manner social institutions have come about, (b) what causes have given rise to them, and (c) to what useful ends they correspond.[49] In this manner, his conception of sociology as a natural science grapples with the dilemma which springs from the fact that social phenomena are both natural, hence determined, and axiological, hence involve consideration of human ends and values.

The task of sociological analysis truly involves, we believe, both the pursuit of sufficient causes and necessary conditions and the search for functions. The first of these tasks identifies sociology with the body of the sciences in general; the second one links it more closely with the sciences of life. But as Durkheim taught, and as we have tried to illustrate in our discussion of *Le Suicide*, each realm of nature is, to some extent, *sui generis*. We may therefore inquire whether in dealing with social matters we exhaust all the possible kinds of obtainable significant knowledge when we determine the causes and functions of social phenomena. Is there not some additional element, distinctive of the social realm, perhaps, that we may also investigate? Is our sociological knowledge complete when we have determined origins and developments and have established causes and functions?

Durkheim in practice inclined towards answering this last question in the affirmative. But contemporary sociology, at least to the extent that it takes cognizance of the contributions of Max Weber, cannot agree with the French theorist. Without prejudicing the accuracy of Durkheim's schema of social analysis, as far as it goes, we have to declare it incomplete. For Max Weber has taught us that in addition to causes and

49 09e, p. 278; *cf.* 37a, p. 532.

functions, we may single out, in social life, the kind of knowledge that is summed up in the concept of *verstehen*. We use the term " verstehen analysis " to refer to the investigation of a social situation or process from the viewpoint of the motivations of the human agents involved. Verstehen analysis consists in relating the actions of these human agents to their motives, in establishing what ends the agents pursue and how they relate means to ends in their social activities. It involves, in short, the seeking out of the *becauses* of human action as they affect social phenomena, situations and processes.

Thus, in studying the division of labor in society, we may establish (a) its cause, which Durkheim believed to be the increased moral density of societies as it effected an increasing severity of the struggle for existence and as it necessitated a mitigation of that severity, (b) its function, which Durkheim regarded as being a socially integrative one, and (c) its *becauses*, i. e. how, in a situation in which moral density makes the struggle for existence more severe, human agents apply means to ends, how, in other words, their behavior, motivated by their effective valuations, brings about a division of labor, whether that be their directly willed intention or not.

This third aspect Durkheim ignored, except as he approached it negatively by assuming that human individuals, who are already members of a group and are attached to one another and to the group as such, would, in the face of an increased severity of social life, seek a solution that did not impair their group, their common values, and their own existence. But Durkheim did not treat the matter systematically. He committed the serious blunder of not following his own methodological precept of specificity. Nowhere in *De la Division* do we find a picture of a specific society actually undergoing the change from a segmentary to a functional structure. Durkheim, surprisingly, and unfortunately, did not think such a specific analysis necessary for his purpose. He believed it possible to study the " general fact " of the progressive advance of the division of labor in the course of social evolution, abstraction made of the specific manifestations of the phenomenon as influenced by particular conditions of time and place.[50]

This lack of specificity had serious consequences. First of all, it made it impossible for Durkheim to test empirically his crucial, and to many, his questionable assumptions that the division of labor mitigates the severity of the struggle for existence and that it can do so without interfering with the common and individual values enumerated in the discussion above.[51] On these points, Durkheim either is purely conjectural or he relies on an analogy from plant ecology, citing evidence from no less eminent biologists than Darwin and Haeckel.[52] He thus raised, but did not empirically answer the question of the relation of the division of labor to the struggle for existence. An answer, at least as regards human social life, would have required the study of a specific society in the throes of the process under consideration. Durkheim, however, did not undertake such an analysis.

Secondly, the lack of specificity rendered verstehen analysis impossible. Not that Durkheim would have undertaken such an analysis on principle, but his material, had it been specific and processually arranged, might have led him to it. As it was, his exclusive concern with the " general fact " forced him to consider only the " impersonal forces " in the situation, and hence only the causes and functions. At the moment of writing his dissertation, Durkheim did not conceive of sociological analysis other than in terms of cause, function, origin and development. His opposition to the psychological method of social explanation,[53] made him wary of the efforts to interpret social phenomena by means of individual motivations or in terms of means-ends analyses. But in the pamphlet on *"Who Wanted War?"* written in 1915,[54] we find him asserting that

50 *De la Division*, p. 211.
51 See above, pp. 93-94.
52 *Cf. De la Division*, pp. 248-249 ff.
53 See below.
54 15b.

in analyzing a social event we must distinguish the impersonal forces which brought it about from the will of the human agents concerned. It is this will, we are told, that renders these impersonal causes operative. Had Durkheim full appreciated, or more accurately, had he lived to appreciate, the implications of the position taken in this pamphlet,[55] he would have been led to perceive the incompleteness of the type of sociological analysis which deals exclusively with causes and functions. If there is any sense in which it is true that Durkheim neglected the individual it is in this failure to take into account the specific manner in which human agents behave in social situations.

As sociologists operating on the social level we must determine not only the causes and functions of social phenomena, but also their *becauses*. Sociological knowledge can be " understandable " as well as etiological and functional. These three types of social knowledge are neither identical nor mutually exclusive; they supplement one another. It is erroneous to assume, for instance, that verstehen analysis can ever be a substitute for causal interpretation, or that the search for functions excludes the pursuit of causes. One type of knowledge complements the others.

3. OBJECTIVITY: DEFINITIONS AND INDEXES

Similar difficulties arise with reference to establishing sociology as an *objective* science. Here, as in the case of " natural," the adjective is ambiguous. Just as there can be no " unnatural " science, whatever that may mean, so there can be no subjective science. However, this does not mean that a science of subjective phenomena is impossible; all the efforts of psychology in the last half-century point to just the opposite view.

---

55 The pamphlet, it must be remembered, bears a double signature, Durkheim's and Denis'. While Durkheim may not actually have written the remarks in question, he at least gave his assent to them by allowing them to appear over his name.

It is important to distinguish the two ways in which the qualifying adjectives are used. When we say that a science is natural we do not refer to the nature of the science, but rather to the nature of the matter with which the science deals. We call that subject matter natural if the principle of determinism is applicable to it. Obviously, the science itself cannot be " natural "; on the contrary, it is rational and man-made, a human construct.[56] On the other hand, in the phrase "objective science," the adjective does not refer to the subject-matter of the science, but to the science itself, that is, to the nature of the body of rules and principles of procedure which we generally call the scientific method. We say that a science is objective when its procedural apparatus includes rules for universal verification and validation, when, in other words, it provides a means by which its empirical results may be accurately and reliably checked by any physically and mentally competent observer who cares to do so. It is only this that Durkheim had in mind when he insisted on an objective method for sociology. Social science, he felt, must meet squarely the apparent paradox of studying objectively subjective phenomena. He always categorically opposed the atomistic behaviorists who, confusing the nature of science with the nature of its subject-matter, discarded subjective data altogether, and thus rejected that which in social facts is social.[57] He likewise excluded from sociology all mystical and literary approaches, and refused to accept, as validated truths, the knowledge arrived at solely by insight, intuition, sympathetic understanding, empathy, and other such introspective psychological processes. Instead of immediately admitting this knowledge into the company of the established verities, he assigned to it a more humble, but perhaps a more fecund, position among the raw

56 This does not preclude the possibility of viewing science as natural when it itself is the subject-matter of a science. There is a science of science or a sociology of science which treats scientific behavior as determined.

57 Cf. MacIver, R. M., *Society: Its structure and changes* (New York: Long and Smith, 1933), pp. 530-31.

materials of science—the body of tentative and working hypotheses. Between this raw material and the final product of scientific investigation (which in reality is never final) there is a distance comparable to that between the roots of a plant and its fruit. The fact that the latter receives its nourishment from the former hardly warrants our confusing the two. Without healthy roots a tree indeed may be barren; but, again, its roots are not its fruits. We emphasize this last point because some contemporary sociologists, in their eagerness to combat the preposterousness and the conceit of behavioristic philosophy, have tended to assign to the personal experiences of the social scientist an ultimate instead of a root position. One may accept MacIver's statement that " the understanding of society *begins* from our personal experience as members of society," [58] if, as we have done, one underscores " begins " and keeps in mind that beginning is not ending. Similarly, we may subscribe to Znaniecki's remark that " the scientist's personal experience is the primary and most reliable source of information in sociology," [59] provided that the word " source " be limited to its primitive meaning of " beginning ", " start ", " spring ". Start and finish, however, are not identical; a river's source is not its mouth. Science stands ready to utilize information from no matter what source, but its end-product is not all knowledge however derived, but only that knowledge which can be, and is, scientifically sifted, treated, and tested.

How are we to deal objectively with subjective phenomena? This is the problem that the *science* of sociology must resolve.

The question is indeed a vast one. We should like here to discuss only the two aspects of it to which Durkheim has

58 *Ibid.*, p. vii. Italics ours.

59 Znaniecki, *Method*, p. 157. Znaniecki himself warns against the method of unchecked introspection. Culture, he writes, consists of numerous systems, " all with a specific objectivity and an intrinsic order of their own. Though human activities construct and maintain such systems, these activities are not what they appear in introspective analysis: what matters about them is not their ' subjective ', ' psychological ' aspect, but how they manifest themselves in this objective cultural world." (*Social Actions*, p. 6.)

given most explicit and extended consideration. We refer to the role of definitions and the use of indexes in the process of scientific objectification.

Definitions are assigned an all-important function by Durkheim. They are for him the first and most indispensable condition of scientific proof and verification.[60] To define the things he is dealing with is the very first task of the sociologist. But the method of definition must be rigorous and objective. The scientist should under no circumstances use in unadulterated and unpurged form the vague, indefinite, and uncertain concepts of common-sense and every-day experience, for these lack the discriminatory properties necessary for valid reasoning. Physics, for example, employs concepts of heat, pressure, and mass which diverge widely from the popular notions of these phenomena. Sociology, Durkheim insists, must adopt the same procedure; and what will be lost in popularity will be gained in clarity.

Durkheim's aim is laudable; precision is without question an ideal of science. However, his specific views on the function of definitions in scientific analysis are erroneous and constitute one of the weakest parts of his methodology. His misconceptions of the role and nature of definitions can be traced, we feel, to his failure to appreciate the vital part played by initial hypotheses and a priori assumptions, i. e. by rational considerations generally, in scientific reasoning. True, Durkheim was too much a part of the French tradition to be a raw empiricist. Nevertheless, his positivism did lead him to overemphasize the "articulations of reality", the "nature of things", the given, the data and to minimize, almost to the point of complete neglect, the rational actions of the scientist, the taken, the capta. Thus, his theory of definition ignores the crucial role of the definer, and seems to imply that somehow or other things define themselves.[61] If phenomena are to be

60 Règles, pp. 54, 44.
61 Règles, p. 44.

objectively delimited, he maintains, they must be defined in terms of some property which is inherent in them. They must be characterized by " an integral element of their nature." But, it may be asked, inasmuch as definition, in Durkheim's conception, is to be the *starting* point of social investigation, how can one know in advance what these inherent properties and integral elements are? Our author replies by granting the point and then dismissing it. At the beginning, he claims, it is not at all necessary to know—and as a matter of fact we cannot know—what the essential features of a phenomenon are. This, however, doesn't really matter, since we can discover all that we need to start with; namely, some characteristics of the phenomenon that " are external enough to be immediately visible." These external traits may not be the most significant that we can abstract, but they will have to suffice. The traits " which are more profoundly situated are, no doubt, more essential, their explicative value is higher, but they are unknown at this (beginning) phase of the science." Our definition, therefore, is to be drawn up on the basis of external and immediately visible characteristics of the phenomenon under study. Of course, the class of phenomena so defined will have to comprise " without exception or distinction " all things which have the defining properties, since there is no criterion for making *a priori* distinctions among them. Hence, the following rule of method: "Always take as an object of research only a group of phenomena previously defined by certain external characteristics that are common to them, and include in the same research all phenomena which correspond to this definition." [62] By observing this rule, the sociologist will immediately gain a firm foothold on reality, Durkheim promises, because " the way in which facts are thus classified does not depend on him, on the particular twist of his mind, but on the nature of things." [63]

62 *Ibid.*, p. 45.
63 *Ibid.*, p. 46; *cf.* p. 53.

His promise, alas, is illusory, and impossible to fulfill. It rests on the credit of the long-since bankrupted assumption that scientists are the passive and facts the active agents in the attainment of knowledge. Facts, our popular language notwithstanding, do not speak for themselves, nor do they qualify and define themselves. We cannot approach facts without some notion of what we are looking for.

Durkheim would have us develop objective definitions by determining the traits common to the whole of a given class of phenomena. But if the class has not been previously delimited, how can one know what phenomena belong to it? Let us consider, by way of illustration, Durkheim's first effort to define socialism " objectively ".[64] His point of departure is the set of doctrines which either people call socialistic or are thus labelled by their authors. He then proposes to establish whether or not one can find some characteristic or characteristics common to all these doctrines. If such common traits are discovered they will constitute, in his opinion, a scientific definition of socialism. However, he does not realize that he is not thereby defining an unknown, undetermined class of things, but is merely describing the common properties of a class already selected: the class of doctrines which are called socialistic. But the very basis of his whole discussion is that we cannot know what socialism is by referring to what people say it is. His definition, therefore, rests on an implicit assumption which he explicitly denounces. In his course on the history of socialism, given two years after the publication of the preliminary definition, his procedure is somewhat modified.[65] Here, instead of starting with the word and then describing the class, he first delimits the class and then applies the word. He starts with the entire body of doctrines which deal with social matters, and, proceeding to observe and compare them, he classifies together those which present common characteristics.

---

64 93c. *Cf.* R P, XXXV, p. 672; XXXVI, pp. 182-189, 631-635.
65 28a, pp. 3-25.

Then, examining the social theories thus grouped, he finds a particular class whose distinctive traits resemble to a large extent those which are ordinarily designated as socialistic. He thereupon decides to call the doctrines comprising this class socialism.[66] Thus, in the corrected as in the first definition, resemblance to the avowedly inadequate popular notion is a criterion of selection and an implicit class is the starting point.

The method is also defective in that it does not offer any criteria whatever by which one may decide how a class should be delimited. Hence, there is complete arbitrariness in the manner in which the various classifications and sub-classifications are determined. Durkheim, in his course, first divides social doctrines into two main categories: scientific and practical, and assigns socialism to the latter. Practical doctrines are sub-classified according to whether they aim at political, educational, administrative or economic reforms, and socialism is placed in this last sub-class. Having already arrived at this point, there remains only the matter of determining whether, among the economic transformations demanded by the various reformist groups, there are not some which are distinctive of socialism.[67] When Durkheim discovers these socialistic principles of economic reform we are not surprised, for it is evident that he has known all along what his definition of socialism will be. For how can he possibly determine whether or not certain demands are distinctive of socialism if he does not have an idea of what socialism is? And how can he know with such alarming immediacy that socialism is practical, not scientific; economic, not political? Surely, such knowledge would not be available to him if he were able to follow his own precept to discard prenotions and forget previous experiences.

Or consider his definition of suicide. Durkheim defines this phenomenon broadly enough to include acts of sacrifice. Halb-

66 *Ibid.*, p. 20.
67 *Ibid.*, pp. 21-22.

wachs, however, prefers to exclude sacrificial acts from the class of suicides. Who is right? Who is more "objective"? Is Halbwachs less objective because he wishes to take into account the attitudes of people towards suicide and sacrifice? Obviously, these are questions which cannot be settled in advance of intensive analysis of the phenomena under consideration.[68]

Thus, because he failed to make explicit the prior rational considerations with which an investigator approaches his subject matter, Durkheim was led to attribute to definitions rather amazing powers of objectification. He did not realize the essentially tentative nature of the first definition. Instead of regarding it as a working tool, to be remodeled or discarded when proved to be inadequate, he accepted it as rather permanent. True, he may never have said that this beginning definition is an acquired truth—though he does refer to it at one point as fundamental as well as initial,[69]—and may even have stressed its approximative character, but there is the objective evidence that in no one volume of his did he ever modify the definition with which he began. He did introduce slight modifications into his first definitions of socialism and religion in later works on these subjects, but as he himself remarked apropos of his new definition of religious phenomena, "these modifications imply no essential change in the conception of the facts." [70]

Definitions are an essential part of our scientific apparatus, but they need not be rigidly established in advance. They may well serve as tentative hypotheses, as guide-posts to investigations; however, when they are so used, it is necessary to bear

68 *Le Suicide*, pp. 2-5; Halbwachs, M., *Les Causes du Suicide* (Paris: Alcan, 1930), pp. 451-480. Halbwachs, it should be noted, reserves the question of definition for his conclusion, while Durkheim introduces his study with it. *Cf.* also, Lacombe, R., *La Méthode Sociologique de Durkheim* (Paris: Alcan, 1926), pp. 105-106.

69 *Règles*, p. 44.

70 12a, p. 31 footnote 1.

in mind Znaniecki's warning that "we cannot avoid the responsibility for our classifications by claiming that they are merely instrumental for future study," for, as the Polish sociologist notes, "whether we want it or not, every classification is already a theory and involves theoretical conclusions about reality which are the result of previous study." [71] But definitions are also the end-products of research and as such can be constituted only after intensive analysis. Far from categorically assigning them a position at the beginning of study, it appears to be more fruitful to place them at the conclusion. Znaniecki's plea for the method of analytical induction in which no definition of a class " precedes the selection of data to be studied as representatives of this class " has much to commend it.[72]

Obstacles abound, too, in Durkheim's effort to study subjective data through the use of objective indexes. It is of the essence of science to attain the highest possible degree of objectivity compatible with the nature of the subject matter it treats. The scientist, therefore, endeavors to substitute for the personal, indecisive impressions of the individual observer rationally and theoretically constructed instruments and techniques whereby standardized, reliable observations may be made. Instead of relying on the unguided sense impressions of the individual, he consults thermometers, spectroscopes, micrometers, and other such measuring devices. However, the corrective function of making observations more accurate is not the only one these instruments of measurement perform. In many instances, they render possible any kind of observation whatsoever. They widen the realm of experience, bringing within the range of empirical knowledge the vast section of the universe which cannot be directly observed. Neither the speed of light, nor the density of a star, nor even the mode of living of the Ancient Egyptians is given to direct observation. In all

71 Znaniecki, *Method*, p. 254.
72 *Ibid.*, Chap. 6.

cases of this sort, science necessarily has to have recourse to what may be termed the method of indirect observation.

By indirect observation, we mean the rational process whereby a directly observable phenomenon is linked, on logical, theoretical, and empirical grounds, to some other phenomenon which is not amenable to direct observation. The relation between the two is so established that one may legitimately infer from some manifestation, behavior, property, or symptom of the former to knowledge concerning the properties, characteristics, or behavior of the latter. By observing a line on the spectrum we infer the presence of a gas; from our observation of the movement of a column of mercury we infer changes in atmospheric pressure, etc. Indeed, indirect observation is one of the most characteristic features of science. In the physical sciences it is extremely useful. In sociology it is indispensable.

The phenomena with which our science is concerned are not, for the most part, directly observable. States of emotion or of mind, feelings, sentiments, attitudes, ideas, beliefs, desires, motives—if such be the stuff of which social life is made— cannot be perceived directly. They may be experienced, in fact, *must* be, but they cannot in themselves be observed. What we do perceive, what we can observe are certain modes of behavior and activity from which the presence and nature of these subjective phenomena are inferred. To use a succinct formula, we may say that sociological data are data of inner experience, not of direct observation.[73]

Science, however, since it is a rational system utilizing *empirical* data, cannot dispense with observation; otherwise there are no controls and checks, and verification and validation become impossible. Without observation, science loses its objectivity, and instead of establishing real relations between phenomena, is reduced to confirming what Pareto has called the accord of sentiments. It is therefore incumbent upon it, whenever its subject matter does not lend itself to immediate

73 *Cf.* MacIver, *Society* (1931), pp. 529-533 and Durkheim, 06b, 11b.

observation, to resort to observing indirectly. This is the situation of sociology. The sociologist is required to establish between the subject matter which is his particular concern and directly observable, overt phenomena rationally derived relations of a nature that will permit him to obtain from the latter relevant knowledge about the former. He must, as Durkheim says, adopt the principle of Descartes which requires every scientist to get the " scientific slant " of his subject matter.[74] This he can do by finding some aspect of his data which, without prejudicing the nature of that data, permits of exact demonstration, and if possible, of measurement. The particular aspect may be some overt manifestation of the phenomenon in question or some observable necessary expression of it; or it may be some other, more overt phenomenon with which it is invariably connected. If we call this manifestation, or expression, or concomitant an index, we may say that our task in analyzing social phenomena involves discovering indexes of them that are amenable to scientific manipulations.

Finding a suitable and utilizable index is not an easy matter. It does not suffice merely to choose or develop one; its adoption must be justified. This justification involves making explicit the theoretical grounds on which the connection between the index and the phenomenon indexed is established, and on which one reasons from the former to the latter. In other words, before an index can be properly used, one must investigate its nature, and theoretically substantiate its adoption. For theoretical considerations are involved in all indexes.[75] The thermometer, the barometer, the spectroscope, aye, all scientific instruments are constructed on the basis of theoretical principles. If our theories of heat, pressure, or light were radically different from the ones that are at present accepted in physics, the measuring devices which rest on these contem-

74 *De la Division*, p. xlii; *cf. ibid.*, pp. 30-31 and *Règles*, pp. 57-58.

75 *Cf.* Cohen, M. R., *Reason and Nature* (New York: Harcourt, Brace, 1931), pp. 92-96.

porary theories would have either to be discarded or to be remodeled along different lines.

It is important to stress the theoretical foundations of measuring devices because it is sometimes assumed by American sociologists who believe that instruments of measurement are necessary for valid theories, that these instruments are, in some inexplicable manner, theory-free. The failure to examine the logical and theoretical grounds on which instruments rest has led to the development of indexes whose construction involves either untenable rational principles or improper logic or both.[76] No one will deny that some of the indexes at present extant in American sociology are veritable scientific monstrosities. But from the discrediting of particular indexes it does not follow that the whole method of index should be abandoned. Our errors should counsel not despair but correction. It is necessary that more careful attention be paid to the logic of measurement and to the rational foundations on which indexes stand. The use of indexes is another outstanding feature of Durkheim's methodology. To him finding the proper index and operating it rationally are the necessary conditions of sociological objectivity. His most famous and most penetrating use of the method of index or of indirect observation is found in *De la Division*. It will be profitable to examine the manner in which he employs it in this volume. Our concern shall be less with the validity of the particular index used than with the mode of its establishment, less with the accuracy of the rational and theoretical principles on which it rests than with the way in which it rests on them.

In undertaking a comparative and classificatory study of social solidarity, Durkheim is confronted with the fact that solidarity " is a completely moral phenomenon which, by itself, is not amenable to exact observation, nor, especially, to measurement." It is therefore necessary for him to " substitute

76 See Alpert, H., *Social Distance: A Problem in Sociological Measurement* (M. A. essay, manuscript; Columbia University Library), 1935.

for the internal fact which escapes us, an external one which symbolizes it, and to study the first through the second." [77]

This "visible symbol" or external index of solidarity he believes to be law, the body of juridical rules. This index is justified on the following grounds. The greater the sentiment of solidarity among the members of a given society, the greater will be the number, frequency, and intensity of the diverse relations they maintain with one another. Furthermore, the number of these social relations is necessarily proportional to the number of juridical rules which regulate them. This last proposition follows from the principle that "social life wherever it exists in a durable manner, tends inevitably to assume a definite form and to be organized; and law is nothing other than this very organization in its most stable form." Another assumption of Durkheim's is that "the general life of society cannot expand without its juridical life expanding at the same time and in the same proportion." If all these propositions are valid, he concludes, "we may be certain to find reflected in law all the essential varieties of social solidarity." [78]

But how valid are they? Some appear to be quite dubious. One may object that many, if not most, social relations are regulated not by law but by customs, folkways and mores and that consequently law can reflect only a part of social life. Moreover, it is well known that the mores are often not in agreement with the law. Durkheim anticipates these objections and attempts to dismiss them. As regards the conflict between the law and the mores, he claims that such a condition is "completely exceptional" and that "normally, the mores are not opposed to law, but, on the contrary, are its basis." As for the relation of law to social life in general, he accepts as perfectly true the belief that there are social relations "which are subject only to that diffuse regulation which derives from the mores." But these relations, he argues, "normally lack

77 *De la Division*, p. 28.
78 *Ibid.*, pp. 28-29.

importance and continuity" and therefore "if it is possible that there are types of social solidarity which the mores alone manifest, they certainly are very secondary" and may be ignored since it is with the important and the essential that we are concerned.[79]

Thus, convinced that he has adequately demonstrated a rational connection between law and social solidarity, Durkheim proposes to study the latter through an analysis of the various types and species of juridical rules and of the relative prevalence of each of these types in a given society. He has arrived at his index by making explicit the implications of solidarity and deducing their consequences.

However, there is a dangerous pitfall in this procedure, and Durkheim was not always on guard against it. We refer to the tendency to conjure up propositions summarily and arbitrarily, almost in the manner of a magician drawing rabbits out of a hat. Is there a logical objection to one of our propositions? Hokus-pokus, and we have a principle, invented *ad hoc,* which melts the objection away. Note, for example, the cavalier fashion in which Durkheim dismisses the objection that the mores as well as law may reflect solidarity. Since it serves his purpose, he introduces for the occasion a totally arbitrary distinction between the "secondary" and the "essential". Surely this is rather flimsy material with which to lay the groundwork for a sociological edifice.[80] The foundations of science require much more substantial matter. This tendency to create general principles out of whole cloth unfortunately vitiates also a good number of Durkheim's other efforts to develop indexes. It is in *Le Suicide,* we believe, that this tendency is found with greatest frequency.[81]

Another reason for his being rather unsuccessful in the creation of indexes is his too narrow and too rigid interpre-

79 *Ibid.,* pp. 29-30.

80 *Cf.* Merton, *op. cit.,* pp. 326-327.

81 *Cf.* Lacombe, *op. cit.,* pp. 75-80.

tation of the principle of objectivity. It is not to be forgotten that on this score Durkheim's views evolved and that as his sociological thought matured his original excessive objectivity became tempered with considerable reasonableness. Nevertheless, in his early writings, those that belong to his juridico-regulatory phase as distinguished from his later religioso-valuational stage,[82] an extremely limited conception of objectiveness is present. In these first works the notion of getting an " objective slant " on social phenomena is equated with the idea of approaching them " independently of their individual manifestations."

When *Les Règles* first appeared in article form the rule relative to objective observation was formulated as follows: " When the sociologist undertakes to explore any order whatsoever of social facts he must endeavor to consider these facts from an angle whereby they present a sufficient degree of objectivity (*consolidation*)." [83] Since the last phrase means simply " sufficiently fixed and stable to be amenable to observation and verification," there can be no difficulty with the rule in this general form. However, Durkheim had posited as a matter of principle that " the more completely social facts are separated from the individual facts which manifest them, the more they are capable of being objectively represented," and consequently changed the phrase " sufficient degree of objectivity " to read " isolated from their individual manifestations." [84]

In this last form, the rule, as interpreted by Durkheim in practice, imposes upon sociology a totally unwarranted limitation of its effective data and hence does not lead to the most

82 These terms refer to the fact that Durkheim's first interests were in juridical phenomena and in the regulatory (order and constraint) aspect of society whereas he later concentrated on religious phenomena and emphasized the ideal and valuational aspects of social life.

83 94a, p. 497.

84 *Règles*, p. 57.

truitful results.[85] By confining the field of social study to such phenomena as " juridical rules, moral rules, popular sayings, facts of structure, etc." [86] it so restricts the scope of the science of society, that the latter finds itself in a sort of rigid straitjacket. That sociology can well profit from a liberation from these narrow confines, recent developments of the science make evident. To take but one example, we may compare the manner in which Durkheim, on the one hand, and one of his students, Professor Bayet, on the other, undertook to analyze suicide as a moral phenomenon.[87]

The founder of the *Année Sociologique*, in conformity with the rule we are discussing confined himself almost exclusively to juridical evidence.[88] Decrees of religious councils, legislative acts, penal codes, biblical commandments and the like constitute his data. Bayet's more thorough investigation of the subject, based on a truly remarkable documentation, is not only more subtle and more plastic than Durkheim's narrowly limited study, but also more accurate. The former does not restrict itself to legal evidence of a people's moral judgment of suicide. It includes in addition such data as customs, popular beliefs, mores, philosophical pronouncements, the moral maxims officially taught in the schools, and, for literate societies, the opinions expressed in newspapers, novels, poetry, drama, etc. True, Bayet's use of this more extended documentation is not as systematic as it might be, but this is another matter. We are concerned here only with illustrating the fruitfulness of giving a much wider interpretation to Durkheim's rule of objectivity than did its own promulgator. It is surely not in keeping with the scientific ideal to adopt the position of Professor Bouglé who, resorting to the Durkheimian distinction

85 We reserve for later a discussion of the concept of " independent existence."

86 *Ibid.*, p. 56; *cf.* 88c.

87 Bayet, A., *Le Suicide et la Morale* (Paris: Alcan, 1922) and 97a, pp. 370-379.

88 *Cf.* his bibliography, 97a, p. 369.

between essential and non-essential obligations, and subscribing to the view that " in a sense, juridical sociology is all of sociology," seems ready to dismiss Bayet's efforts with an " It doesn't matter." [89]

There is no justification for regarding juridical evidence as any more " objective " than the other types of data just mentioned. It is difficult, particularly in the light of current discussions in this country of the Supreme Court, to subscribe to Durkheim's statement that " a rule of law is what it is and there are no two ways of perceiving it." [90] But any one accepting this proposition would have to apply it with equal cogency to other types of social facts. Would one not have to admit that the precepts of a text-book used in classes in morals and civics " are what they are and there are no two ways of perceiving them "? And is this not also true of " biographies, newspaper records, reports of all sorts, historical explorations, statistical researches " [91] and the other materials which reveal the full richness of social life?

Thus, while accepting, as we necessarily must accept, the general principle adopted by Durkheim that social phenomena must be studied by the method of indirect observation or of objective index,[92] we at the same time feel that the French sociologist's specific rules for how this should be done are shackles from which contemporary sociology may well free itself. Durkheim's strictures may have admirably served the purpose of convincing philosophers and scientists that sociology can be established as a positive discipline, but they need not, on that account, be made part of our permanent methodological baggage. Even Durkheim freed himself from them.

89 Bouglé, *Bilan*, pp. 97-98.

90 *Règles*, p. 56.

91 MacIver, *Society* (1931), pp. vii-viii.

92 An index, we should like to mention in passing, should not be used without the limits of its relevance being recorded, for there generally are points beyond which the index becomes inoperative. Thus, if one uses income as an index of status, one must make explicit at what point the index is no longer indicative.

4. SYNTHESIS AND SPECIFICITY

As regards the Durkheimian conception of sociology as a specific, yet synthetic science, no extended treatment is necessary. No twentieth century writer has ever, to our knowledge, maintained that sociology is a one-problem science. We have become too deeply immersed in empirical investigations of specialized questions to be able to believe that sociological research will lose its *raison d'être* the moment we shall discover *the* nature of society, or *the* course of social evolution, or *the* pattern of social change. We are too keenly aware of the infinite diversity and complexity of social life to think that there is a single key that opens all the locks. We are wary of what Cooley has aptly termed particularisms. If there is any one feature that sharply differentiates twentieth from nineteenth century sociology, it is precisely the specialized, specific, investigatory and research nature of our contemporary science. Some of the eminent sociologists who lived through the transitional period from the era of generality to that of specialty reflect this transformation in their own lifework. We need mention but two such outstanding examples as Giddings and Tönnies. A comparison of the Columbia University Professor's *Principles of Sociology* with his *Scientific Study of Human Society* is indeed a commentary on the changes wrought in American sociology during the third of a century that elapsed between the appearance of the two volumes. The development of the author of *Gemeinschaft und Gesellschaft* from an earlier phase of philosophical studies to a later one of specialized statistical researches is likewise characteristic.[93] Would we be far from wrong in adding the case of Durkheim? The wealth of ethnological documentation in *Les Formes élémentaires* as against the relative paucity of precise empirical evidence in many sections of *De la Division* does, perhaps, justify our doing so.

93 *Cf.* Heberle, R., "The Sociology of Ferdinand Tönnies," A S R, II (1937), pp. 9-25.

However, it must not be assumed that this transformation in emphasis from the general to the specific, simply because it has stimulated a vast amount of productive research and has widened the empirical base of our science, has not also had its undesirable consequences. One of these has been an intransigent reaction against all types of generalizations and systematization. The spark engendered by the excesses of the nineteenth century masters was inflamed by the winds of radical and raw empiricism and resulted in a huge fire of contempt for rational theorizing. A cult of fact-worshippers appeared, by whom, to use Durkheimian expressions, facts were relegated to the realm of the sacred and the hallowed, while theories were treated as profane objects, things to be ignored, despised, or ridiculed.

Durkheim was among the foremost to warn against the dangers of unsystematically gathering facts. While pointing out that a science could not long survive without factual evidence, he at the same time insisted that facts alone were hardly a substantial diet on which a scientific discipline could exist.

We must be specific. Instead of philosophizing on the nature of contemporary morality, we should examine a specific moral problem such as suicide and determine its nature, extent, causes, and relation to other social phenomena. Instead of writing huge volumes on the nature of society, we should undertake the investigation of a more limited question, as for example, how the meaning of words is affected by changes in social structures, or how the social position of women is transformed by their increasing participation in business and industrial activities. The future of sociology, Durkheim believed, lies in turning our attention to specific problems and in thoroughly nourishing ourselves on facts. As Professor Lynd has recently stated apropos of the community survey, " social research seems to make larger gains by digging vertically rather than by raking together the top-soil horizontally." [94]

94 Lynd, R. S. and Lynd, H. M., *Middletown in Transition* (New York: Harcourt, Brace, 1937), p. ix.

But facts have no place in science, Durkheim repeated time and again, unless they are made rationally significant, that is, are related to other facts within a systematic framework. This is what is meant by saying that sociology is a specific, yet synthetic science. That contemporary American sociology would be well rewarded if it adopted the Durkheimian conception, a critical survey such as Michael and Adler's *Crime, Law, and Social Science*, makes quite clear. As Veblen is said to have remarked, the most painstaking collection of information is, without guidance and theoretical analysis, " irrelevant, incompetent, and impertinent." [95]

5. COOPERATION

Nor need we linger long on Durkheim's insistence that sociology requires the active and conscious cooperation of a large number of workers, and hence must be a collective enterprise. Again, there is no one who maintains that sociological science is a one-man affair. The day when thinkers spin sociological theories out of whole cloth or weave them out of thin air, when each writer is a system of sociology all by himself seems definitely past. Even Vilfredo Pareto, isolated in his country retreat, enjoying scarcely any company other than that of his Angora cats, and haughtily impervious to the activities of his fellow-workers, wrote only a *general* sociological treatise, that he hoped others would supplement with special sociologies.

An objective index of the present-day realization that sociology is and must be a cooperative, collective endeavor is the ever-increasing number of sociological societies, international, national, and local. It is significant that scarcely any of these groups antedates the last decade of the nineteenth century. The vast majority of them are less than twenty-five years old.

95 *Cf.* Michael, J. and Adler, M., *Crime, Law and Social Science* (New York: Harcourt, Brace, 1933). Of present day sociologists, we may mention MacIver and Znaniecki as among the outstanding leaders in the fight to stem the excesses and wastes of the raw empiricistic position.

The *Institut International de Sociologie*,[96] perhaps the oldest of associations of sociologists, is coeval with Durkheim's *De la Division*. Of particular significance is the "team" of the *Année Sociologique* whose successful experiment in sociological cooperation is an ever-present reminder of the advantages of group activity. The *Année* collaborators became the nucleus of the *French Institute of Sociology* which today carries on the Durkheimian tradition in France.

6. INDEPENDENCE: RELATIONAL SOCIAL REALISM

The Durkheimian position which has evoked the greatest amount of controversy is, no doubt, his view of sociology as an independent science. Much of the polemics on this question rests, however, on misunderstandings arising out of terminological difficulties.

By an independent science one does not in any way mean a discipline which severs all connections with other sciences, or which refuses to utilize the findings of the latter. Such independence would be illusory and self-defeating, since it would be based on ignorance, not on knowledge, and as a matter of principle, would have to neglect many fields of interaction. In this connotation of the term, it is interdependence, and dependence, rather than independence, that characterizes the various sciences, for the specific aspects of reality that each of them investigates have points of contact and interaction with one another. This, obviously, is not at all the Durkheimian sense of "independent."

In claiming independence for sociology, the French social theorist did not attribute any special quality to the particular science to which he was devoted; he merely applied to it the general principle that any science, if it is to exist at all, must exist independently. And by independent existence he implied only two things: (a) a science must have a field of its own and (b) it must contain within itself its own principle of ex-

96 For a brief history of the Institute, see A S R, I (1936), 449-454.

planation. The second of these propositions follows from the first, i. e., *if* a science has a field of its own, then it must contain its own explanatory principle. Put into Durkheimian language and applied to sociology, these statements express the ideas that (1) there is a social reality *sui generis* and (2) social facts must be explained sociologically, i. e., in terms of other social facts. It is difficult to understand how a science which is not merely a sub-section or branch of some other discipline can possibly exist without affirming these principles. Deny them in their general form ((a) and (b)) and there is no means by which the sciences can be distinguished from one another. Refuse to accept the specific propositions ((1) and (2)) and the science of sociology disappears.

The sciences are not distinguishable from one another by the things they study. Science, in fact, does not study things; Durkheim's use of the word "*chose*" is extremely unfortunate. It necessitated a good deal of explanation and re-interpretation that would have been obviated had he chosen a different term. Things are concrete, specific entities presenting in their empirical completeness such an infinity of aspects that a thorough study of them is, humanly speaking, inexhaustible. Science, rather, studies phenomena, i. e., processes, or, to use a much abused word, behavior. It is concerned not with things as such but with relations between, and aspects of, things. Thus, it is not by the concrete objects which they investigate that the sciences are distinguishable from one another. This proposition can be clearly demonstrated by asking which science studies trees, or rocks, or human beings. Obviously, the only intelligible answer is to inquire, which aspect of trees, or rocks, or human persons, or to ask what it is about these things one wishes to know. A recent textbook writer defined sociology as the study of individual men, women, and children. As if biology, or psychology, or even chemistry isn't! No, the distinction between the sciences is determinable on rational, not purely empirical grounds. It is determined by the aspect of things we wish to single out for investigation and by the kind of knowledge about them that we want to know. A tree, for example, has physical and chemical properties, and if our interest is in this aspect of it, it is studied by physics and chemistry. But it also has certain life functions, that is, some aspects of its behavior are directly derived from the fact that it is an organic entity. To study it from this angle is the task of the biologist. Of course, there is a chemistry of life, as there is a chemistry of inorganic matter, and hence we have the sub-science of bio-chemistry; but life and its manifestations and derivatives when studied as such fall within the province of biology. The latter we regard as an independent science, since it has a field of its own which we may approximately delimit as life as such.

The reasons for asserting that biology has a domain of its own are numerous. There is, first of all, a vast amount of negative experiential and experimental evidence that the processes of life cannot be completely accounted for in chemical and physical terms alone. These can explain only the chemical and physical aspects of living things. Then, there is the more positive evidence that the principle that life as such can adequately be explained only in terms of life has had fruitful experimental consequences. Therefore this principle, rather than an atomistic, reductionistic one, should be adopted, if for no reason other than its proven heuristic value. All one needs to show to justify the assertion that a science has a field of its own is that this science deals with an aspect of reality which has properties *sui generis*. And there are empirical, logical, and pragmatic grounds for believing that biology is such a discipline.

What of sociology? It is not sufficient to argue by analogy; analogies must be demonstrated, not asserted. The case for sociology must be built up independently. Does it too analyze some aspect *sui generis* of reality which is not completely explained by being treated merely as the subject matter of some other science?

The accumulated data of anthropology, ethnology, and sociology make it unnecessary for us to consider here the possibility of reducing such phenomena as marriage rites, political parties, or courts of law to purely physical, chemical, or biological terms. We know of no attempt at such reductions that has been able to withstand rigorous logical criticism.[97] We may therefore concentrate our attention on the relations between sociology and psychology, since the latter is the only other possible field within which the data usually assigned to the former may fall. This, indeed, is the very problem which consumed so much of Durkheim's energy and which has remained a focal one in French sociology.[98]

The manner in which this question is resolved depends, obviously, on the way one defines the field of psychology. We must, therefore, determine what Durkheim's conception of this science was. But first, two preliminary considerations are necessary.

It is not always easy to interpret Durkheim's thought, as the very fact that he was frequently misunderstood bears witness. His analyses are often, and not on the least important points, couched in ambiguous and highly equivocal terms. It becomes necessary, as a consequence, to recast his none too felicitous terminology in order to get at his intended meaning. We have already mentioned his unfortunate use of the word " *chose* " and the misleading nature of his adjective " mechanical." Equally lamentable is his manner of employing the term " *fait* " (fact). He seems constantly to use it in a concrete sense, which makes it difficult for him to convey the meaning of " aspects or elements of things." Thus, he speaks of " social facts " and " psychical facts " whereas what he has in mind is the social *element* of a given phenomenon, or its psychical *aspect*.

97 *Cf. Le Suicide*, Book I, and Bain, R., " The Concept of Complexity in Sociology," S F, VIII (1930), 376-378.

98 *Cf.* Mauss, M., " Rapports réels et pratiques de la psychologie et de la sociologie," J P, XXII (1924), 892-922; and Essertier, D., *Psychologie et Sociologie* (Paris: Alcan, 1927).

This difficulty renders ambiguous a statement such as " a social fact must be explained by another social fact." If " fact " refers to a concrete entity, the proposition is dubious, if at all meaningful. However, it is clear from its context that Durkheim means simply that the social element or aspect of a phenomenon must be explained socially.

The second point we wish to make is that one of the best clues for ascertaining Durkheim's position on a particular problem is to determine to what doctrines and views he is opposed. In the early phase of his sociological career, he assumed a severely hostile attitude towards those theories and beliefs that did not coincide with his own. His first writings consequently have the character of fiery and war-like polemics. Durkheim took up the doctrines of others chiefly in order to demolish and dismiss them. It is scarcely possible, as Blondel has pointed out, to find a single smile in the writings of this austere and serious sociologist. Thus, to get a clear picture of what Durkheim is *for*, it is valuable to find out what he is *against*.

Keeping in mind, then, that we are sure to meet difficulties of phraseology, and that his position will be, more likely than not, polemically stated, we may take up now Durkheim's conception of the relations of sociology and psychology. What we have just said about his unfortunate use of expressions is particularly true of such crucial terms as " individual," " psychical," and " psychological." An examination of the first of these words will prove revealing.

The human individual may be regarded from several angles. Since we are not at this moment interested in him as a physical mass, or as an equilibrium of energies, or as a system of chemical reactions, we may omit reference to him from these points of view, and turn immediately to some of his other aspects. The term " individual " may be used to refer to: (1) the biological individual, the individual as an organic entity, the life aspect of the person; (2) the psychological individual, the individual as a psychical entity, psychic man-in-general, the mental aspect of the person; (3) the isolated, organico-psychical individual, the individual *qua* individual, but considered as he would be were he to live in complete isolation; (4) the social person, the social aspect of the human personality, the individual " as he is made by others and by himself to appear in their experience and his own in the course of his social relationships "; [99] (5) the organico-psychico-social individual, the real person, the individual as he really is, as a member of society and as a complete personality, the real social being considered as such.

Now, in which of these senses does Durkheim use the term? Almost invariably, when he speaks of the individual he has in mind the individual in our sense 3, the isolated, organico-psychical being. However, when he specifically uses the qualification " as he really is," the reference is generally to sense 5, and sometimes to sense 4. Thus, when he says that social phenomena cannot be explained in terms of the individual, or that the individual is an abstraction, he means the isolated individual (3), but when he asserts that sociology endeavors to know the individual as he is presented to experience, he has in mind the complete social personality, man as a member of society (5). When he speaks of the duality of human nature, it is the human nature of person 5 that he is thinking of, the dual elements being person 4 on the one hand, and individuals 1 and 2 on the other. " Individual " pertains, also, to man-in-general, to the psychical behavior of man in its most universal aspects (sense 2). Thus when it is said that " the social " is more complex than " the individual," the reference is often to the contrast between the specific nature of 5 and the very general properties of 2.

Sometimes, too, " individual " has the connotation of " individual persons taken severally," as in the statement that a group is not a simple sum of individuals, the meaning here being that the group as a group is a plurality of individuals

99 Znaniecki, *Method*, p. 120.

considered jointly, i. e., in their associative aspect, and not severally. At other times, "individual" means "any one individual taken alone," as in the proposition that a social fact (substitute: the social element of a phenomenon) is never explained by an individual fact (substitute: by reference to any one individual alone). Thus, an invention may be attributed to an individual genius, or a reform to a particular statesman, but such questions as what led the inventor or the statesman to work in this direction, what elements of the social heritage did he exploit, why did the invention or reform receive widespread acceptance, whence come the authority and prestige that the inventor or statesman enjoys, are, obviously, problems which require analysis in terms of more than just a single individual taken alone, no matter how great his personal talents.[100]

This inconsistent use of the important term "individual" is, of course, regrettable, but in the light of the fact that the word does have the diverse meanings we have singled out, it is incumbent upon text book writers who employ such stereotypes as "Durkheim neglects the individual" to make more explicit and precise the particular connotation of the term they have in mind.

Why this confusing variety of meanings attributed to "individual"? This question makes relevant the second of our preliminary points, for to answer it one must determine the doctrines in opposition to which Durkheim attempted to establish his position as a sociologist. The French social theorist came to sociology with the hope of being able to develop a well-founded, realistic, and comprehensive theory of human nature. Man, he maintained in keeping with the Aristotelian tradition, is by nature a social being for whom the society of other persons is a necessary and natural environment. Man cannot live outside of society and, as his social milieu is, so is he. To know him, then, one must know society. These

100 Cf. Règles, p. 137, footnote 1.

principles, which Durkheim regarded as giving sociology its *raison d'être*, were propounded by the French theorist in vigorous protest against those doctrines which viewed society as an artificial mechanism deliberately invented by human beings. Whether the doctrine was a social contract theory and held that these beings were free individuals who had compacted to live together with a view towards enjoying severally the fruits and advantages of cooperation or whether it was the political philosophy that explained society as the conscious contrivance of a few strong individuals who hoped thereby to dominate their weaker fellow beings, it didn't matter. The essential point was that these theories, however divergent their specific Hobbesian, Rousseauan, utilitarian or individualistic form, were in agreement in viewing society as fundamentally a post-individual phenomenon. In the beginning there were individuals, " isolated," " independent," " free," " natural," " solitary." Then these individuals, already endowed with such qualities as reason, emotion, sympathy, foresight, egoism, altruism, desire to dominate, love of war, wish for peace, etc., etc.—endowed indeed with whatever psychological elements a particular philosopher thought most necessary to give his theory the logical and consistent allure that, in our culture, men of learning demand — got together and formed society. Now this type of social theory, and the consequences supposedly derived from it: utilitarian in ethics, laisser-faireism in economics, and rugged individualism in political science, inspired in Durkheim a great distrust which led him to wage mortal and unremitting combat against them. *De la Division du travail social* for which *Anti-utilitarianism* would have been as appropriate an alternative title as the one we suggested in Part I, was the first major battle in this war of ideas. *Le Suicide* was an ingeniously planned surprise attack that caught the individualists off their guard, so to speak — " Even our egoism is in large part a product of society," Durkheim purported to show therein.[101]

101 *Le Suicide*, p. 411; *cf.* 06b.

More frontal in its approach was *L'Education Morale*. The incompleted *Ethics* would no doubt have announced utilitarianism's complete surrender.

For the arms, weapons, and materials with which to wage this doctrinal battle against social compact and utilitarian theories, Durkheim turned to sociology. This science, he believed, was the only one capable of furnishing the correctives for the flagrant inadequacies of the various individualistic views. His efforts to establish an independent science of sociology were, then, directed chiefly against those doctrines which imply that there were individuals who existed prior to, and were responsible for, the creation of society.

However, in his relentless opposition to such theories, Durkheim committed a grave error of tactics; he endeavored to combat these doctrines on their own grounds. This, we feel, explains the terminological difficulties of all sorts into which he got himself and, in particular, accounts for the variety of ways in which he employed the term " individual." The fundamental fallacy of the views he was opposing was readily perceived by him. He clearly realized that individuals cannot exist as such prior to, and apart from, society. Men were not first " isolated and independent " individuals who only afterwards became social beings. Rather, it was only as social beings that they became individuals. It is society, as Aristotle said, that is prior to the individual.[102] Thus, the basic mistake of the individualistic view was to confuse the individual as we know him, i. e., as a product of his social milieu (our sense 5) with the isolated organico-psychical individual (our sense 3). To the latter, a meaningless abstraction, were attributed the qualities and traits of the former. Durkheim understood all this, and persistently argued against confusions of this nature. However, instead of rejecting and dismissing the concept of the isolated, organico-psychical individual as an illogical

---

102 This does not mean that society existed before there were individuals. Aristotle used prior in a logical, not a chronological, sense.

and illusory construct, *he accepted it for polemic purposes* and set up his own sociological conceptions *in opposition to it*. Hence, his constant and invariable use of the word individual in sense 3. Hence, too, his frequent tendency, whenever he wishes to emphasize the fundamental difference between the organico-psychical isolated individual, and the socially developed human being, to set up a dichotomy between " the individual " and " the social," to announce the heterogeneity of the two, and to oppose the latter to the former.

These considerations go a long way in clarifying Durkheim's conception of sociology as an independent science. Let us briefly follow his reasoning on this point, starting, as he does, with the difference between individual 3 and individual 5. To study the former [103] one must take a human being and make abstraction of those aspects of his behavior which relate to, or derive from, his association with other human beings. Individual 5, on the other hand, is analyzed not only as an organico-psychical entity, but, in addition, as he is affected by the set of influences constituted by his fellow-men and the products of their fellowship. Now, from such evidence as feral cases and the effects of isolation and solitary confinement on human beings, we know that 5 has certain characteristics and properties (e.g., possesses ideals and values) which 3 lacks and which the former too would lack if he were in the isolated position of the latter. These distinctive properties of 5 we may attribute to the fact of human association, since it is the only thing that distinguishes him from 3. In other words, man as a member of society, as an associative entity, has characteristics which he would not have if he were an isolated individual. It is necessary, therefore, to distinguish, on the one hand, those aspects of human activity which relate either to the phenomenon of association itself or to its consequences, and, on the other, those that refer to the individual taken in isolation.[104]

103 The appellation " organicô-psychical isolated being " is, it should be noted, not ours but Durkheim's.

104 *Cf. De la Division*, p. 342, footnote 3, and *Règles*, p. 126.

The former we may call the associational, or, as is more common, the social, aspects of human behavior; and we may term the plurality of associated individuals who maintain more or less stable relations with one another a social group. Social life, then, " is constituted by a system of facts which derive from positive and durable relations established among a plurality of individuals ";[105] and the term " social facts " refers to those phenomena, processes, and actions, or to those aspects or elements of them, which are directly attributable to the fact of association, which are, as Tylor put it, acquired by man as a member of society, or which, to use Durkheim's language, are because human associations are, and are *what* they are because society is what it is.[106] Reduced to these terms, the proposition that there is an aspect of reality that we may name the social and which we may designate as the distinctive field of sociology seems hardly disputable. Contemporary anthropologists and sociologists, in fact, have no difficulty in speaking of a science of society, or a science of culture, or a science of social relations, or a science of custom, yet all these expressions imply acceptance of the principle just enunciated.

Implicit in the argumentation just presented is Durkheim's conception of the relation between psychology and sociology. The clue to his view of the connection between the two sciences lies in the above-mentioned differentiation between the aspects of human activity that relate to the single individual taken in isolation, and those that refer to the phenomenon of human association and its consequences. For, if sociology includes the associative aspects of human life, psychology deals with the purely individual elements of behavior.

But what does "purely individual" mean? Whenever Durkheim employs the terms " psychical " and " psychological " in contradistinction to " the social " and " the sociological," they relate almost invariably to the mental behavior of the isolated,

105 *De la Division*, p. 329.

106 *Cf.* 09e, p. 268; 00c, p. 136; and Fauconnet, P. and Mauss, M., article " Sociologie," G E, XXX, pp. 165-176.

organico-psychical being. Psychology, he urges, should be restricted in its meaning to denote exclusively "individual psychology" and should be specifically defined as it always has been defined, as the science of the mental life of the individual.[107] But what individual? Durkheim can only have in mind either the isolated and independent individual (3) or, possibly, the psychological individual (2), since it is to another science, which he calls socio-psychology, that he assigns the study of the socially formed person, the real 'social being. Socio-psychology, he tells us, will study those individual, psychical facts which "result from social causes," i. e. from the action of phenomena which are directly or indirectly derived from the fact of human association.[108] Unhyphenated psychology, then, studies only those individual, psychical facts over which social facts exercise no influence.[109] Since social forces are all-pervasive, these purely individual psychical facts can only relate either to a situation in which there are no social actions, as in the case of the isolated individual, or to those very general, universal, and hence limited aspects of our mental life which are not affected by social factors. Thus, when Durkheim opposes social and sociological data to psychical and psychological facts, he is thinking for the most part of the distinction between the phenomena that are derivatives of association and those that pertain either to the societyless, isolated person or to man in his most general aspects.

What he means by "the psychological method" in sociology and the reasons for which he so vehemently rejects it must be understood in somewhat the same manner. "Every time that a social phenomenon is *directly* explained by a psychical phenomenon, one can be assured that the explanation is false" is one of Durkheim's most famous battle-cries.[110] It

107 24a, p. 47, footnote 1.

108 *De la Division*, p. 341.

109 The reader is asked to bear in mind our strictures on the use of the term "fact" and to interpret these statements accordingly.

110 *Règles*, p. 128. It is we who underline. In citing this sentence there is a

sums up his opposition to the psychological method of sociological explanation. This method may be defined, to parallel
Durkheim's words, as the approach to social phenomena which
explains them directly in terms of psychological phenomena.[111]
It consists, essentially, of two steps. First one posits a certain
kind of human nature inherent in all individuals and made up
of psychological entities such as faculties, attitudes, ideas, sensations, instincts, tendencies, desires, wishes, etc. These one
accepts as irreducible and self-sufficient elements, that is, as
units which require no explanation other than the fact that
they exist and are " given " to experience. Then, one proceeds
to " explain " a given social phenomenon by relating it to one
or several of these already posited psychological elements.
Does one wish to explain the custom of blood-revenge? One
consults the table of psychological elements that one has prepared and picks out, let us say, the instinct for revenge, or, if
one's table omits instincts, perhaps the desire to kill or the
wish for new experiences will do. Is exogamy the order of the
day? The elements are ever plentiful: the instinct of racial
purity, the desire for novelty, the feeling of guilt, etc. Is one
puzzled by religion? One need not be for long. Consult the
elements and one will " discover " the fear of the dead, the
fear of nature, the desire for immortality, the instinct for
myth-creation, etc. It is only this kind of *ad hoc* legerdemain
that Durkheim is dismissing when he dictatorially banishes
psychological explanations from the social realm. It is only
this particular hypothetical being who is pre-socially and extra-
socially equipped with all the baggage necessary to live a complete life as a human personality whom he is demanding that
we get rid of when he " discards the individual " as a suffi-

---

tendency to overlook the important word we have italicized. Durkheim, as
we have attempted to show, by no means excludes psychical factors from
sociological explanation; he dismisses them only as direct and self-sufficient
causes. *Cf. ibid.*, pp. 130-132.

111 *Cf. Règles*, pp. 120-137.

cient explicative factor of social data.[112] Indeed, how else can the social element of social phenomena be explained other than in terms of the associational behavior of socially developed associated beings? *Cultura ex cultura, societas ex societate;* there is no alternative except to deny reality altogether to culture and society.

Yet the proponents of the psychological method as above described must necessarily adopt this alternative, for they, like the advocates of social contract and individualistic views, implicitly accept the assumption of a pre-societal individual, i. e., of man existing as man prior to society. In fact, the psychological approach to sociology may be regarded as only the methodological consequence of these socio-political philosophies. For, if independent beings existed in full maturity as isolated persons before entering into social relations, social phenomena can only be the expression of the individual human personality. Consequently, the nature of social facts may be essentially deduced from the nature of the individual (pre-societal) human being. To know society, then, one need only know the individual person. Moreover, inasmuch as the science of the individual is psychology, and since the phenomena we call social are explicable directly in psychological terms, sociology is, in reality, only a phantom science.

Such are the implications of the psychological method, whose inadequacies Durkheim spared no effort in exposing. Man, he repeatedly proclaimed, is a product as well as a creator of society, and hence a theory of human nature, far from being the starting point of a science of sociology, must necessarily be one of its end results. In opposition to the view that social life is deducible from the inherent elements of the individual personality, he adopted what Professor Faris has properly termed the histrionic or dramatic theory of human nature. This view, Professor Faris summarizes: " conceives the per-

112 *Ibid.,* p. 125. The distortions to which the phrase " *l'individu écarté, il ne reste que la société* " has been subjected have been infinite, yet in its context there can be no doubt of its meaning.

sonality as a role, a part to be played, and the role of an actor depends on the play that is being enacted. Institutions and customs precede individuals and personality results from participation in these ongoing social processes. Human personality, arising in communication, is the result of conduct which takes place in the presence of others and in contacts with friends and enemies, allies, and opponents. Personality is mobile, self-developing, self-organizing. Groups precede babies and children are born into communities with customs. To assume fixed points of origin or stable elements which are combined into a personality is to reverse the order of development. Ideas, sensations, and wishes occur, but they are events and consequences, not elements. They must be defined in terms of the social process, not the process in terms of them." [113] Sociology, therefore, must reverse the psychological procedure and explain these elements as derivatives of cultural and associational life. It is blood-revenge, as anthropologists have so frequently pointed out, that accounts for " the instinct of revenge," religion that explains the fear of the dead, and not the opposite. The cart does not pull the horse.

We see, then, that Durkheim builds his sociological structure polemically. It is in opposition to individualism, to utilitarianism, to psychologism (if we may thus refer to what he calls the psychological method of explanation) that he endeavors to erect an independent sociology. One must bear this constantly in mind if one wishes to interpret aright the various dichotomies he establishes; individual vs. social, psychical vs. social, psychological vs. sociological. The first terms here refer to abstractions of which he himself did not approve but which he nevertheless adopted from opposing views because of his

---

113 Faris, E., " Of Psychological Elements," A J S, XLII (1936), 175-176. It is significant that in pursuing his study of social actions Znaniecki found it necessary to try " to get rid of the assumption that the whole variety of the social actions of men has to be deduced from a few permanent and fundamental psychological forces—essential attitudes, wishes, desires, or what not." (*Social Actions*, p. viii).

predilection for the polemic style of cogitation. It is essential to remember that the pre-societal, extra-social, but nonetheless fully matured, human individual invented by the individualist philosophers was the central target against which he directed his sociological darts. To this phantom and illusory individual, to his would-be behavior and to his pretended psychology, he opposed real social beings, social conduct and sociology.

Polemic ratiocination, like the method of elimination which is one of its components, has both the advantage of being psychologically convincing and the disadvanage of being logically precarious. It tends to make one accept a given problem in the terms in which it is set by one's opponents, even though the manner in which they pose the question may be false, misleading, or illogical. Unfortunately Durkheim did not avoid this danger, as is seen in the set of propositions that comprise what is generally referred to as his " social realism." [114]

The utilitarian, individualistic, and social compact philosophers, failing to perceive such basic sociological truths as that " the individual is neither beginning or end, but a link in the succession of life," that " only in society do we become individuals," and that " individuality and society are in fundamental harmony," [115] constantly posed their problems in terms of a dichotomy and conflict between " society " and " the individual." The individual *versus* society, individual welfare *versus* social welfare, individual rights *versus* the oppressive action of society, no matter what the particular question the fundamental, irreconcilable dichotomy between the two terms was always present. The spiritualistic, Hegelian thinkers reversed the emphasis, stressing Society as against the Individual, but they in no way altered the logical form of the problem; to them, too, it was a matter of a conflict and dichotomy.

114 Deploige, S., *Le Conflit de la morale et de la sociologie* (3rd ed., Paris, Nouvelle Librairie Nationale, 1923), Chap. V, and Simpson, G., " Emile Durkheim's Social Realism," S S R, XXVIII (1933), 3-11.

115 MacIver, *Society*, pp. 20, 21, 24; *cf*. Chap II, sec. 2, and the same author's *Community*, esp. Book III, Chap. III. *See also*, Durkheim, *De la Division*, pp. xliii-xliv, 318 footnote 1, and item 98c.

As long as social philosophy conceived the question in this form, it was inevitable that the advocates of the individualist theses should propound such principles as, "There are only individuals; there is no society," "Society is composed only of individuals," "Only individuals are real; society is chimerical," and that their spiritualist opponents should counter with such statements as "Society alone is real; individuals are only its parts," "Society is a reality over and above the individuals who comprise it," "Society is a real entity; individual consciousnesses are only reflections of the great social consciousness." In such terms was the problem of the relations of society and the individual being debated in the last half of the nineteenth century, at the very moment that sociology, beginning to be recognized as a special and distinct discipline, was endeavoring to establish itself as a positive science. Some sociologists rallied to the individualist cause and became known as "social nominalists" while others adopted the spiritualist views and were termed "social realists." [116] Perhaps the most eminent of the nominalists was the outstanding English individualist, Herbert Spencer. This philosopher of economic liberalism was torn, it is true, between his individualism and his biologism, and hence between a social contract and a naturalistic view of the origin of society. Nevertheless, he allowed

---

[116] The *social* nominalism—*social* realism debate is not to be confused with the philosophical nominalist-realist controversy. The former refers to the question of the relation of the individual to society, while the latter is concerned with an ontological problem. Thus, Fouillée's formulation of the *social* nominalist-realist problem as involving the question as to whether society is a word or a thing is completely misleading. A *sociologist* cannot possibly be a nominalist if this means accepting society as only a word. Neither Spencer nor Tarde were nominalists in this sense of the term. As the former has said, the issue is not whether society is a word or a thing, but rather what kind of a thing it is. See Spencer, H., *The Principles of Sociology* (3rd ed., N. Y.: Appleton, 1923), Vol. I, pp. 447-448; Fouillée, A., *Les Eléments sociologiques de la morale* (2nd ed., Paris: Alcan, 1905), pp. 159 ff.; *cf.* Deploige, *op. cit.*, pp. 138 ff.; and Park, R. E., and Burgess, E. W., *Introduction to the Science of Sociology* (2nd ed., Chicago: University of Chicago Press, 1924), Chap. I.

his laisser-faireism to conquer his organicism, and subscribed to the nominalist position. The individual human being is the initial factor of sociology, he maintained, and even if society *is* an organism, it must not be presumed that it has a common sensorium. "As, then, there is no social sensorium, the welfare of the aggregate, considered apart from that of the units is not an end to be sought. The society exists for the benefit of its members, not its members for the benefit of society." [117]

The realists, it seems, were more numerous. They comprised two major groups. On the one hand, they included the sociologists who espoused the organicist position and who, consequently, regarded society as an organismic entity of which individuals were, in the biological sense of the term, only members. Lilienfeld was, perhaps, the most extreme of them, but not far removed from his position were Schäffle, Espinas, and Worms. On the other hand, there were realists who, under Hegelian influences, propounded what Hobhouse has termed " the metaphysical theory of the state," i. e., the theory which views society as " the incarnation of something very great and glorious, indeed, as one expression of that supreme being which some . . . thinkers call the Spirit and others the Absolute, and according to which society is an end in itself," an

---

117 Spencer, *op. cit.*, pp. 461-462. Note the characteristic dichotomous mode of statement; *cf.* the title of his famous *The Man Versus the State.* See also Rumney, *op. cit.*, p. 20. Rumney defends Spencer against the charge of nominalism. "Spencer," he writes, "does not set up that false antithesis —*the* individual and human society." (*Ibid.*) Yet, on the very same page, he admits that Spencer derives society from a pre-social state and quotes him to the effect that "it is much more true that Society is created by its units, and that the nature of its organization is determined by the nature of its units. The two act and react; but the *original* factor is the character of the individuals, and the *derived* factor is the character of the society." (Italics ours.) And further on, Rumney states that "Spencer makes Society a mechanical collation of units" and asserts that "the other extreme" of this view is to postulate a social mind (p. 235). Admittedly, there is an inherent contradiction in Spencer, but when pressed hard and forced to choose, he generally adopts a social nominalist view. Spencer, of course, was not a philosophical nominalist.

end to which the lives of men and women are merely means. They believed, to parallel Spencer's language, that the welfare of the aggregate, considered apart from that of the units is an end to be sought, since " the happiness of the individual is to be valued by the perfection of the whole to which he belongs." [118] Then, those thinkers who were impressed with the recent and novel analyses of crowds, mobs, and mass movements, and who as a consequence adopted the concept of a group or collective mind, were also realists. To this group of mystical realists belong the names of Gumplowicz and Le Bon.[119]

The nominalism-realism controversy is one of those eternal questions that will never become superannuated. Nevertheless, we have no great difficulty today in perceiving that, if the individualistic or nominalistic position implicitly assumes that meaningless abstraction we have called the pre-societal individual, the spiritualistic or realist view rests on the no less fallacious proposition that a pluralistic whole is of the nature of its elements, i. e., that a unity of organs is itself an organ, a unity of trees itself a tree, or a unity of minds itself a mind.[120] But what is more important is the fact that we have come to realize that the very question to which these conflicting views purport to be the answer is itself falsely stated. The relation of the individual to society is not a matter of having to decide in favor of one of two conflicting and contrary forces, but rather a problem which involves viewing two different aspects of the same thing. Self and society are twin-born, a generation of American sociologists has learned from the wise Charles Horton Cooley.[121] It is significant that this eminent American social scientist begins his discussion of social organization by

118 Hobhouse, L. T., *The Metaphysical Theory of the State* (N. Y.: Macmillan, 1918), pp. 18-19. *Cf.* MacIver, R. M., *The Modern State* (Oxford: Clarendon Press, 1926), pp. 447-454.

119 Gumplowicz, in his later writings, modified his realism.

120 MacIver, *Modern State, loc. cit.*

121 Cooley, C. H., *Social Organization* (N. Y.: Scribner's, 1909), p. 5.

dismissing immediately any dichotomous view whatsoever of the relation of society to the individual. Such a view, he asserts, is neither necessary nor reasonable. " Mind is like the music of an orchestra, which is made up of divergent but related sounds. . . . No one would thing it necessary or reasonable to divide the music into two kinds, that made by the whole, and that of particular instruments, and no more are there two kinds of mind, the social mind and the individual mind." [122]

Now, when Durkheim definitely decided to embark on a sociological career he had the individualistic theories, then widespread in France, with which to contend, and, as we have seen, he oriented his own social thinking with reference to them. Since, in his efforts to combat the utilitarian solution to the problem of the relations of the individual to society, he accepted, for polemic purposes, the dichotomous formulation of the question, he could do naught else but take over the individualist propositions and turn them around by emphasizing the social, in opposition to the individual, term. Consequently, his own principles tend to be couched in " realistic " language. His phraseology is, in fact, decidedly that of the realists. " Social facts have their own existence, independent of their individual manifestations "; " Society is a specific reality which has its own characteristics distinct from those of the individuals who comprise it "; " Collective tendencies exist external to individuals "; " There is heterogeneity between individual states and social states," etc.[123] To which we may add such Durkheimian appurtenances, to borrow a word from Lévy-Bruhl, as the concepts of collective consciousness, collective representation, social current, collective mentality, etc. It is no wonder, then, that Durkheim is usually classified as an outstanding representative of the school of social realists.[124] Is this a valid classification, and, if so, in what sense?

122 *Ibid.*, p. 3.
123 01c, pp. xiv-xix, 19, 57; 97a, pp. 348-363; 93b, p. 341; 24a, pp. 45-48.
124 In addition to the Deploige and Simpson references above, see Park

Realism, in philosophy, pertains to a doctrine expressing a relation between knowers and things known. It is the view that holds that " some or all known objects owe their being to conditions different from those to which they owe their being known." [125] In this epistemological sense of the term, Durkheim is a confirmed realist. His insistence on the naturalness of social data, on the necessity of treating them as things, and his realistic definition of what things are, allow of no other interpretation. However, *social* realism, as we have seen, is not so much concerned with this particular epistemological view as with the question of the relation of the individual to society. As such, it has been defined as the doctrine that maintains that " society, its facts and products, exist outside of, and above individuals, that the existence of social facts, in short, is not dependent upon individuals." [126] This position we should like to call substantialist social realism inasmuch as it implies that society is an ontological reality, a substantial entity having corporate existence apart from, or, to use the traditional phrase, over and above, the individuals who comprise it.[127] *In this substantialist connotation of social realism, Durkheim is not, never was, and never became a realist.* It is surely misleading, if not erroneous, to classify him as such.

There is much evidence to support this contention. We may, first of all, mention the fact that Durkheim himself persistently and categorically denied ever believing in society as a tran-

and Burgess, *op. cit.*, p. 36, Rumney, *op. cit.*, p. 235; Gehlke, *op. cit.*, pp. 84-87; Sorokin, P., *Contemporary Sociological Theories* (N. Y.: Harper & Bros., 1928), p. 465; and Perry, R. B., " Des Formes de l'Unité Sociale," in *Congrès des Sociétés Philosophiques américaine, anglaises, belge, italienne et française, Communications et Discussions* (Paris: Colin, 1921), pp. 445-470, and the same author's *General Theory of Value* (N. Y.: Longmans, Green, 1926), p. 471.

125 Perry, R. B., quoted by Simpson, *op. cit.*, p. 3.

126 Simpson, *op. cit.*, p. 3.

127 The view that " society is an indivisible and substantial unity " is called by Professor R. B. Perry the doctrine of " social substance." See his *General Theory of Value* (N. Y.: Longmans, Green, 1926), pp. 402-403.

scendental, hypostatized, and substantial entity.[128] It is therefore incumbent upon those who attribute this belief to him to
maintain that he was a realist of this order in spite of himself,
and that he unconsciously espoused a doctrine to which he was
deliberately and explicitly opposed. Exegesis based on this
assumption is patently absurd. Many are the occasions on
which Durkheim insisted that " individuals are the only active
elements in society," that " it is an evident truth that there is
nothing in social life which is not in individual consciousnesses," that " society is not possible without individuals," that
" society can exist only in individual consciousnesses and
through them," that " society exists and lives only in and by
individuals . . . (and) has reality only to the extent that it has a
place in human consciousnesses." [129] In anticipation of the possible objection that Durkheim's views on this question evolved,
and that his realism is manifest only in his later works, we
should like to point out that the dates of the statements just
quoted are, in order, 1898 (repeated 1901), 1893, 1897, and
1912 (twice). Thus we find an explicit stand against substantialist social realism even in such a sociologismic work as *Les
Formes élémentaires*, the last of Durkheim's volumes to appear
in his lifetime. It is, therefore, not at all legitimate to dismiss
his earliest published views on this subject as merely youthful
aberrations indicative of a thought not yet matured. However
else Durkheim's views may have changed, on this particular
score he was quite consistent. He was no less vehemently opposed to a transcendental group-mind or group-entity doctrine
in 1912 than in 1885. If, just before the World War, he
asserts that society can exist only in and through individual
consciousnesses, he is merely echoing a view that he propounded
twenty-seven years previously in almost the same language.

128 *Cf. Règles*, p. 127, footnote 1; *Suicide*, pp. 361-362; *Les Formes élémentaires*, p. 299.

129 *Cf. Règles*, p. xiv, footnote 1; *De la Division*, p. 342; *Le Suicide*,
p. 362; *Les Formes élémentaires*, pp. 299, 496; *Sociologie et Philosophie*,
p. 40, footnote 1, p. 85.

In 1885, in a review of Gumplowicz's *Outlines of Sociology* he objected to the Austrian sociologist's mystical conception of society in the following terms: "Society has nothing metaphysical about it. It is not a more or less transcendental substance. . . . Since there are only individuals in society, it is they, and they alone who are the factors of social life." [130]

Moreover, the social realist position, as defined above, contradicts the fundamental thesis that Durkheim endeavored to demonstrate in *De la Division*. Disciple of Renouvier, he made human individuality or personality the highest moral value in contemporary society. However, instead of accepting this ethical principle on neo-Kantian grounds, he tried to show that this conception of the high moral worth of the human personality is itself a product of social evolution, that it is only in and through society that the human being acquires his individuality, and that the more complex the society, i. e., the more it is founded on mutual functional differences, the greater is the degree of individuality developed. The very starting point of Durkheim's dissertation was the problem of how it came about that sociality and individuality, to use MacIver's formulation of the question, develop *pari passu*.[131] Now, this principle of the dignity of the individual human personality always remained focal in Durkheim's ethical thought. The human personality has become the highest social value of European societies, he repeatedly remarked, and thus, " far from there being any antagonism between the individual and society, as has so often been maintained, in reality, moral individualism, the cult of the human individual, is the handiwork of society." [132] Now, on social realistic premises, this

130 85c, p. 632.

131 *De la Division*, p. xliii; MacIver, *Community*, p. 220. *See also*, Cooley, C. H., *Human Nature and the Social Order* (N. Y.: Scribner's, 1902), p. 7.

132 24a, p. 84. See *ibid.*, p. 131. This was written in 1906, yet it has been asserted that "after *Le Suicide* (1897), Durkheim became a thoroughgoing realist and left little place for the individual." (Simpson, *op. cit.*, p. 4.) *Cf.* also 25a, Part I, and 98c.

principle of " moral individualism " cannot be defended. For, how can one attribute moral dignity to the individual if he has no significant existence? Thus, once again one must choose: either Durkheim was a social realist in direct contradiction to his most fundamental social and ethical principles, or it is erroneous to attribute the doctrine of social realism to him. Simpson, for instance, accepts the first alternative. However, he is forced constantly to accuse Durkheim of " straying from his views," of "doing strange things," of " misunderstanding what he himself was proving," of " going off to belie his own doctrine," of achieving in his later works " a complete denial of the very valid conclusions " he reached earlier, etc.[133] But it is inadmissible, as we have seen, to distinguish between Durkheim's earlier and later works *on this particular point.* It is really remarkable how unnecessary all these mental contortions become the moment one ceases to misrepresent the French theorist's views. The square peg simply doesn't fit into the round hole. Perhaps, after all, it isn't Durkheim who does strange things.

On the basis, then, of his replies to critics, and of his own positive assertions, and on the evidence of what may be called the inner consistency of his system, we may conclude that if social realism is the view that posits the existence of a collective mind as an ontological reality beyond and above, and independent of individual consciousnesses, Durkheim is not by any means a social realist.[134] Yet a number of difficulties re-

133 Simpson, *op. cit.,* pp. 4 ff.

134 *Cf.* Blondel, *op. cit.,* p. 51 ; Davy, G., *Sociologues d'hier et d'aujourd'hui* (Paris: Alcan, 1931), p. 168; Bouglé, C., *Bilan,* pp. 10-12; Marjolin, R., "French Sociology—Comte and Durkheim," A J S, XLII (1937), p. 695, as corrected by the author, *ibid.,* p. 901 ; Ginsberg, M., *Studies in Sociology* (London: Methuen, 1932), pp. 28-29; " It is doubtful whether even Durkheim thought of these collective representations as inhering anywhere save in individual minds," says Professor Ginsberg. *See also,* Jerusalem, W., *An Introduction to Philosophy* (tr. by Sanders from tenth edition, revised; N. Y.: Macmillan, 1932), pp. 371-373 and Fauconnet's remarks in *Congrès des Sociétés Philosophiques américaine, anglaises, belge, italienne et française, Communications et Discussions* (Paris: Colin, 1921), pp. 471-472.

main. If Durkheim is not a social realist, in the above sense of the term, is he then a social nominalist? What meaning can we assign to such sentences as " Social data exist independently of individual facts " and " Collective consciousness is independent of individual consciousness "?

If one accepts the dichotomy between society and the individual, the only alternative to substantialist social realism is social nominalism. For, if there is no real, corporate collective entity or mind, only the separate individual minds can be real. However, the presentation of these two alternatives in this manner is essentially beside the point and does not meet the issue. It is not imperative that we choose between collective entities, on the one hand, and separate individual minds, on the other. There is a third alternative which this mode of stating the problem ignores completely. If we reject the antithesis society *versus* the individual as " false and hollow whenever used as a general or philosophical statement of human relations," [135] we may perceive that our concern is neither with social minds nor with separate individual minds taken distributively, but rather with minds in association and reciprocal relationship; and thus, a third approach to the question becomes feasible.

We must start with the fundamental and primitive fact of human association. Human life is associative life. Human beings are always found in pluralities, in relationship with other human beings. Man, in short, is ever in the company of fellow-men. However, to speak of association as a fact is inexact; what we mean by " the fact of human association " is more accurately rendered as " it is a fact that human beings are associated." For, association itself is not so much a "fact" as it is a process, a procession of activities, a come-and-go of actions, interactions, reactions, and counteractions. It is an interplay of forces, a drama of interacting influences. Now, this activity and interaction is not just idle and unproductive

135 Cooley, *Human Nature*, p. 7.

" sound and fury signifying nothing "; it is generative, stimulative, creative. It gives rise to ideas, sentiments, and actions which would have been other than they are, if they were at all, had there been no association of individuals, and hence, no interaction and interstimulation among them. Association, then, creates ways of thinking, feeling, and acting which would not have come into being without it; and the specific ideas, beliefs, sentiments, and modes of activity to which it gives rise depend on the organization of association, i. e., on the manner in which individuals are associated. In brief, the process of association and its particular mode of organization have a direct effect on the associated individuals, transforming them, in a sense, and determining many aspects of their behavior. Consequently, the associated persons are other than they would be were they not associated.

The doctrine that the process of association is creative, that it engenders phenomena for which it is causally responsible, i. e., which arise from the interaction and intercommunication of individuals, we may call associational or relational realism. This associational or relational realism, so termed because it claims that association is a real, generative process and that society as a system of relations is a reality *sui generis*, is not to be confused either with social nominalism or with what we have called substantialist social realism. In contradistinction to the former, it insists that " society " does not refer to a plurality of independent beings who are complete in and by themselves and who derive nothing from their "pluralitiness", but rather that it is a term connoting a distinctive reality: a plurality of associated individuals who are in reciprocal relationship, who are bound to one another in an organization of interrelations, and whose characteristics and behavior are directly affected by the fact that they constitute a network or reticulum of relationships. Relational realism is also opposed to substantialist realism, for, unlike the latter, it refuses to accord transcendent reality to the whole as against the parts, and conceives society as being in its members, not over and above them. Associational realism, as here defined, is the only kind of realism that Durkheim ever espoused. The two other doctrines with which we have contrasted it were explicitly repudiated by him. If he is to be termed a realist, clarity demands that the precise sense of the appellation be indicated." [136]

With the distinction between associational and substantialist realism in mind, we are in a position to interpret what Durkheim means by social facts "existing independently" of individual facts. If the notion of independent existence is taken in an ontological sense, it is pertinent to ask, as Fouillée does, [137] where it is that social facts enjoy this independent existence. However, since Durkheim specifically tells us that social phenomena exist only in individual consciousnesses, this can hardly be a fair interpretation of his principle. That he does not have ontological existence in mind is also evidenced by his constant reference to the connection of the social to the individual in terms of the parts—whole relationship. Now, a whole cannot be an existential reality apart from, or outside of, its parts. Water doesn't exist in one place, and its constituent elements in another, nor does a painting exist somewhere other than where the brush strokes that comprise it are; and neither does society have a location in time and space different from that of its individual components. Durkheim asked his critics to spare him the humiliation of even suspecting him of such a manifest absurdity. "To exist independently," then, cannot be given this meaning. Rather, it must be understood as signifying "being qualitatively different from," "having characteristics other than," "being of a nature different from." In Durkheim's own words: society, i. e. the group formed by a plurality of associated individuals, must be understood as a "personality" *qualitatively different* from the individual per-

---

136 *Cf.* Park and Burgess, *op. cit.*, p. 36, who give a definition of realism similar to the relational one here presented, and who classify Simmel, Ratzenhofer, Small, Cooley, and Ellwood, as well as Durkheim, as realists.

137 Fouillée, *op. cit.*, p. 160.

sonalities that comprise it.[138] In this sense the phrase has no
ontological implication. We may say that the nature of the
whole is qualitatively different from that of the elements of
which it is composed, without in any way thinking of the
whole as existing apart from these elements. Thus, water has
properties of a nature different from that of either hydrogen
and oxygen when these elements are not combined in a specific
manner to form water. But it makes no sense to say that water
exists beyond and above its component elements, and has reality independently of them. It has properties that these do not
have when not in combination. This, however, is another
matter. Similarly, when Durkheim speaks of a social phenomenon existing independently of its individual manifestations,
he means only that as a product of human association and
interaction (for that is what we mean by social) the phenomenon has properties which, since they result from the action
and the mode of association, are different from what they
would have been had the particular phenomenon been developed
separately by non-associated individuals, or by individuals who
were differently associated.[139] When he says that there is a
collective consciousness which is independent of individual
consciousnesses, he refers only to the fact that the ways of
thinking, feeling, and acting that are characteristic of a plurality of associated individuals, are, because of the creative nature
of the associational process, different from what they would
have been had these individuals not been in communication
with one another or if they had communicated in a different
manner. The " independent existence of social facts " has, in
Durkheim's thinking, a relational, not a substantialist, connotation, for to him society is only an associational reality. As
for the " realistic " proposition that " *la société dépasse l'individu* " which persistently recurs in Durkheim and which is
frequently seized upon as convincing evidence of his social

138 24a, pp. 52-53.
139 *Le Suicide*, pp. 350, 362.

realism, it must be emphasized that there is invariably left understood in this statement the completing phrase "considered purely as a biological organism." Society, Durkheim means, makes demands on the individual which, purely as a biological being, he would not make on himself. To live in society, the individual *qua* organism must *se dépasser;* the human infant must become acculturated, the human animal must become a civilized being.

Durkheim's position is not as antithetical to Professor Perry's "composite and interactive" approach to society as the latter seems to believe. Perry is careful to point out that his conclusion that "society is analyzable into men . . . in no way invalidates the view that the social man differs from the non-social man or that society differs from man. It is not a *reduction* of society to men, in the sense of denying that society has peculiarities of its own, any more than the analysis of a liquid such as water into gases such as hydrogen and oxygen is a denial of the peculiar physical properties of a liquid. On the contrary, the composite and interactive view of society implies that its members compose something, and that they act upon, and thus modify, one another."

"They compose," Professor Perry continues, "that which may properly be termed a *whole,* possessing properties *as* a whole, which cannot be attributed to the members severally. They compose that which may properly be termed a *system,* possessing an orderly structure that persists when its members change. A social whole or system possesses, furthermore, an *individuality* of its own, which renders it unique within the class of such wholes or systems.[140] It is difficult to see how assertions like "society differs from man," "society has peculiarities of its own," and is "a whole possessing properties *as* a whole which cannot be attributed to the members severally," differ in any important respect from such Durkheimian propositions as "man as a social being is other than the individual

140 Perry, *General Theory of Value,* pp. 460-461. Italics in text.

taken in isolation," "society has properties *sui generis*," "there are properties in a whole which it has as a whole and which are not those of its parts taken severally." True, there are terminological differences, and on this score Perry's clear language has distinct advantages over Durkheim's equivocal phraseology.

Although we find ourselves in sympathy with much of the Harvard philosopher's judicious discussion of the nature of society,[141] we differ with him categorically in our understanding of Durkheim. Whereas we attempt to get at the intended meaning behind Durkheim's admittedly confusing and ambiguous terminology, it seems to suit Professor Perry's purpose to take Durkheim's propositions " *literatim et verbatim.*" [142]

The proper equivalent of the latter's concepts of collective consciousness and collective representation is not group mind, or social mind, or collective being, but rather public opinion and public consciousness as the terms were used by Cooley. The renowned Michigan sociologist's characterization of public opinion, for example, reads like a paragraph out of Durkheim. Public opinion, Cooley wrote, is " no mere aggregate of separate individual judgments, but an organization, a cooperative product of communication and reciprocal influence. It may be as different from the sums of what the individuals could have thought out in separation as a ship built by a hundred men is from a hundred boats each built by one man." [143] Is it not significant that Professors Fauconnet and Mauss, in an article written as an expression of the sociological position of Durkheim, employed the concept of public opinion as the equivalent of what Durkheim termed the system of collective representations? [144] In the same article, these disciples and successors of Durkheim speak of institutions as the specific subject matter

141 *Ibid.*, chaps. 14-17.

142 *Cf. ibid.*, p. 431.

143 Cooley, *Social Organization*, p. 121.

144 Fauconnet and Mauss, *op. cit.*

of sociology and remark that social institutions are made up of representations, i. e. have their basis in public opinion. On this point, too, Cooley's view is strikingly similar. An institution, he writes, " is simply a definite and established phrase of the public mind, not differing in its ultimate nature from public opinion." [145] It is indeed to a Cooley that one must turn for the Anglo-American equivalent of Durkheim's conception of the relations of society and the individual.

Thus, the Durkheimian concepts of collective representations and collective consciousness have nothing mysterious about them. They are representations and consciousnesses that exist nowhere else than in individual minds and individual consciousnesses. Yet they merit the adjective " collective," or better still, for ears accustomed to English, " public " or " social," because they are the direct results or end-products of human association.

There are at least two reasons why Durkheim had great difficulty in making himself clear on this point. First of all, he confused many readers by using exteriority or externality as an immediately visible symbol of social facts, and hence as a good objective criterion of them. This externality, however, does not mean that social facts exist apart from human individuals, but only that social phenomena assume such external and visible embodiments as codes of law, statutes of incorporation, monuments, buildings, rules of etiquette, books, statistical regularities, etc., from which vantage point, according to Durkheim, they can be most fruitfully studied. But these material manifestations, he always insisted, (although, perhaps, with varying degrees of emphasis) are only the overt index of internal, subjective states — representations and sentiments— which were for him the more basic stuff of social life. The fact that he adopted a particular criterion as an " exterior sign " of social data does not mean that he ignored the fact that this external symbol was only " the material and apparent

145 Cooley, op. cit., p. 313.

expression of an internal and deep-seated fact." [146] Social facts, he repeatedly remarked, are only the products of human activity. They are "realized" only by men, and are the creations of human intelligence and will.

Secondly, he obscured his true position because of his polemic style. In his fight against individualism, he accepted, as we have seen, the notion of "the isolated organico-psychical being," and was therefore led to oppose the "social" to the "individual" although such a dichotomy poorly expressed his thought. Thus, in contrasting the individual and the collective consciousness, he frequently meant by the former not the consciousness of the fully developed social person but only that of this isolated abstract being. At one point, he justified the distinction between the two types of consciousness, individual and collective, by saying that the states of the former derive from the "nature of the organico-psychical being taken in isolation," while those of the latter result from "the combination of a plurality of beings of this kind." [147] Davy, interpreting Durkheim on this matter, relied on the same sort of differentiation. We may speak of the collective consciousness of the group, he wrote, "by analogy with the individual consciousness of the isolated individual." [148] This manner of viewing the problem may have had its polemic advantages, although even this is questionable, but it surely did not make for clarity. Durkheim would have been spared a vast amount of self-exegesis, perhaps, had he announced at the very outset of his sociology, as Cooley did, that "a separate individual is an abstraction unknown to experience, and so likewise is society when regarded as something apart from individuals," or if he had reserved the concept, "individual" to refer not to the isolated organico-psychical being, but to man, member of society, social animal. Then, he, too, could have clearly asserted as

146 *Les Formes élémentaires*, p. 298, footnote 2. *Cf. Règles*, pp. xxi, 24; and 95e, p. 696.

147 *Règles*, p. 127, footnote 1.

148 Davy, *Emile Durkheim*, p. 14.

did the American sociologist, that Society and Individual are but "the collective and distributive aspects of the same thing." [149]

We see, then, in what manner Durkheim conceived of sociology as an independent science having a field of its own and a subject matter that is explicable in its own terms. Such an independent science does not necessitate postulating a group-mind or evolving a transcendental " realistic " theory of society. All that it is necessary to posit is that human life presents a distinctive and creative associational aspect which cannot be explained in terms of pre-social or non-social individuals. If this is so, a complete theory of human nature is impossible without a study of the associational or social phases of human behavior.

7. UNITY: SOCIOLOGY THE CORPUS OF THE SOCIAL SCIENCES

Man is a social being whose associational life is diverse and multiple, presenting a richness and complexity which, as experiencing individuals, we may admire, but of which, as social scientists, we can give a systematic account only with great difficulty. Should we view the social life of human beings in all its diversities and modalities as a whole, or should we have special disciplines to investigate specific phases of it? Should there be, in other words, only one social science or several social sciences, and if several, what should be the relations among them? These questions require us to examine more precisely what the scope of sociology is and what its relations to the other disciplines of the social and cultural life of man are.

It is hardly doubtful that, pragmatically speaking, the most fruitful of Durkheim's principles has been his conception of sociology as a unitary social science. We refer to his view of sociology as not *a* social science, but as social science itself, or, to use his own terminology, as the system or corpus of the social sciences.

---

149 Cooley, *Human Nature*, pp. 1-2.

The unitary nature of social science is revealed in (1) the interrelatedness of the subject matter of the special disciplines, (2) the cooperative contributions of each of the disciplines towards a common goal: a unified philosophy of man, member of society, and (3) the common focus of the social studies: the social being. Unitary social science must be conceived as the body of the social disciplines sociologically treated, that is, studied from the sociological point of view, approach, and method.

The fecundity of this point of view is everywhere evident. The manner in which it has transformed and renovated such disciplines as economics, jurisprudence, religion, ethics, linguistics, esthetics, etc. is revealed in the studies of those who have been affiliated with, or influenced by the *Année Sociologique*. Davy and Fauconnet have brought the sociological approach to the study of contracts, law, and responsibility. Simiand and Halbwachs have demonstrated the feasibility of treating the data of political economy as the facts of economic sociology. Meillet has shown how the study of linguistics is transformed when one considers the phenomena of language in their social aspects. Lalo has developed a sociology of esthetics. Contributions of real importance have been made by Bayet and Halbwachs to the sociology of moral facts. And so forth. In every field that deals with man as a member of society sociology has wrought a veritable revolution.[150] Outside of France, however, the Durkheimian conception of the social sciences as constituting a unitary discipline has not received the widespread acceptance that its proven fecundity would lead one to expect. In Germany and in the United States it seems to have fallen on unattentive, if not altogether deaf, ears. In these countries, sociologists, concentrating their efforts on establishing their science as a special discipline, independent of, and

150 *Cf.* Bouglé, *Bilan*; Mauss, M., " La Sociologie en France depuis 1914," in *La Science Française* (Nouvelle édition, Paris: Larousse, 1933), Vol. I, pp. 36-47; Essertier, D., *La Sociologie* (Paris: Alcan, 1930) ; Marjolin, *loc. cit.*

separate from, the other social sciences, have failed to appreciate the possibility that all social science is one, that there is an essential unity of the social sciences which permits us to regard them as a single, and hence unitary, science. Of the various attempts to develop sociology as a special study alongside of the other social sciences, the endeavors of the German formalist school seem to be the most notable, and, alas, the most unsuccessful. Neither Simmel, nor Vierkandt, nor Von Wiese can be said to have justified and vindicated his position. The criticisms that Abel and Sorokin have levied against the formalistic approach have gone essentially unanswered for almost a decade.[151] Especially important is the fact that in actual practice the formalists did not themselves adhere to their own definitions of the field of sociology; largely, as their critics correctly aver, because they simply could not. Their subject matter—fortunately—was other than their formal, and in this case, formalistic definitions supposed it to be. As Sorokin has said, if the works of the formalists have not become a purely scholastic, dead, and almost useless catalogue of human relations, " it is because of the fact that they themselves have not followed the ' formal pretension.' The best parts of their works are exactly those in which they forget this pretension and plunge into an investigation of the ' content ' phenomena." [152]

This inconsistency between formal definition and actual content is also found among other sociologists. Max Weber, for instance, defines sociology as the science which aims to understand " social behavior," i. e. human behavior related to the attitudes of other individuals, yet his concrete investigations imply a conception of the *scope* of sociology not unlike Durkheim's.[153] Similarly, although MacIver states that " the subject matter of sociology is social relationships as such," a much

151 Abel, T., *Systematic Sociology in Germany* (N. Y.: Columbia University, 1929), and Sorokin, *op. cit.*, Chap. IX.

152 Sorokin, *op. cit.*, p. 513.

153 *Cf.* Salomon, A., " Max Weber's Sociology," So R, II (1935), 60-73; and Mauss' comment, A S, n. s., II, p. 186.

better guide to his conception of the science than this somewhat Simmelian formula, is his more detailed statement of
what the aims of sociology are. "Sociology," he writes, "seeks
to discover the principles of cohesion and of order within the
social structure, the ways in which it roots and grows within
an environment, the moving equilibrium of changing structure
and changing environment, the main trends of this incessant
change and the forces which determine its direction at any
time, the harmonies and conflicts, the adjustments and mal-
adjustments within the structure as they are revealed in the
light of human desires, and thus the practical application of
means to ends in the creative activities of social man." [154]

Giddings is perhaps the outstanding representative of American sociology who, independently of German influences, endeavored to justify a special place for sociology *among* the
social sciences. The Columbia professor conceived of his discipline as the *fundamental* social science, and hence as the most
general of the social studies. A general science must deal with
the attributes of a class that are common to all its sub-classes,
he maintained, and consequently, " general principles are fundamental " and a general science is " a science of elements and
first principles." This general science, however, is to precede
the special sciences and is to serve as their basis. "An analysis,
then, of the general characteristics of social phenomena and a
formulation of the general laws of social evolution should be
made the *basis* of special study in all departments of social
science," he wrote.[155] Thus, a general science is not to be confused with a summary science. " Sociology is the inclusive
and coordinating science only as it is the fundamental social
science. So far from being merely the sum of the social
sciences it is rather their common basis "; and its " far-
reaching " principles, Giddings added, are the postulates of the
special sciences. According to this view, sociology is confined

154 MacIver, *Society* (1931), pp. 3, viii.

155 Giddings, F. H., *Principles of Sociology* (3rd ed.; N. Y.: Macmillan,
1898), p. 33. Italics ours.

to study only the most analytical, the most extensive, and the most indeterminate aspects of social life, since its data are expected to be sufficiently abstract to cover all particular cases. Giddings himself, however, could not stay within the bounds of this definition of sociology. We may say of him what has been said of the German formalists: his most valuable contributions, even in the *Principles*, are those concrete, special, and thoughtful studies in which he investigated phenomena that he would have had to exclude, had he followed his own criterion for selecting sociological data.[156]

A recent attempt to establish sociology as a special social or cultural science with an empirical field of its own is that of Znaniecki.[157]

Frankly, we do not comprehend what exactly it is that Znaniecki rejects when he dismisses the conception of sociology as a general theory of cultural data. Although he at first defines this theory of culture as one which studies *" cultural phenomena viewed as social phenomena,"* [158] his arguments are directed not against this particular conception, but against the one which conceives the general theory of culture as the study of cultural systems as such.[159] The distinction between these two definitions of the theory of culture is fundamental. We agree with Znaniecki that cultural systems like Shakespeare's Hamlet or the theory of relativity are *as such* nonsocial. But this does not preclude the possibility and the feasibility of viewing them not *as such*, but as *social phenomena*. A bank is a financial system, true, but it is also a social institution and can be studied from this angle. A factory is an economic system, but it may be viewed also as a reticulum of social relationships, a determinate form governing the manner in which men enter into relations with other men. *Hamlet* is

---

156 *Cf.* Durkheim and Fauconnet, 03c, pp. 476-479.

157 Znaniecki, *Method*, Chap. 3.

158 *Ibid.*, p. 101. Italics in text.

159 *Ibid.*, pp. 102-104.

beyond doubt a literary system. Nevertheless, sociologically relevant questions may be asked about it. For example, does it reflect the mores of Elizabethan England? Or more generally, the question, does literature reflect the mores of an era, may be posed; and surely, it is a sociological problem we are raising. As sociologists we are not concerned with the history of literature or the history of science as such, but with the *sociology* of literature or the *sociology* of science.

Durkheim made this quite clear in his critique of Spencer's analysis of ecclesiastical institutions.[160] The English philosopher, he felt, tended to treat sociology not as *a* science but as Science, the totality of human knowledge. Consequently, Spencer's study of religion failed to distinguish that which is sociologically relevant from that which is not. There are non-social aspects of religion, Durkheim observed. " The sociology and the history of religions are and should remain distinct things." The sociologist, for example, might study religion in its social role, that is, as a social institution regulating the behavior of individuals in society. This, however, constitutes only one aspect of religion. Religious phenomena are too complex to be studied in all their ramifications in a single book, however large. " Each writer must choose his point of view." The sociologist is interested in religion as a human institution, as a complex of social behavior, and as having a definite function in social life.[161]

It is important, therefore, to differentiate that which Znaniecki confuses. The science of cultural phenomena viewed as social phenomena is one thing, the theory of cultural systems as such is another. Only the former conception can be correctly attributed to Durkheim.

Moreover, the Polish sociologist explicitly states that he is " far from denying that a general positive science of cultural phenomena . . . is possible " and admits that " if such a general theory of culture is founded, then indeed, all the special sci-

160 86a.

161 *Ibid.*, pp. 66-69.

ences will be dependent upon it." [162] His objections to such a view of the field of sociology are based not on theoretical but only on practical considerations. " It can be founded only by a slow process of induction," he says, and " is a tremendous task needing the cooperation of many specialists perfectly acquainted with their respective domains and at the same time able to rise above the limitations of their specialities." [163] It is difficult to understand why sociologists should be condoned for shirking " tremendous tasks " or why it should not be demanded of them that they " rise above the limits of their specialties." Whatever is, is not necessarily right and the fact that sociologists *do* so shirk and *do* so fail to rise is no basis for not requiring them or training them to change their ways. A deplorable condition should not be made an ideal simply because it is a fact. All of Durkheim's efforts were dedicated to the very task of getting sociologists to undertake what Znaniecki says is a slow process and a tremendous enterprise. Is not all science slow in its development and tremendous in its endeavors? Should we throw out the baby along with the bath because he is a long time in getting cleaned?

In rejecting the conception of sociology as a science of cultural phenomena in general or of what has been called " the totality of cultural facts considered in relation to the total social situation," [164] Znaniecki claims that he is simply accepting the " unmistakable verdict of the history of science." This is hardly a legitimate basis for rejecting the conception. First of all, it should not be assumed that unmistakable verdicts of history may not be mistaken verdicts. Secondly, the verdict cannot be so unmistakable if, on the basis of the same kind of empirical investigation that Znaniecki offers as authority for his assertion, another writer pronounces this verdict to be something altogether different. Sorokin, for example, after a

162 *Ibid.*, pp. 104-105.

163 *Ibid.*, p. 105.

164 Marjolin, *loc. cit.*, p. 698.

study of the development of sociological theories for the past fifty years concludes that sociology " seems to be a study, first of the relationship and correlations between various classes of social phenomena (correlations between economic and religious, family and moral; juridical and economic; mobility and political phenomena and so on); second, that between the social and the non-social (geographical, biological, etc.) ; third, the study of the general characteristics common to all classes of social phenomena." [165]

In a recent paper on " The Place of Sociology " [166] Mannheim makes a brilliant plea for the necessity of a general sociology. Sociology, as he sees it, " has as its *raison d'être* the construction of a consistent general theory of society." [167] It should establish the much needed cooperation among the social sciences by coordinating their problems and by comparing their results. It should, therefore, be " on the one hand a clearing-house for the results arrived at by the specialized social sciences and on the other hand, a new elaboration of the materials on which they are based." [168] Mannheim's arguments on the need for a synthesis of the social sciences and for cooperation among them are convincing. We cannot, however, accept his view that this general sociology should exist " outside of the separate social sciences." [169] We feel, rather, that general sociology belongs within the corpus of the social sciences and that it should be elaborated not as a specialized study by a particular set of individuals known as general sociologists, but as a cooperative endeavor engaged upon by social

165 Sorokin, *op. cit.*, pp. 760-761. *See also* the list of " sociological specialisms " given by Professor Ginsberg on the basis of an inductive survey of what sociology actually studies. Ginsberg, M., " The Place of Sociology " in *The Social Sciences: Their Relations In Theory and In Teaching* (London: Le Play House, 1936), pp. 190-192.

166 *The Social Sciences: Their Relations In Theory and In Teaching* (London: Le Play House, 1936), pp. 164-189.

167 *Ibid.*, p. 179.

168 *Ibid.*, p. 188.

169 *Ibid.*, p. 181.

scientists representing all the social disciplines. General sociology should in no case be allowed to stray too far from the special sociologies. As Professor Ginsberg warns in the same volume, it is important " to resist the tendency of the social sciences to become isolated from one another and from general sociology which can surely only flourish by their systematization." [170] But it is likewise necessary to resist the efforts to isolate general sociology from the body of the particular social disciplines.

Thus, despite the efforts of certain sociologists, there appears to be little ground for rejecting the more than thirty-year-old conclusion of Durkheim that the attempts to establish sociology as a special science by separating it from the other social sciences, can result only in reducing it to " a formal and vague philosophy." [171] The Durkheimian principle that sociology is nothing if it is not the system of the social sciences, that it can only be the unitary science of cultural and social life considered in its organization, functioning and becoming, is tending more and more to correspond to what in practice contemporary sociology actually is. In England, for example, Professor Ginsberg has adopted a conception of the scope of sociology which, he recognizes, " is in general conformity with that held by such great thinkers as Durkheim and Hobhouse." [172] He regards the chief functions of sociology as follows: "(1) It seeks to provide what may be called a morphology or classification of types and forms of social relationships, especially of those which have come to be defined in institutions and associations. (2) It tries to determine the relation between different parts or factors of social life, for example, the economic and political, the moral and religious, the moral and the legal, the intellectual and the social elements. (3) It endeavors to disentangle the fundamental conditions of social change and persistence. Since social relationships depend pre-

170 *Ibid.*, p. 217.
171 03c, p. 484.
172 Ginsberg, M., *Sociology* (N. Y.: Holt, 1934), p. 14.

sumably on the nature of the individuals and their relationships (a) to one another, (b) to the community, (c) to the
outer environment, sociology seeks to pass from its preliminary
empirical generalizations to the more ultimate laws of biology
and psychology, and possibly to distinctive sociological laws,
that is laws *sui generis* not reducible to the laws which govern
life and mind in individual organisms. . . . Sociology must
stand in friendly relation to such specialisms as history, comparative jurisprudence, anthropology, which are themselves
within the social field, and to others more general, such as
biology and psychology. Its object is throughout to determine
the relation of social facts to civilization as a whole, and this
involves the bringing together of results which cannot be
attempted by the special sciences as such." [173]

In the United States, Sorokin has insisted that sociology
" has been, is, and either will be a science of the general characteristics of all classes of social phenomena, with the relationships and correlations between them, or there will be no
sociology." [174] As the generation of American sociologists
who, in the last decade or so, came directly under the influence
of the cultural anthropologists, and who were thus nourished
in their sociological cradles, so to speak, on the various culture
concepts and cultural approaches, grows to maturity, it is to be
expected that the Durkheimian conception of sociology as the
corpus of the social sciences, as the unitary discipline of social
life, will gain more widespread acceptance in this country.
But to be truly in the Durkheimian tradition, cultural sociologists will have to make more sharp than many anthropological
students are at present wont to do the *social focus* which makes
the various aspects of man's cultural activities sociologically
relevant. [175]

173 *Ibid.*, pp. 17-18.

174 Sorokin, *op. cit.*, p. 761.

175 Durkheim, 03c, p. 481 ; 00c, p. 136; 86a, review of Spencer. *Cf.* Mac-
Iver, R. M., *Society: A Textbook of Sociology* (N. Y.: Farrar and Rinehart,
1937), pp. v-viii.

The sociologist is concerned with the science of culture only to the extent that it is or can become a *sociology* of culture. Social anthropology, the functional study of social systems, as it is defined by Radcliffe-Brown,[176] can only be a comparative sociology.

176 Radcliffe-Brown, *op. cit.*, p. 401, footnote 8.

PART III

SOCIETY, EVOLUTION, PERSONALITY

1. Introduction

From the discussion of the nature of our science, its method and scope, we may turn to a consideration of the nature of our subject matter, society. But in directing our attention to this problem, we involve ourselves also in an analysis of the human personality. There are two reasons for this: sociology, the science of societies, cannot study human groups "without in the end arriving at the individual, the final element of which these groups are composed;"[1] and secondly, it has been definitely established that vast segments of human behavior are socially conditioned and determined. Furthermore, since the interrelations between society and the individual have evolved historically, it is essential that we view these interrelations as closely linked to, and indeed, determined by, the course of social evolution. Thus, in analyzing society, we cannot escape taking into consideration the problems of evolution and personality. This proposition we have tried to express in the title of this Part. Using Durkheim as our guide, we shall endeavor to describe society and to show how the human personality is molded and affected by the dynamically changing patterns of social cohesion.

2. Society as Unity: Social Solidarity

Durkheim, we have said, based his sociology on the premise that to know man one must first know society, for as the latter is, so is he. But what is society? In part, Durkheim's answer to this question is that society is (1) unity, (2) regulation, and (3) source of life and expression.

Society is a unity. It is neither a mere plurality of individuals, nor a simple mechanical juxtaposition of human beings,

---

1 Durkheim, 14a, p. 206.

although, of course, it could be nothing if it were not at least this. Society is an organization, a more or less definite, and more or less permanent system of relationships. It is an association, interaction, and communication, but of a sort that permits us to conceive of it as system, and hence as organization and unity. Men throughout history have been deeply sensitive to this fundamental truth of sociology. They have expressed it, however, in myriad ways. Our ordinary language experiences no difficulty in using society as a collective noun requiring only a singular verb. This linguistic fact reflects the feeling of oneness, of togetherness which the term suggests. Some thinkers have sought to convey this idea by conceiving society as a whole, as, for example, Aristotle. Others have expressed the same thought by substantializing society, i. e., viewing it as an entity or as a being. A Herbert Spencer, pursuing the matter further and inquiring whether this entity is of the nature of organic or inorganic things, found it necessary to assert that society is an organism, since " a whole of which the parts are alive, cannot in its general characters, be like lifeless wholes."[2] What permits us to think of society as a social organism, the English philosopher explained, is that between society and all other organisms, there is " community in the fundamental principles of organization." [3] Others have sought to express the unity of society by conceiving it as a Greater Mind (Gumplowicz) or as a General Will (Rousseau). The same notion is reflected in the view of those, who, like Pareto, think of society as an equilibrium, or who with Giddings conceive it as an organization.

Thus, the history of social thought offers ample evidence that man has perceived the oneness of society. In fact these theories

2 Spencer, *op. cit.*, p. 448.

3 *Ibid.*, p. 592. Spencer, it may be noted in passing, "rejected the conception of Plato and Hobbes that there is a likeness between social organization and the organization of a man; saying that ' there is no warrant whatever for assuming this.'" Such an analogy, he felt, is " far too special." (*Op. cit.*, pp. 591-592.)

of society as Whole, Entity, Being, Organism, Social Mind, General Will, Equilibrium or Organization are but variations on a fundamental theme: the unity of social life. Durkheim, too, was keenly aware of this unity which he sought to express by referring to society as an entity, an "*être*," a whole, an organism.

The reality of social unity is one of the firmly rooted generalizations of contemporary sociology. Social science has amassed much evidence to show that society is an integration, that is, a state of being whole, an "integer". If the concept of social unity is at all challenged it is because of the tendency to confuse the *relation* of unity or integration with the *ethical or aesthetic norms* of union and harmony. Thus, the discussions of social unity are often conducted on an ethical plane. Because of the confusion of the relation with the norm, social unity is identified with peace, cooperation, and friendliness, whereas disunity or disintegration is associated with war, conflict and antagonism.

Such identifications however, are completely unwarranted, as such eminent pre-war representatives of modern sociology as Simmel in Germany and Sumner in America have demonstrated. Conflict and antagonism, opponent, foe and stranger are as much integrating factors in social life as cooperation, friendliness, neighbor, and ally. Closed groups, to use Bergson's term, are "agin'" groups, and their unity is derived in part from their "agin'ness." Consequently, the question of social integration cannot be resolved simply by examining the amount of cooperation or conflict that is present in a particular group. Rather, the test of social integration is the capability of a group to function as a whole.

That groups are capable of such *integral* activity is everywhere in evidence. The clearest case, perhaps, is the situation of inter-group conflict. But no less indicative of group organization is the existence of the modern state which reveals the capacity of communities to organize for the regulation of internal as well as external affairs, for peace-time as well as war-time activities. These, however, are only the extreme examples. The whole institutional and cultural patterning of a society is a manifestation of its organization and systematization. Of course, groups reveal varying degrees of integration. In a recent study of primitive social systems, it was found helpful to distinguish three types of societies according to the degree of social integration represented by each:

(1) the *simplest* societies, those possessing a culturally defined recognition of group unity, but lacking the political forms necessary for group action.

(2) *corporate* societies, those having "(a) the capacity for corporate action as a group and (b) continuity of existence over a period such that at any moment it is possible to distinguish who is and who is not a member of the group."

(3) *true political* societies, which are corporate societies that (a) maintain in some way a local or territorial continuity, usually by exercising dominion over a definite territory and (b) manifest some form of corporate action on the part of the group in (1) maintaining its rights against invaders from outside and in (2) exercising control over its own members.[4]

This classification may not be useful for the study of contemporary societies, but it does serve to bring out the fact that groups are differentially integrated.

Thus, to the question: is society a unity? our comparative sociological and anthropological data compel an affirmative reply. This, however, doesn't settle the matter; it merely sets the problem. We have still to inquire into the nature of that unity, its types and kinds. What, in other words, is the nature of social bonds? What are the modes of social cohesion?

The focal concept that Durkheim used in answering these questions was " *solidarité* ". This term has unhesitatingly been translated as " solidarity "; and it would be only confusing to depart from that procedure here. We should like to point out,

4 Mead, M., ed., *Cooperation and Competition Among Primitive Peoples* (New York: McGraw-Hill, 1937), p. 467. For the definition of " social system " underlying this study see pp. 458-459.

however, that the cognates are not exact equivalents. The English word has, at least in its current usage, more of an ethical, evaluative connotation than the French term had at the time Durkheim employed it. The latter used *solidarité* in an objective and even biological sense to refer to a type of *relation* between a whole and its parts. But within four years of the appearance of Durkheim's study, Leon Bourgeois published a short volume entitled *La Solidarité* in which he laid down the principles of the political and ethical movement that came to be known as solidarism. Bourgeois was one of the leaders of this movement and "*La Solidarité*" became its manifesto. The term thereupon acquired a very definite moral tone which, up to the time of its use by the solidarists, was foreign to it. It became necessary to distinguish *de facto* solidarity, i. e. solidarity as an objective relation, from the ethical ideal of solidarity as it was developed by Bourgeois as a principle of moral action. To the latter, solidarity was an ethical duty and a social obligation implying the notion of "social debt." It is important not to identify Durkheim with the solidarist movement. Although he too was immediately concerned with moral questions, and attempted to develop the ethical consequences of social unity, he used the concept "*solidarité*" in its pre-Bourgeois, objective, relational, and non-ethical sense. Because of the manner in which the term has been evaluatively weighted by the solidarists and because of the ethical implication of the English word solidarity, we prefer to substitute for it some more neutral word such as "cohesion." But perhaps we are only suggesting a choice between two evils. For is there any word that does not carry some emotional charge? Having made these considerations explicit, we feel free to continue the sociological tradition which admits the term solidarity.[5]

5 *Cf.* Bourgeois, L., *La Solidarité* (7th ed., Paris: Colin, 1912) and Bourgeois, L., Croiset, A., *et al.*, *Essai d'une philosophie de la solidarité* (2nd ed., Paris: Alcan, 1907). A brief history of the term solidarity is contained in Croiset's preface to the latter volume. On solidarity as a slogan, note the comment of H. La Fontaine in the same volume: "If solidarity is

In Durkheim's thinking, the nature of social cohesion was " the initial problem of sociology." With it, he began his university teaching of the subject.[6] What are the bonds that unite men and determine the formation of social aggregates? By a progressive development of his thought, Durkheim came to perceive that an answer to this question was indispensable to an understanding of the nature of the organization of contemporary societies. It was necessary, he realized, to determine first the various bases on which societies rest. One had to know what their principles of integration were, what called them into being, and what maintained them. In short, one had to classify and compare the different types of social solidarity.

How shall we study such an elusive and subjective phenomenon as solidarity? Our method, it follows from what we said in Part II, must be that of objective indexes. The particular index of solidarity that Durkheim uses is law. The various categories of law will reveal to us the types of solidarity corresponding to each. The basic types of law are: (1) Repressive or penal law, i. e. the system of juridical rules with organized repressive sanctions, and (2) Restitutive law, i. e. the system of juridical rules with restitutive sanctions. Our method is now clearly established; we have only to ask what are the bonds of social solidarity corresponding to each of these two categories of laws.

Let us consider first repressive or penal law. The bonds of solidarity which this type of law expresses can be understood only if we know the nature of crime and punishment. A crime is an act which offends strong and definite dispositions of the collective consciousness and which, as a consequence, evokes a

---

the ideal of socialism, socialism is the politics of solidarity " (p. 272). Weill traces the solidarism movement back to Renouvier and Fouillée whom he regards as its precursors. Weill, G., *op. cit.*, p. 470. For social solidarity as the philosophy of social legislation see Henderson, C. R., " Social Solidarity in France," A J S, XI (1905), 168-182.

6 See 88a, pp. 257 ff.

punishment.[7] Punishment is an emotional reaction of graded intensity which society exercises, through the intermediary of a tribunal, on those of its members who have committed crimes, that is, have offended strong and precise sentiments of the common consciousness by violating certain rules of conduct.[8] Common or collective consciousness is a name that Durkheim gives to the sum total of social similitudes, that is, to the complex whole of ways of acting, thinking, and feeling which, on the whole, are characteristic of the members of a group. It is the fund of social likenesses or resemblances; the system of those values which are alike unto all.[9] The analysis of crin.e and punishment [10] shows us that " the rules which punishment sanctions express the most essential social similitudes." [11] Thus, penal law reveals a type of solidarity or social cohesion which is derived from the fact that individuals are attracted to one another because they resemble one another, because they have a fund of beliefs and practices common to them all.[12] This we may call similitudinous solidarity, or, to use the curious alternative expression offered by Durkheim, mechanical solidarity, i. e. the social cohesion based on likeness.

Turning to restitutive law, we cannot fail to notice that the solidarity to which it corresponds is of an altogether different nature. The rules of conduct which it regulates lie in the realm of differences, outside of the common consciousness. The sentiments evoked by the violation of these rules are not sufficiently violent nor severe enough to lead to a demand for punishment;

7 *De la Division*, pp. 47, 52.

8 *Ibid.*, p. 64.

.9 *Ibid.*, pp. 46-47.

10 An analysis, incidentally, which has been recently restated in essentially the same form and only with terminological differences, by Znaniecki (*Social Actions*, pp. 354-358). A crime, the latter writes, is " behavior which the collectivity regards as an aggression against some socially valid system" and is a crime " if its author is an object of active collective opposition."

11 Durkheim, *op. cit.*, p. 73.

12 *Ibid.*, p. 155, footnote 1.

a restoration of order is all that is necessary. The social relations governed by restitutive law imply, on the part of individuals, either an abstention from conflict or a positive collaboration, a cooperation which is derived essentially from the division of labor. We see, then, that restitutive law is a manifestation of the type of social solidarity that is based on mutual and complementary differences, hence, on the division of labor. This solidarity is " organic."

We thus uncover two fundamental and radically different principles of social integration, one based on the attraction of like for like, the other organized on complementary differences. Whether the cohesion of a society is achieved along the lines of the one or the other of these principles is most crucial in determining the major structural features of that society. In a society that is held together by similitudinous (mechanical) solidarity, the bond between the individual and society is a direct one, that is, the link is between the unit and the whole and not between the unit and other units. The individual is a member of such a society only as he acquires the habits, and attitudes, beliefs and values which constitute the common consciousness of the group. Society is, thus, merely the more or less organized whole of beliefs, feelings, and values common to all the members of the group. The strength of this kind of society varies inversely as the development of individual personality. Mechanical solidarity is at its maximum when personality is near the zero point and when individuals are only reflections of the collective type. This type of bond, however, is quite brittle, and is easily broken. Consequently the unity it establishes is not firm and, indeed, is quite unstable. These summary remarks may suffice to indicate why the solidarity based on likeness is called *mechanical*. The cohesion it creates is like that existing in the realm of inorganic matter. In a society bound together by similitude, the relation of the individual to the group is analogous to that between the molecules of a body of water, let us say, and the body of water itself. For the parts (molecules or individuals) have no distinctive and characteristic properties of their own and the whole can function only to the extent that they do not have them.

Of an altogether different nature are the structural features of a society based on complementary differences or organic solidarity. Here, the bond between the individual and society is indirect; the individual is bound to society only to the extent that he is bound to specific institutions and to other individuals within it. In other words, the direct bond is the one of interdependence among the units; the bond between the unit and the whole is indirect. This society is a system of distinctive, specialized, differentiated and precisely coordinated functions. Its strength varies directly as the development of individual personality. The more distinctive the individuals, the more cohesive is the solidarity based on the division of labor. This solidarity is at a maximum when personality is most fully expressed. Because it is rooted in functional differences and is functionally maintained, organic solidarity is relatively strong and enduring. The bonds it creates are broken only with difficulty. We call this solidarity *organic* because it resembles that of the organs of the higher animals. In complex organisms, the whole is capable of functioning even though the parts have distinctive properties. Each organ has its own characteristics, yet, the more marked the individuality of the parts, the greater is the unity of the organism. The same is true of contemporary societies, which, for the most part, are integrated on the basis of functional interdependence.

This last remark must be understood in the light of the following. These two types of solidarity, or as we prefer to think of them, these two principles of social integration, are not mutually exclusive. Strictly speaking, there is no society in which both of them are not present.[13] Nevertheless, we may legitimately refer to a given society as being integrated on the basis of the one or the other of these principles, if we are able to establish that that particular type of cohesion is the functionally

13 88c. p. 258.

significant one in the society under consideration. By the functionally significant type of solidarity we mean the one that operationally insures the cohesion of the group, the one to which the group cannot be indifferent without its very structure being threatened with dissolution. Consequently, to determine the integrating principle that is rooted in a given society, it is irrelevant to apply a purely quantitative test; our criterion must be functional, and our analysis must be operationally qualitative. The mere existence or appearance in a society of a certain amount of division of labor does not of itself tell us anything about the relation between this division of labor and the social cohesion of the group; that connection remains to be determined. It is therefore beside the point, and it constitutes no effective critique of Durkheim, to indicate that one can distinguish, as Dr. Walter Watson has done on the basis of a study of thirty primitive groups, 1,485 different occupations of primitive peoples. Once more, we must not be beguiled by Durkheim's " objective " terminology. Although he purports to demonstrate his thesis by quasi-quantitative methods, he makes it clear that in asserting such a proposition as: primitive groups are " mechanical " while contemporary societies are " organic " he is leaving understood the qualifying adverb *significantly*. His thesis is simply that communal unity, that is, integration based on participation in a community of beliefs and sentiments, is the focal, essential, and significant type of cohesion in primitive societies, whereas functional unity, that is, integration in terms of functional interdependence is, in such groups, only incidental, secondary, and merely concomitant. On the other hand, in modern societies, the functional roles of these two types of solidarity are reversed. It is functional unity that is essential in contemporary social life, and communal unity that is secondary.[14] It is therefore misleading to attribute to Durkheim the proposition that " there is no division of labor among primitive people," if this is to be taken in either an absolute or

14 *De la Division*, pp. 261, 373. Note the words "essentially" and "especially."

a quantitative sense.[15] The French theorist's viewpoint is more accurately expressed as follows: functional differentiation is not the significant source of social cohesion among primitive peoples. This is not a mere verbal quibble; Faris' proposition and the one just given have different theoretical import and require different kinds of evidence for validation.

Furthermore, the two modes of integration are not only not mutually exclusive, but functionally considered, there is a genetic relationship between them. The unity based on likeness, on what Giddings has termed consciousness of kind, is genetically prior to the development of the unity based on complementary differences. The latter, it may be said, develops within the limits set by the former. The division of labor and functional interdependence imply the prior existence of a group within which they arise and this group, if it be a group, must already be possessed of some form of cohesion.[16] Thus, Durkheim's analysis of the nature of the social bond does not contradict the work of Giddings; it merely supplements and complements it. It is wrong, the former wrote, to view the division of labor as the fundamental fact of *all* social life. Associational living, and hence group solidarity and " likemindedness " exist prior to the time when the division of labor can become an effective bond of social solidarity.

The discovery of two fundamentally different principles of social unity—one based on the community of ideas and sentiments, on resemblances, and resulting in a social structure wherein the individual is more or less completely absorbed by the group and wherein tradition and custom are king, and the other, resting on mutual and functional interdependence and creating a social structure wherein the individual human personality comes to be invested with a sort of sacredness—and of the genetic connection between them constitutes one of the major achievements of modern sociology. Here again we are

15 This proposition is attributed to him by Faris, A J S, XL (1934), 376.
16 *De la Division*, pp. 260-261.

in the presence of one of the basic and recurrent themes of social thought. Durkheim's analyses represent but a single, albeit illuminating, variation on a sociological idea-motif. There have been numerous thinkers besides the French theorist who have found it necessary to grapple with the same problem of social cohesion. Without attempting to be exhaustive, we may mention in this connection such eminent students of society as Sir Henry Sumner Maine, Herbert Spencer, and Ferdinand Tönnies. It is of great significance that althought these writers had varying starting points and different approaches, and although their interests and valuations (often reflected in their particular terminologies) were divergent, they nevertheless arrived at solutions which, in spite of internal differences, are markedly similar.

Some of the above mentioned writers would no doubt object to this statement. They themselves were more wont to emphasize their differences than their resemblances. And this is natural, since these differences bore on vital ethical and evaluational issues. Thus, Durkheim, who owed so much to Spencer, spent section after section, and even a whole chapter of his book to underscore the points on which he differed from the English philosopher. On the other hand he acknowledged his fundamental agree with Tönnies, taking exception only to the latter's analysis of contemporary society. The German sociologist, however, was less gracious, insisting that his analysis of the two types of social structure was "*ganz und gar verschieden*" from that of Durkheim.[17] As for the two Englishmen, we learn from Pollock that Spencer gave "courteous treatment" to Maine. We do not wish to minimize in any way the divergencies inherent in the views of these thinkers; we wish merely to dwell on the convergent aspect of their theories.

17 For an interesting exchange of reviews between Durkheim and Tönnies, see 89b and Tönnies, F., *Soziologische Studien und Kritiken* (Jena: Fischer, 1929), vol. III, pp. 215-217.

The parent theory, at least as far as modern thought is concerned, is Sir Henry Maine's distinction between societies based on status and those based on contract and his view that social evolution has been a movement from status to contract.[18] To Maine, this evolutionary change resulted in a liberation of the individual personality. "Starting, as from one terminus of history, from a condition of society in which all the relations of persons are summed up in the relations of Family, we seem to have steadily moved towards a phase of social order in which all these relations arise from the free agreement of individuals." [19] Of Maine it has been said that he was the founder of the study of social history,[20] and it is certainly true that he gave direction to the social thought of the nineteenth century.

Maine's contemporary, Herbert Spencer developed a rather similar view and even adopted the former's terminology. In his study of political institutions, Spencer distinguished " two fundamentally-unlike kinds of political organization, proper to the militant life, and the industrial life, respectively." [21] Adopting the method of ideal types,[22] Spencer describes the militant society as one in which the individual is " owned by the state " and which involves " a close binding of the society into a whole." It is a form of society characterized by *status,* " a society, the members of which stand one towards the other in successive grades of subordination." [23] Militant organization is regimentation; its fundamental principle of integration is " compulsory cooperation." Its structure is keyed to resist

18 Maine, H. S., *Ancient Law* (4th American ed.; New York: Holt, 1906), p. 165. The first edition appeared in 1861.

19 *Ibid.,* p. 163. For a brief discussion of Maine's formula by Pollock, see *ibid.,* appendix L, pp. 422-425.

20 Starcke, C. N., *Laws of Social Evolution and Social Ideals* (Copenhagen: Levin and Munksgaard, 1932), p. 294.

21 Spencer, *op. cit.,* vol. II, p. 568.

22 *Ibid.,* pp. 569, 606.

23 *Ibid.,* pp. 571-573. It is to be noted that Spencer's is a social definition of status whereas Maine's is essentially juridical. Spencer, *op. cit.,* p. 573, Maine, *op. cit.,* pp. 163-165.

change, and to allow centralization of power. The individual in such a society is subordinated to his group in " life, liberty, and property." Since " a necessary relation exists between the structure of a society and the natures of its citizens," [24] it is to be expected that the militant type of society will create a congenial personality type in whom the " military " virtues will be highly developed.

Likewise, industrial society, which contrasts sharply with the early militant type, will engender its own " industrial " personality pattern. The industrial type of society is based on the system of *contract,* not on that of status. In it the individual is liberated. The citizen's individuality " instead of being sacrificed by the society has to be defended by the society." The industrial social order gives the individuality of each man " the fullest play compatible with the like play of other men's individualities." It is, in short, a regime of contractual cooperation. Between the two types of structures there exists a genetic relationship. Industrial societies arise by modification of pre-existing military structures.[25]

The resemblance between Spencer and Durkheim is evident. It must be remembered, however, that the latter corrected the former by stripping the English philosopher's views of their utilitarian and individualistic biases.

Turning to Tönnies, we have the German sociologist's explicit acknowledgment of the influence directly exercised upon him by Maine to whom he refers as " ein soziologisch denkender Jurist." The idea of his *Gemeinschaft und Gesellschaft* came, Tönnies tells us, from his reading, in 1880, of Maine's *Ancient Law.*[26] There are two ideal types of social systems (*soziale Wesenheiten*), says Tönnies, each having its own concomitant type of individual will-pattern (*Willensgestalt*). The first, the more primitive, and the genetically prior type of social

24 Spencer, *op. cit.,* p. 592.

25 *Ibid.,* pp. 603-615.

26 Tönnies, *op. cit.,* vol. I, p. 54; *cf. ibid.,* pp. 43, 51.

unity is *Gemeinschaft* (community), a natural social bond of which the family tie is one of the purest examples. *Gemeinschaft* implies a principle of integration whereby the whole is an absolute unity, and the parts are hardly distinguishable from one another. It derives from communal living, intimate contact, and participation in a common set of values, traditions, and memories. A *Gemeinschaft* type of society rests on *status,* not on contract, and in it customs and traditions dominate. It is in this mode of social life that the temperament—affective type of individual will (*Wesenwille*)[27] receives its fullest development and achieves its richest expression. *Gesellschaft* (society), on the other hand, is a highly individualizing and differentiating pattern of social unity. In it, individuals are distinct and essentially isolated from one another. The parts are hardly unified; between them there is scarcely more than physical juxtaposition. *Gesellschaft* relationships, which characterize large social aggregates, give rise to the rationally oriented type of individual will (Kürwille). Empirically speaking, all societies are admixtures of the *Gemein-* and the *Gesellschaft* principles, although the former predominates in primitive societies and the latter is overwhelmingly characteristic of modern social life.[28]

There have been still other variations on the theme. Hobhouse, following the English liberal tradition, has used " freedom " and " mutuality of service " in addition to scale and efficiency as criteria of social development.[29] And MacIver has attempted to trace the pattern of social change from the primitive type of functionally undifferentiated society wherein social life is of a communal nature, to the more evolved, functionally diverse, and institutionally and associationally differentiated social group wherein the basis of individual relationships is less

27 This concept is, according to Heberle, derived from Schopenhauer's " *Bewüstloser Wille.*" Heberle, *op. cit.,* p. 14, footnote 20.

28 Tönnies, F., *Gemeinschaft und Gesellschaft* (2nd ed., Berlin: Curtins, 1912). First published in 1887.

29 Hobhouse, L. T., *Social Development* (N. Y.: Holt, 1924), pp. 78 ff.

communal and more associational, and wherein personality becomes more developed and more expressive.[30]

Giddings made the same point in his distinction between social *composition* and social *constitution* and in his view of social evolution as a movement from an " ethnogenic " stage wherein social composition prevails to a " demogenic " level at which we find " a thorough subordination of the social composition to the social constitution." [31] The distinctions between primary and secondary groups, to take a final example, and between their concomitant primary and secondary attitudes, sentiments, and *Weltanschauungen* represent the manner in which American sociology has developed the same theme. We see, then, that Durkheim's theses that society is unity and that there are at least two fundamental principles by which that unity is achieved are scarcely isolated points of view. They are deeply imbedded in the history of social thought and constitute part of the solid foundations on which sociology rests.

Durkheim admirably demonstrated the heuristic value of his analysis of social solidarity in his study of suicide. It enabled him not only to explain the social rates of suicide in terms of the degree of integration of an individual in his social groups, and not only to develop two types of suicide depending on whether they stem from excessive or deficient integration, but also to account for the decline in the suicide rate during periods of political crises, such as revolutions, wars, and elections. This decrease in the relative number of suicides is due, Durkheim thought, to the revitalization of collective sentiments and hence to the stronger social integration which political events of this sort bring about. When men unite in the face of a common danger the group unity becomes more firmly knit.[32]

Durkheim's explanation, however, is too simple, for it rests on a naive quantitative interpretation of the notions of lesser

30 MacIver, R. M., *Community*, pp. 219 ff.; *Society: Its Structure and Changes*, pp. 431 ff.

31 Giddings, *op. cit.*, p. 299; *cf.* pp. 153 ff., 171 ff.

32 *Le Suicide*, p. 222.

or greater integration. By introducing a qualitative analysis, as Halbwachs has done, and thus recognizing that in conflict situations the type of group integration is qualitatively different from its peace-time unity, we are able to explain the decline in the suicide rate during a period of war not only in the belligerent, but also in the neutral countries. A war situation requires a more simplified social structure, a change, so to speak, in the very basis of unity. Halbwachs rightly invokes here Spencer's distinction between the militant and industrial modes of integration. Moreover, a modern war is not purely an army affair; the entire population is more or less directly involved. Normal economic and occupation activities are in part paralyzed. Individuals are in many regards somewhat released from the strict and overpowering demands of the group. The opportunities for frustration are fewer.[33] Durkheim might well have contributed one more subtle explanation to a volume in which ingenious interpretation of statistical data abounds, had he considered social integration, in peace-time and in conflict, in terms of his own analysis of the two major principles of social cohesion.

3. SOCIETY AS REGULATION: NOMIA, LAW, RITUAL

Society as organization is not only unity, but also regulation. It is a system of order, a régime of discipline, and hence, in its regulatory aspect involves both a complex of rules by which order is maintained and a complex of forces and mechanisms whereby these rules are enforced. Social life is *nomic* life, (if we may use this adjective in its primitive connotation of " pertaining to rules or laws "), and society is a state of *nomia*. The antithesis of, and the alternative to social living is, as political philosophers such as Hobbes so clearly understood, lawlessness, the " state of nature " characterized by the *bellum omnium contra omnes*. Who speaks of society, then, must speak of control. Social order is disciplinary and restraining.

33 Halbwachs, *Les Causes du Suicide*, pp. 325-328.

Durkheim laid great stress on the regulatory functions of society. This, however, was not so much because of any personal ethical valuation of social control on his part, as because such emphasis served well his mission of convincing the French philosophical public of the possibility of a positive science of sociology. The disciplinary (*contrainte*) aspect of social data was, he felt, easily identifiable, an " immediate datum of experience." [34] Consequently, it could be used along with " externality " as an objective and readily perceptible index of these data. By means of this overt characteristic one would be able to recognize and " get at " the social. But it is a distortion of Durkheim's views to assume that he ever meant that discipline or restraint is the exclusive and sole feature of social facts; it is only one of their many properties, and not necessarily an important one. It is helpful, however, as a tool of identification.[35] Stripped of its exclusive connotation, which in Durkheim's thinking it never had, the proposition that the social is regulatory is hardly disputable.

Once again we must remark on Durkheim's unfortunate terminology. The ambiguity of the term " *contrainte* " has been clearly demonstrated by Lacombe who was able to discern three distinct connotations that the word has in Durkheim's writings.[36] It sometimes refers to the pressure that stems from prestige and authority, and at other times it means the need to conform to social standards as a condition of group existence. In addition, it not infrequently has reference to the notion of mechanical necessity. But one should not exaggerate the significance of the inconsistent usage of a term; the specific meaning of the word, can for the most part, be fairly easily gleaned from its context.

One must also question the accepted use of the English cognate " constraint." This term has too psychological a connota-

34 *Règles*, p. 16, footnote 1.

35 *Ibid*., p. xx, footnote 1 ; o3c, p. 472, footnote 2.

36 Lacombe, *op. cit*., pp. 40-48.

tion to serve as an accurate equivalent of " *contrainte* ". We prefer the noun *regulation* and the adjective *regulatory* as being more faithful to Durkheim's meaning. These terms are fairly sociological, if not exactly juridical, in their significance. And it is in juridical phenomena that Durkheim saw one of the clearest manifestations of *la contrainte sociale?* For technical discussions we should like to advocate the terms nomia and nomic. Durkheim, surprisingly, employed only the negative concept of anomia.

To understand why the author of *Les Règles* insisted on the notion of " social constraint " we must recall what we said in Part II about his defiant, polemic style, and about his severe stand against utilitarianism. Durkheim no doubt adopted the concept of *contrainte* as a protest against the doctrines of natural rights, natural freedom, and inherent individual liberty that were being fostered by the individualistic philosophies. Society, he urged against the individualists, is not a thing of whim and fancy to be entered into at will or on one's own terms. Man belongs to it willy-nilly and willy-nilly he is shaped by it.

Of Durkheim's various contributions to an understanding of the regulatory aspects of social life, we should like to mention two as especially revealing: (1) his analysis of juridical evolution and (2) his theory of the social functions of ceremony and ritual.

The study of juridical evolution presented in *De la Division* [37] is, in a sense, only incidental to the major theme of social solidarity. It is, nevertheless, a significant piece of empirical research, quite apart from its relation to the problem of social integration.

One of the stumbling blocks to a proper understanding of legal evolution and especially of primitive law has been the tendency to view all forms of social control as legal control, to regard all social sanctions as juridical sanctions, and to classify all sanctioned rules of conduct as law. Confusions of

37 See esp. Book I, Chap. IV.

this sort were carefully avoided by Durkheim. He properly distinguished organized from diffuse sanctions, and regarded only the former as juridical in nature. In this manner he could differentiate law, on the one hand, from customs, mores, and conventions, on the other.[38] The latter are maintained by the diffuse sanctions, i. e. those like ostracism and shame, for instance, which are at the command of, and are used by, everyone in the group. Legal rules, on the other hand, are supported by the organized sanctions i. e. those which are inflicted on violators in accordance with a regularly established procedure by a " definite organ " of the community, be it the group as a whole or one or some of its duly authorized agents.[39]

Now, examining the body of organized sanctions, we discover that there are two major types, corresponding to two different modes of group reaction to the violation of a legal rule. Sometimes the wronging party is made to suffer by being deprived of something he enjoys, as for example, life, liberty, honor, fortune, or privilege. The violator, we say, is punished. At other times, a violation is adjudicated not in order to punish the wronging party, but solely with the intention of restoring the troubled relations between the parties involved to their former, normal state. This generally takes the form of making the wronger pay " damages " to the wronged. Sanctions of the first kind, involving punishment, are *repressive* and the body of rules the violation of which evokes organized sanctions of this nature constitutes the *repressive law*. The second type of organized sanction, aiming at the restoration of troubled relations to normalcy, is *restitutive* and is applied to support the body of juridical rules comprising the *restitutive law*.

Such, then, are the cornerstones of Durkheim's legal evolutionary structure: a clear distinction between law and the other social rules of conduct based on the difference between organ-

---

38 A confusing table appearing at the end of Book I, Chap. I of the first edition of *De la Division* was omitted by Durkheim in subsequent editions.

39 *De la Division*, pp. 33, 81.

ized and diffuse sanctions; and a differentiation, within the corpus of organized sanctions, of two basic types: the punitive or repressive sanctions, and the restorative or restitutive ones. These conceptual tools resemble, but should not be confused with, the concepts used by other writers. The distinction between organized and diffuse sanctions corresponds fairly closely to the fundamental differentiation in American sociology between law and the mores. But repressive and restitutive law are categories for which " criminal law " and " civil law " are only approximations. The latter concepts are applicable only with the greatest difficulty to primitive societies.[40] Such application was attempted, however, by Malinowski,[41] in spite of the fact that he recognized that in applying such concepts to savage law one was using " modern and hence necessarily inappropriate " labels.[41] Denying that all savage law is criminal law, he asserted that there exists a body of positive commandments " the breach of which is penalized but not punished and the machinery of which can by no procrustean methods be stretched beyond the line which separates civil from criminal law." [43] By civil law among the Trobrianders, Malinowski means the " body of binding obligations regarded as a right by one party and acknowledged as a duty by the other, kept in force by a specific mechanism of reciprocity and publicity inherent in the structure of their society." [44] Durkheim would hardly have denied the existence of such a body of " positive commandments " or " binding customs " although he no doubt would have agreed with Seagle that Malinowski " has somewhat over-

40 Cf. Radcliffe-Brown, A. R., " Primitive Law," E S S, (1933), vol. IX, p. 202.

41 Malinowski, B., *Crime and Custom in Savage Society* (N. Y.: Harcourt Brace, 1932). For a critique of this volume see Seagle, W., " Primitive Law and Professor Malinowski," A A, n. s., XXXIX (1937), 275-290.

42 Malinowski, *op. cit.*, p. 58.

43 *Idem.*

44 *Idem.*

worked the system of reciprocity." [45] The essential question, however, is: do these binding customs constitute a body of *law?* In answering affirmatively, Malinowski has committed, in the words of Seagle, "what may be described as the pathetic fallacy of primitive jurisprudence. He has transferred to primitive law the legal emotions of his own culture. He has simply sought in primitive society those institutions which *in the modern world have come to be the subject matter of legal obligation.* He has selected the *customs* relating to marriage, inheritance, and property, and pronounced these to be primitive law." [46] MacIver has raised the same objection, pointing out that what Malinowski terms "legal mechanisms" are only "primitive *equivalents* of our legal institutions." [47]

Closer to Durkheim's concepts is the distinction made by Radcliffe-Brown between the law of public delicts and the law of private delicts. [48] Public delicts are those that invoke penal or repressive sanctions; private delicts are subject to restitutive sanctions. But Durkheim explicitly rejected the differentiation between "public" and "private" law as having only a practical and not a scientific value, and as obscuring the proper role of society even in "private law." [49] Radcliffe-Brown's analysis is, however, essentially Durkheimian and raises the question whether the differences between the anthropologist and the French sociologist are not merely terminological. It is important, in any case, to inquire into the accuracy of the former's identification of penal sanctions with public law and of restitutive sanctions with the law of private delicts.

Accepting Durkheim's conceptual tools, we may view legal evolution in a two-fold manner. We may examine the changing roles assumed in the course of social evolution by the organized and the diffuse sanctions. And we may also investigate the

45 Seagle, *loc. cit.*, p. 280.

46 *Ibid.*, pp. 282-283. Italics in text.

47 MacIver, *Society* (1937), p. 333.

48 Radcliffe-Brown, *loc. cit.*, pp. 202-206.

49 *De la Division*, pp. 32-33, 96.

changing relative positions of repressive and restitutive law within the total body of law. A complete analysis would, of course, consider both these problems. Durkheim, however, devoted himself only to the latter question. He attempted to establish the historical law that the more primitive a society, the more predominant is the role of penal law in relation to restitutive law within it. This proposition is not absolutistic, but proportional. Stated in another way, it affirms that the degree of predominance of penal over restitutive law varies directly as the degree of primitiveness of a society.

To support his general proposition, Durkheim adduced the empirical data summarized in the following table. It should be noted that although throughout his study Durkheim speaks of law in " primitive society " (*dans les sociétés inférieures*) he is really dealing not with *primitive* law as anthropologists understand the term today, but rather with what more closely corresponds to *ancient* and *feudal* law. The distinction between primitive and ancient law and Durkheim's immediate concern with the latter should be borne in mind before attributing to the French theorist extravagant propositions concerning law " in primitive society." [50]

The general law of legal evolution above formulated represents, in our opinion, one of the more solid generalizations proposed by Durkheim.[51] Its empirical foundation is firm. Its theoretical import, however, would have been greatly enhanced had it been supplemented by a study of the concomitant changes

[50] See *De la Division*, p. 44, but note the societies referred to.

[51] See, however, the strictures on Durkheim's views suggested by Sorokin in *Social and Cultural Dynamics* (N. Y.: American Book Co., 1937), vol. II, chap. xv, pp. 609 ff., esp. footnotes 69 and 74. To the extent that Sorokin's arguments pertain to the severity of the penalties imposed in accordance with the laws of the Twelve Tables, they do not affect Durkheim's characterization of this code as predominantly repressive in nature. Moreover, Sorokin fails to consider the possibility that the post-war twentieth century " orgy of executions, banishments, bodily punishments " may be due, in accordance with Durkheim's theories, to a heightened intensification of collective consciousnesses (nationalism, totalitarianism) in so many countries.

TABLE IV

The Relative Proportions of Repressive and Restitutive Laws in the Codes of Four Societies. Based on Durkheim, E., *De la Division du travail social,* Book I, Chap. IV, Par. II. (Page references are to this volume.)

Society: ranked in descending degree of primitiveness [a]	Code	Number of laws included	Number repressive	Number restitutive	% Repressive	% Restitutive
1. Ancient Hebrews	Last four books of Pentateuch	4000-5000 verses	4365 [b]	135 [c]	97	3
2. Franks	Salic Law	293 articles	268	25	91	9
3. Burgundians	Burgundian Law	311 articles	213	98	68	32
4. Romans of 5th Century B.C.	Twelve Tables	115 fragments	49 [d]	66	43	57

(a) " In saying of a social type that it is more advanced than another, we do not mean that the different social types are arranged in a single ascending linear series, more or less elevated, according to the historical period. It is certain on the contrary, that if the genealogical table of social types could be completely drawn up, it would have, rather, the form of a tufted tree, with a single trunk, no doubt, but with divergent boughs. But in spite of this arrangement, the distance between two types is measurable : they are more or less high " (p. 112, footnote 2). A social morphology is broached in Book I, chap. VI, par. I (see also *Règles*, pp. 26, 94-109). For justification of the rankings in the table see pp. 112-113, 116. We can only conjecture Durkheim's intended ranking of the Burgundians. They are less primitive than the Franks who are more primitive than the 5th century Romans, he asserts. But he makes no direct comparison between the latter and the Burgundians.

We omit the Visigoths because Durkheim's evidence concerning them (pp. 116-117) does not lend itself to statistical tabulation.

(b) Using 4500 as basis of calculation.

(c) At the very most. See p. 110.

(d) Keener analysis, however, permits one to conclude that even here the penal law actually constituted the major part of the law (p. 114).

in customs and mores and in the relation of these to the total body of law.

Juridical phenomena, in the strictest sense, are only one phase of the regulatory aspect of society. The legal code is but one of many social codes, and legal sanctions comprise but a part of the total body of social sanctions. There are social rules of conduct other than laws, and mechanisms of social control other than the machinery of law enforcement. A student of society cannot ignore, for instance, the far-reaching social functions, including regulatory functions, of ceremony and ritual.

Durkheim inquired into the nature and functions of ceremonial and ritualistic institutions in Book III of *Les Formes élémentaires*. His mode of analysis here follows his general theory of religion which he perceives as an expression, in symbolic form, of social realities. He first determines the religious functions of ceremonial and ritualistic behavior and then tries to get behind the symbolic beliefs and behavior to the social realities which they are purported to express. In thus " substituting reality for symbol " he brings religion down to earth, so to speak, and hence is able to ascertain the social functions of the religiously symbolic conduct.

A study of the *proscribing* rites, i. e. taboos and interdicts ("the negative cult ")[52] and of the *prescribing* ones such as sacrificial, imitative, commemorative, and piacular rites ("the positive cult ")[53] reveals that ritualistic institutions have a number of vital social functions which vary, of course, with the nature of the particular ceremony being performed. The following are four social functions of ritual to which Durkheim pays special attention.[54]

[52] *Les Formes élémentaires*, Book III, Chap. I.

[53] *Ibid.*, Book III, Chaps. II-V.

[54] We list them without regard to the specific rites which especially foster each. Durkheim, we feel, tends to classify as separate rites what are in a sense only elements found in varying degree and with varying frequency in almost all ceremonies. Thus a "piacular rite" such as mourning is frequently not devoid of sacrificial, commemorative, or imitative elements; nor is the taboo aspect entirely absent.

1. *A disciplinary and preparatory function.* Ritual prepares an individual for social living by imposing on him the self-discipline, the " disdain for suffering," the self-abnegation without which life in society would be impossible. Social existence is possible only as individuals are able to accept constraints and controls. Asceticism is an inherent element in all social life.[55] Ritual, being formal and institutional, and hence to some degree prohibitive and inhibitive, is necessarily ascetic. " In fact," Durkheim observes, " there is no interdict, the observance of which does not have an ascetic character to a certain degree. Abstaining from something which may be useful or from a form of activity, which, since it is usual, should answer to some human need, is, of necessity imposing constraints and renunciations." [56] But abstinences, he adds, " do not come without suffering. We hold to the profane world by all the fibres of our flesh; our senses attach us to it; our life depends upon it. It is not merely the natural theatre of our activity; it penetrates us from every side; it is a part of ourselves. So we cannot detach ourselves from it without doing violence to our nature and without painfully wounding our instincts. In other words, the negative cult cannot develop without causing suffering. Pain is one of its necessary conditions." [57] Moreover, the positive cult is possible " only when a man is trained to renouncement, to abnegation, to detachment from self, and consequently to suffering." [58] Ascetic practices, therefore, are " a necessary school where men form and temper themselves, and acquire the qualities of disinterestedness and endurance without which there would be no religion." [59] Substitute, in the above quotations, " social rule " for negative cult, " social life " for positive cult, and " society " for religion and one has a clear picture of the disciplinary function of social ritual.

55 Durkheim, *ibid.*, p. 452.
56 *Ibid.*, p. 444.
57 *Ibid.*, p. 446.
58 *Ibid.*, p. 451.
59 *Ibid.*, pp. 451-452.

2. *A cohesive function.* Ceremony brings people together and thus serves to reaffirm their common bonds and to enhance and reenforce social solidarity. " Rites are, above all, means by which the social group reaffirms itself periodically." [60] Ceremonial occasions are occasions of social communion. They are necessitated by the inevitable intermittency of social life.[66] The work-a-day, immediate, private, and personal interests of an individual occupy much of his every-day life. His social ties to his fellowmen, their common pool of values, tend to become obscure, indistinct, and even to lapse from consciousness. But since society is a necessary condition of human civilized living, it is imperative that this condition be remedied, that periodically at least, man be given the opportunity to commune with his fellow social beings and to express his solidarity with them. Ceremonial institutions afford just such opportunities. Whatever their stated purpose, " the essential thing is that men are assembled, that sentiments are felt in common, and that they are expressed in common acts." [62] Closely related to this cohesive function of ritual is its:

3. *Revitalizing function.* If society is to be kept alive, its members must be made keenly aware of their social heritage. Traditions must be perpetuated, faith must be renewed, values must be transmitted and deeply imbedded. In this task of vitalizing and reanimating the social heritage of a group, ceremony and ritual play an important part. Men celebrate certain rites in order to " remain faithful to the past, to keep for the group its moral physiognomy." [63] A large number of ceremonies include rites whose object is " to recall the past and, in a way, to make it present by means of a veritable dramatic representation." [64] These rites serve to sustain the vitality of the social heritage and to keep its essential parts from lapsing from

60 *Ibid.*, p. 553.
61 *Ibid.*, p. 493.
62 *Ibid.*, p. 553.
63 *Ibid.*, p. 530.
64 *Ibid.*, p. 531.

memory and consciousness. In short, they "revivify the most essential elements of the collective consciousness." Through them, "the group periodically renews the sentiment which it has of itself and of its unity; at the same time individuals are strengthened in their social natures." [65] Ceremony functions, then, "to awaken certain ideas and sentiments, to attach the present to the past, the individual to the group." [66] Since it aids in transmitting the social heritage it may also be said to have an educational function.

Viewed from another angle, ceremony and ritual have: 4. *A euphoric function.*[67] We mean by this that they serve to establish a condition of social euphoria, i. e. a pleasant feeling of social well-being. This function takes on special significance when a group is faced with an actual or a threatened condition of dysphoria. All societies are subject to crises, calamities, disappointments, losses of particular members, and other "dysphoric" experiences. In certain cases the very existence of the group may be in jeopardy. These socially adverse conditions tend to disrupt the smooth functioning of the group; they threaten its sense of well-being, its feeling that all's right with the world. The group attempts, therefore, to counterbalance the disturbing action of these dysphoric situations; and in smoothing its way through crises and adversities, ceremony and ritual are of invaluable service.[68] They perform this function by requiring individuals to have and to express certain emotions and sentiments, and by making them express these sentiments and feelings together.

Consider, for example, the mourning ceremonies. " When a society is going through circumstances which sadden, perplex, or irritate it, it exercises a pressure over its members to make them bear witness, by significant actions, to their sorrow, per-

65 *Ibid.*, p. 536.
66 *Ibid.*, p. 541.
67 *Cf. ibid.*, pp. 591, 613.

68 Symbols and slogans are also effective, as the Lynds have well illustrated in *Middletown in Transition.*

plexity, or anger." [69] Thus, in the face of a dysphoric experience such as the loss of a member through death, a group exerts moral pressure on its members to make their sentiments harmonize with the situation. They must show that they have been duly affected by the loss. In any case, the group cannot allow them to remain indifferent. For " to allow them to remain indifferent to the blow which has fallen upon it and diminished it would be equivalent to proclaiming that it does not hold the place in their hearts which is due it; it would be denying itself. A family which allows one of its members to die without being wept for shows by that very fact that it lacks moral unity and cohesion; it abdicates, it renounces its existence." [70]

When someone dies, then, " the family group to which he belongs feels itself lessened, and to react against this loss, it assembles . . . collective sentiments are renewed, individuals consequently tend to seek out one another and to assemble together." [71] This coming together of individuals, this entering into closer relations with one another, and this sharing of a like emotion give rise to " a sensation of comfort which compensates the original loss." Since the individuals weep together, " they hold to one another, and the group is not weakened. . . . Of course they have only sad emotions in common; but communicating in sorrow is still communicating; and every communion of mind, in whatever form it may be made, raises the social vitality." [72]

We see then that ritual and ceremony in general serve " to remake individuals and groups morally." [73] They are disciplinary, cohesive, vitalizing and euphoric social forces.

The above summary sketch of Durkheim's analysis of the social functions of ceremony and ritual can do justice neither to its profundity nor to its wisdom. Durkheim may have been

69 Durkheim, *op. cit.*, p. 589.

70 *Ibid.*, p. 571.

71 *Idem.*

72 *Ibid.*, p. 574.

73 *Ibid.*, p. 529.

mistaken in his interpretation of certain Australian ceremonies, and in his sharp differentiation between magic and religion [74] and no doubt he erred in considering only religious rites to the practical exclusion of secular ritual,[75] and in neglecting in general to give due attention to those phenomena that are social but non-religious; [76] his functional analysis of ceremonial and ritualistic institutions nonetheless remains, we believe, a major contribution to sociology.

4. SOCIETY AS EXPRESSION: TOWARDS A SOCIOLOGISMIC PSYCHOLOGY

The psychological consequence of social nomia is individual frustration. Biologically rooted impulses are bound to be inhibited when men live in an ordered society. Since rules generally exist where there is a tendency to act contrary to their commandments, the price of social regulation is individual constraint. It is onesided, however, to think of society solely as a control mechanism. If society is restraint, it is also expression; if it is restriction, it is also liberation. We must view both sides of the medal. Society is for its members not only regulation but also a source of life and expression. Durkheim expressed this succinctly when he stated that society is not only a system of

74 See Warner, W. L., "The Social Configuration of Magical Behavior" in *Essays in Anthropology Presented to A. L. Kroeber* (Berkeley: U. of California Press, 1936).

75 See, however, 24a, p. 135 and 14a, p. 218. *Cf.* Dr. Benedict's remarks: "The contention of Durkheim and many others that religion arises from ritualism as such must be challenged, for the most extreme ritualistic formalism does not convert the council of elders or affinal exchange into an aspect even of the already existing religious complexes. Durkheim's theoretical position is untenable once it is recognized that ritual may surround any field of behavior and of itself does not give birth to religion any more than it gives birth to art or to social organization." Benedict, R., "Ritual," E S S (1934), Vol. XIII, p. 396.

76 *Cf.* Goldenweiser: "In economic pursuits and in industry, in the ideas and customs clustering about the family or kinship, social factors figure at least as prominently as individual ones, without, however, assuming a halo of sanctity." Goldenweiser, A. A., *Anthropology* (N. Y.: Crofts, 1937), p. 220.

organs and functions maintaining itself against external forces, but also " le foyer " of an internal moral life leading the individual ever beyond himself.[77] Society is the source, the creator of ideas, ideals and values. It has, to pursue a Durkheimian metaphor, not only a body, but also a soul, and this soul is the totality of social ideals.[78] Social phenomena are essentially systems of values and ideals.[79] A comprehensive sociology must therefore view society as giving direction to human life and as developing personality.

It is a commonplace of sociology that it is " our social heritage ", to use Graham Wallas' phrase, that keeps man from sinking to the level of mere bestiality and animality. It is the totality of our socially acquired and socially transmitted techniques, knowledge, beliefs, institutions, traditions, values and ideals that makes all the difference between man the civilized being and man the pitiful, biologically underequipped animal. Durkheim is hardly alone in asserting that " man is human only because he is civilized." [80] Take away from the human being his language, his conceptual apparatus, his categories of thought, his ethics, religion, art, science and philosophy, and what remains? An animal dominated completely by his sensible appetites, a prey to his instincts, impulses, whims and fancies, whose life, as Hobbes foresaw, would be " poor, solitary, nasty, brutish, and short." Graham Wallas has vividly pictured what would happen " if the earth were struck by one of Mr. Wells' comets, and if, in consequence, every human being now alive were to lose all the knowledge and habits which he had acquired from preceding generations (though retaining unchanged all his powers of invention, and memory and habituation)." " They would have no language to express their thoughts, and no thoughts but vague reverie. They could not read notices, or drive motors or horses. They would wander about, led by the

77 24a, pp. 132-133.
78 Ibid., p. 136.
79 Ibid., p. 141.
80 14a, p. 206.

inarticulate voices of a few naturally dominant individuals, drowning themselves, as thirst came on, in hundreds at the riverside landing places, looting those shops where the smell of decaying food attracted them, and perhaps at the end stumbling on the expedient of cannibalism." [81] And the growing literature on feral cases adds empirical and experimental support to the suppositions of these political writers.

Man, then, is a double inheritor. From his biological parents he receives his original nature: his organs, and their capacities, functions, impulses and tendencies. From society, on the other hand, he acquires, through the social processes of education and habituation, his social nature: his culture, his values, in short, his civilization. Culture, however, is not a biological part of man. It is " a post-natal imposition upon his biological organism—that is the real meaning of its being socially inherited." [82] His double inheritance, therefore, makes man a dual creature; it is the source of his never-ceasing, inextricable unrest. *Human* nature, as the resultant of original and social nature can only be an imperfect harmonization of its two component but, in many respects, divergent elements. The exigencies of social life are not always compatible with the immediate urges and pleasures of the organism.[83] As mentioned above, there is necessarily an ascetic, and hence a frustrational element in orderly social living. Human nature, being dual,[84] is inexorably subject to unceasing tensions. " Far from being simple, our inner life has a sort of double center of gravity. There is, on the one hand, our individuality, and more especially our body which is its foundation; on the other, all which, in us, expresses something other than ourselves." [85]

81 Wallas, G., *Our Social Heritage* (New Haven: Yale Univ. Press, 1921), p. 16.

82 Mekeel, H. S., "A Psychoanalytic Approach to Culture," *Journal of Social Philosophy*, II (1937), p. 234.

83 14a, pp. 219-221.

84 See 13b, 14a.

85 14a, p. 209.

Tension may be a severe price to pay for social living but it is a necessary price if we are to live at all as human personalities. For it is from society, and not from original nature, that we obtain the necessary conditions of personality development. It is society that teaches us discipline and self control, the reins without which our personality would run wild.[86] Durkheim has well described the consequences of anomia, that is, the condition in which the social pressures making for self-discipline are rendered impotent. " Imagine a being liberated from all external restraint, a despot more absolute than the ones history tells us about, a despot whom no external power can control and rule. By definition, the desires of such a being are irresistible. Shall we say, therefore, that he is omnipotent? Certainly not, for he himself cannot resist them. They are masters over him as over all other things. He is subject to them; he does not dominate them. In a word, when our desires are freed from all moderating influence, when nothing limits them, they become themselves tyrannical and their first slave is the very subject who experiences them. Moreover, you know the sad spectacle he presents. The most contrary impulses, the most antithetical caprices follow one upon another, leading this self-entitled absolute sovereign in the most divergent directions, so that this apparent omnipotence resolves itself, in the end, into a veritable impotence. A despot is like a child; he has the latter's weaknesses, and for the same reason: he is not master of himself. Self-mastery, then, is the first condition of all true power, of all liberty worthy of the name." [87] Anomia, moreover, is conducive to suicide, for human life can hardly be happy or even possible, unless one's wants approximate one's means.[88] Normally the moderating influence of society serves to check one's wants, to keep them within bounds. Under anomic conditions, however, the social brake gets out of order and indi-

86 See 25a, Part I, pp. 19-62.

87 *Ibid.*, pp. 50-51. *Cf. De la Division*, Book III, Chap. II, and *Le Suicide,* Book II, Chap. V.

88 *Le Suicide*, p. 272.

viduals' wants soar rapidly. A " the sky's the limit " psychology develops. The suicide statistics record the rest of the story.

Thus, in imposing self-discipline on individuals society is creating the condition for personality expression. Expression means systematic action, and this, in turn, implies sustained attention and effort, habits that are developed only under the pressure of social requirements.[89] Society, however, exercises an even more positive action.

As mentioned above, and as Cooley taught,[90] we acquire from our experiences in groups, our sense of values, our ideals, our standards, our sympathies, loves, hates, and fears. Moreover it is society that has created the dignity of man and the glory of his past and future. It is for these reasons that a psychology of human nature must be largely sociologismic.[91] Since much of our *human* nature has a social origin, a comprehensive human psychology must comprise: a sociology of values which traces the social origins and settings of ideals [92] and which analyzes the social factors in ethics [93] religion,[94] law,[95] economic life,[96] and art,[97] a sociology of thought and knowledge; [98]

---

89 *Cf.* 14a, pp. 220-221, and Piaget, J., *Judgment and Reasoning in the Child* (N. Y.: Harcourt Brace, 1928), and the same author's *The Language and Thought of the Child* (2nd ed.; N. Y.: Harcourt Brace, 1932).

90 See both *Social Organization* and *Human Nature and the Social Order*.

91 See Part I for a definition of this term.

92 See 24a, 12a, esp. conclusion, and Bouglé, C., *Leçons de Sociologie sur l'Evolution des Valeurs* (2nd ed.; Paris: Colin, 1929).

93 See 24a, 20a, 25a.

94 See 12a and Granet, M., *Danses et légendes de la Chine Ancienne* (Paris: Alcan, 1926).

95 See Davy, G., *La Foi jurée* (Paris: Alcan, 1922).

96 See Simiand, F., *op. cit.*, and Halbwachs, M., *La Classe ouvrière et les niveaux de vie* (Paris: Alcan, 1912), and by the same author, *L'Evolution des besoins dans les classes ouvrières* (Paris: Alcan, 1933).

97 See Lalo, Ch., *L'Art et la vie sociale* (Paris: Doin, 1921).

98 See 12a and the critical essay by Essertier, D., *Les Formes inférieures de l'explication* (Paris: Alcan, 1927), esp. pp. 258-278.

a sociology of mental states;[99] a sociology of emotions;[100] and a sociology of language.[101] It can scarcely be denied that the developments towards a sociological psychology of human nature which are mentioned in the footnotes to this paragraph[102] and for which Durkheim supplied the impetus and inspiration have borne ample and significant fruit. Of course, in studies of the sociologismic kind, one must guard against ignoring the biological basis of human nature and against reducing the individual to a mere automaton impassively receiving and conforming to his social heritage. Merton is unquestionably right in contending that when French writers " treat the collective representations as hypostatized entities ready to fasten onto individuals who come within their realm they turn to sterile, meaningless psittacism." [103] It can be positively asserted however, that such a criticism is in noway applicable to Durkheim. The latter was keenly aware of the recalcitrant nature of human beings, of the give and take element in the process of acculturation, and of the fundamental tendency of individuals to be refractory to social discipline.[104] It is erroneous to attribute to Durkheim, as Malinowski apparently does,[105] the theory of unswerving, automatic, " slavish, fascinated, passive " obedience to social codes. The former was even quite saddened by the inherent antagonism between social demands and individual inclinations.[106] If society were merely the natural and spon-

99 See Halbwachs, M., *Les Cadres sociaux de la mémoire* (Paris: Alcan, 1925) and the works of Lévy-Bruhl.

100 See Blondel, Ch., *Introduction à la psychologie collective* (Paris: Colin, 1928) and the same author's "Les Volitions," in G. Dumas' *Traité de Psychologie* (Paris: Alcan, 1924), Vol. II, Book I, Chap. V, pp. 333-425.

101 See the late Professor Meillet's "Comment les mots changent de sens," A S, IX (1906), 1-38 and his *Les Langues dans l'Europe nouvelle* (Paris: Payot, 1918).

102 See Bouglé's *Bilan*, esp. chap I, for a résumé of most of these contributions.

103 Merton, R. K., "Recent French Sociology," S F, XII (1934), 542.

104 *Cf.* 13b, 14a, 25a.

105 Malinowski, *op. cit.*, p. 4.

106 14a, p. 220.

taneous development of our organic nature, he wrote, there would be no resistences and no conflicts between our biological and our social selves. These two parts of our nature would harmonize and adjust to one another without friction. Society, however, has exigencies altogether different from the ones implied in our strictly biological nature. Our social and organic natures, while always effecting an adjustment to each other, are nevertheless made up of somewhat different elements and tend to orient us in divergent directions.[107] Such thoughts could hardly be expressed by one who ignored the organic rootings of human life, or who saw in the individual only a passive, psittacistic product of his social milieu.

It is likewise doubtful whether the charge of "cultural determinism" is validly applicable to the Durkheimian brand of social psychologists.[108] If cultural determinism ignores individual differences, if it "views the individual as a passive recipient of the cultural patterns of his group" and if it "pays little attention to original nature, sees no problem in social development, and belittles the possibilities of human beings having unique lines of experience," [109] then it is a distortion to attribute this position, as Blumer does, to writers like Blondel and Halbwachs, or even to Lévy-Bruhl. These French social psychologists have concerned themselves with the social aspects of psychological phenomena, it is true, but in doing so they have not denied that these phenomena possess other aspects. Blondel in particular has insisted on the importance of a psychology of individual differences in which psycho-physiological as well as socio-psychological factors are considered.[110]

107 14a, pp. 219-220.

108 The charge is made by Blumer. See Blumer, H., " Social Psychology," in Schmidt, E. P., ed., *Man and Society* (N. Y.: Prentice-Hall, 1937), pp. 154-157.

109 *Ibid.*, p. 157.

110 Blondel, *op. cit.*, p. 187. *Cf.* Halbwachs, *Les Cadres sociaux de la mémoire*, p. xi, footnote 1, and Lévy-Bruhl, L., *La Mentalité primitive*

A second danger inherent in the sociologismic approach is the tendency to invent one's own psychological principles or to adopt implicitly some outmoded system of psychology. It is well-nigh impossible to study phenomena like primitive mentality or magical behavior, even in their strictly sociological aspects, without adopting some kind of psychological view of the nature of mental processes, of the association of ideas, or of human motivation. It is imperative, therefore, that sociologists keep in constant touch with the developments in psychological science, just as it is incumbent upon psychologists not to ignore what Professor Delacroix has termed the "social dimension" of psychic data.[111] Since their tasks involve some degree of psychologizing, sociologists must become more conscious of their implicit psychological assumptions.[112] One of the most serious defects in Durkheim is precisely this tendency to adopt or invent psychological principles *ad hoc*.

A third risk contained in sociologismic investigations is the hypostatizing of society and social forces. The Durkheimians undoubtedly do not have a clean slate on this score. But if, with Essertier, we may distinguish "pure sociologism," with its literal, unqualified and substantialist acceptance of concepts like "collective consciousness" and "collective entity," from "neo- or moderate sociologism" which, as it is professed by Marcel Mauss [113] and seems to be adopted by Paul Fauconnet,[114] treats "collective consciousness" and "collective representa-

(Herbert Spencer Lecture; Oxford: Clarendon Press, 1931), pp. 10-11. Blumer, we feel, exaggerates the unity and "schoolishness" of these writers. See e. g. Blondel's review in R P, CI (1926), 290-298. Blondel's conclusion contains a warning against "sociological imperialism" and "pan-sociologism" (p. 298).

111 Delacroix, H., *Le Langage et la pensée* (Paris: Alcan, 1924), p. 55.

112 *Cf.* Essertier, D., *Psychologie et Sociologie*, pp. 30-31.

113 See Mauss, M., "Rapports réels et pratiques de la psychologie et de la sociologie," J P, XXI (1924), 892-922.

114 Fauconnet, P., in *Congrès des Sociétés philosophiques américaine, anglaises, belge, italienne et française, Communications et Discussions* (Paris: Colin, 1921), pp. 471-472.

tions " merely as heuristic modes of expressing the reality of associational life, then, we do not hesitate, in the light of our discussion in Part II, to qualify Durkheim's position as neo-sociologismic.[115] If the expression is not too odd, we may say that Durkheim was a moderate Durkheimian.

In conclusion, then, it may be urged that sociologismic studies, provided that they give due consideration to the biological basis of human nature, make explicit their psychological presuppositions, and avoid the tendency towards social hypostatizing,[116] can well serve to present a penetrating and revealing picture of the expressional aspects of social living.

Society is too complex a phenomenon to be described in a simple formula. Three words can hardly convey the vast intricacy of social life. Yet, however incomplete and over-simplified the statement, it can be safely asserted with Durkheim that the science of sociology must reckon with Society as Unity, Regulation, and Expression.[117]

115 The expressions neo-sociologism and moderate sociologism (*sociologisme nuancé*) appear in Essertier, *op. cit.*, pp. 93-94. Essertier seems to regard Davy as representative of the extreme position. See Essertier, D., *La Sociologie*, p. 179, footnote 3.

116 *Cf.* Mauss, M., "Fragment d'un plan de sociologie générale descriptive," An S., Série A, fasc. 1 (1934), pp. 1-56.

117 This study was unfortunately completed prior to the publication of Professor Parsons' *Structure of Social Action* and hence could not avail itself of the stimulating discussions contained therein.

APPENDIX A

A COMPREHENSIVE BIBLIOGRAPHY OF EMILE DURKHEIM

INTRODUCTORY NOTE

How well known a person is and how well he is known are two different things. Dr. Faris is perfectly right in maintaining that " Durkheim has been familiar to American scholars for a generation " [1] In fact, the very first volume of the American Journal of Sociology of which Durkheim was a foreign editor, contained an article devoted in part to an analysis of *Les Règles*.[2] Shortly afterwards the Journal published so excoriating a critique of *Le Suicide* that Durkheim was impelled to defend himself in a letter to the editor.[3] Moreover, it should be remembered that Gehlke's doctoral dissertation is now more than 20 years old.[4] The French sociologist is also given frequent mention in our general textbooks. The corroborative evidence for Dr. Faris' contention is, indeed, abundant. But to be known, referred to, and quoted is one thing, to be understood is another.

On this last score, American social scientists do not perhaps stand up as well as on the first.[5] This miscomprehension is in part attributable not only to the cause implied by Professor Warner, namely that " all the works of this great French social theorist are not available in English," [6] but also to the fact that a comprehensive bibliography of Durkheim's writings has not been readily exploited.

1 Faris, E., A J S, XL (1934), 376-77.

2 Tufts, J. H., "Recent Sociological Tendencies in France," A J S, I (1896), 446-457.

3 Tosti, G., " Suicide in the Light of Recent Studies," A J S., III (1898), 464-478. Durkheim's letter appears *ibid.*, pp. 848-849.

4 Gehlke, C. E., *Emile Durkheim's Contributions to Sociological Theory* (N. Y.: Columbia University, 1915).

5 *Cf.* statement of Professor Warner, A A, n. s., XXXVII (1935), 355.

6 *Ibid.*

Durkheim is known in America—on this point there can be no dispute—but he is known chiefly through his *magna opera: Division, Règles, Suicide,* and *Les Formes élémentaires.* His articles, reviews, notes, discussions and letters, however, are just as valuable source materials for the comprehension of Durkheimian sociology as his major works; and, we may say, sometimes even more important, especially when they serve to supplement, make succinct, and clarify the principles stated in the larger volumes. One is certain to gain new insights and new understandings by consulting these shorter works. They shed light, for instance, on the development of Durkheim's thinking, revealing changes in his point of view and in his emphases. They make explicit his methodological positions and bring out his relations to his contemporaries.

Furthermore, a large number of misstatements and misleading insinuations about Durkheim could easily be dissipated by a comprehensive knowledge of his bibliography. We need mention but three examples. Mitchell's views on Durkheim's philosophy of nationalism,[7] for instance, should not be accepted without consulting the French sociologist's own explicit statements on the subject as recorded in the *Bulletin de la société française de philosophie.*[8] Mitchell nowhere utilizes, nor does he even mention, this reference. Or contrast what Professor Sorokin " cannot help thinking " about the relation of Durkheim to Tönnies[9] with the *Cours de Science Sociale* that the former gave the year of the appearance of *Gemeinschaft und Gesellschaft.*[10] And finally, we should like to call Professor

7 Mitchell, M. M., " Emile Durkheim and the Philosophy of Nationalism," P S Q, XLVI (1931), 87-106.

8 See Bibliography, item 08a1. It is curious, for example, to find Durkheim foreshadowing, according to Mitchell, the " integral nationalism " of Charles Maurras (p. 106). The sharp opposition between these two French writers is clearly stated by Fonsegrive, G., *De Taine à Péguy: L'Evolution des Idées dans la France contemporaine* (Paris : Bloud et Gay, 1917), pp. 298-299.

9 Sorokin, P., *Contemporary Sociological Theories* (N. Y.: Harper and Bros., 1928), p. 491.

10 See item 88a.

House's attention to the fact that Durkheim's Latin thesis on the contributions of Montesquieu to the establishment of political science is *not* " a formal philosophical essay " but an evaluation of Montesquieu's contribution to the constitution of social science and its methodology;[11] nor is House's comment on Durkheim's failure to acknowledge his indebtedness to Robertson Smith correct.[12] In a letter to the editor of *La Revue Néo-scholastique*[13] the author of *Les Formes élementaires* noted that his realization of the capital role played by religion in social life " was due completely to the studies of religious history that I had just undertaken (i. e. about 1895) and notably to the reading of the works of *Robertson Smith* and his school."[14]

But a bibliography, after all, is its own justification. The one presented here, while comprehensive, is *not complete*. It is, however, more thorough than those previously published. Gehlke's, Jyan's and Marica's, the most complete ones thus far available, have, of course, been consulted and exploited.[15] The compiler has personally checked all the items with the exception of the ones preceded by an asterisk. Those so marked were not available to him and are included on the authority of others.

11 House, F. N., *The Development of Sociology* (N. Y.: McGraw Hill, 1936), p. 205. *Cf.* below, items 92a and 37b.

12 House, *op. cit.*, p. 265.

13 Item 07b.

14 07b, p. 613; italics ours. *Cf. Les Formes élémentaires*, p. 63, footnote 1, pp. 126-127, pp. 480-491, p. 584, p. 586 footnote 1, p. 589, footnote 1.

15 Gehlke, *op. cit.*, pp. 185-188; Jyan, Choy, *Etude comparative sur les doctrines pédagogiques de Durkheim et de Dewey* (Lyon: Bosc frères et Riou, 1926), pp. 233-236; Marica, G. E. *Soziologie und Soziologismus*, vol. VI of *Sozialwissenschaftliche Bausteine* (Jena: Fischer, 1932), pp. 170-174. Other bibliographical sources are Deploige, S., *Le Conflit de la morale et de la sociologie* (3rd ed., Paris: Nouvelle Librairie Nationale, 1923), pp. 18-19; Günzel, K., *Die Gesellschaftliche Wirklichkeit: Eine Studie über Emile Durkheim's Soziologie* (Ohlau-i-Schl.: Eschenhagen, 1934), pp. 77-78, and Fauconnet, P., " The Durkheim School in France," S R, XIX (1927), pp. 15-20.

Whenever subsequent editions of a work contain nothing new and amount merely to reprintings, they are omitted. Translations likewise are not listed, unless they have been submitted as original contributions to periodicals.[16] We recommend that Durkheim be consulted in the original whenever possible. However, we may mention that the following writings are available in English: *On the Division of Labor in Society, The Rules of Sociological Method, The Elementary Forms of the Religious Life, Who Wanted War? Germany Above All;* and, of course, items 05c and 05d. In addition, a number of pages of *Le Suicide* appear in English in Sorokin, Zimmerman and Galpin's *Systematic Source Book in Rural Sociology.*[17]

We have departed from the previous practice of Durkheim's bibliographers by listing separately each of the volumes of the *Année Sociologique* (old series), and by specifically mentioning the important prefaces, notes, and introductions as well as the major articles of Durkheim that have appeared therein. We have, furthermore, offered representative samples of the fields covered by the works which Durkheim reviewed in the *Année*. This arrangement serves to emphasize the prodigious productivity of this outstanding French sociologist of the pre-war generation.

It should be noted, too, that we have not followed the usual procedure of numbering the items in the bibliography consecutively. Rather, we have used a system which permits one to refer to the items by number and letter so that one may recognize immediately the year in which a particular reference appeared.

Durkheim is too important a figure, and too rare a mind to be ignored. His writings, even his incidental notes, are among the more precious parts of our sociological heritage.

16 As is the case with items 97b, 97c, 05d.

17 Minneapolis: University of Minnesota Press, 1932, Vol. III, pp. 189-201, corresponding to pp. 149-174, 182-223 of *Le Suicide*.

COMPREHENSIVE BIBLIOGRAPHY OF
EMILE DURKHEIM
(1858-1917)

1885

85a "Schaeffle, A., *Bau und Leben des Sozialem Körpers:* Erster Band," R P, XIX, pp. 84-101 (Review).

85b "Fouillée, A., *La Propriété sociale et la démocratie,*" R P, XIX, pp. 446-453 (Review).

85c "Gumplowicz, Ludwig., *Grundriss der Sociologie,*" R P, XX, pp. 627-634 (Review).

1886

86a "Les Etudes de Science sociale," R P, XXII, pp. 61-80 (a review of works by Spencer, Régnard, Coste *et al.*, Schaeffle).

86b "DeGreef, Guillaume, *Introduction à la sociologie,*" R P, XXII, pp. 658-663 (Review).

1887

87a "La Philosophie dans les universités allemandes," R I E, XIII, pp. 313-338, 423-440.

87b "Guyau, M., *L'Irréligion de l'avenir,*" R P, XXIII, pp. 299-311 (Review).

87c "La Science positive de la morale en Allemagne," R P, XXIV, pp. 33-58, 113-142, 275-284.

1888

88a "Cours de ⸱ ᴜᴇ sociale: Leçon d'ouverture," R I E, XV, pp. 23-48 (Reprin: d separately, Paris, Colin).

88b "Le Program..e économique de M. Schäffle," R E P, II, pp. 3-7.

88c "Introduction à la sociologie de la famille," A F L B, pp. 257-281.

88d "Suicide et Natalité: Etude de Statistique Morale," R P, XXVI, pp. 446-463.

1889

89a "Lutoslawski, W., *Erhaltung und Untergang der Staatsverfassungen nach Plato, Aristoteles, und Machiavelli.*" R P, XXVII, pp. 317-319 (Review).

89b "Tönnies, F., *Gemeinschaft und Gesellschaft,*" R P, XXVII, pp. 416-422 (Review).

1890

90a "Les Principes de 1789 et la sociologie," R I E, XIX, pp. 450-456. (Review of Ferneuil, Th., *Les principes de 1789 et la Science sociale*).

1892

92a *Quid Secundatus politicae scientiae instituendae contulerit* (Bordeaux: Gounouilhou).

1893

93a "Richard, G., *Essai sur l'origine de l'idée de Droit*," R P, XXXV, pp. 290-296 (Review).

93b *De la Division du travail social: Etude sur l'organisation des sociétés supérieures* (Paris: Alcan).

93c "Note sur la définition du socialisme," R P, XXXVI, pp. 506-512.

1894

94a "Les Règles de la méthode sociologique," R P, XXXVII, pp. 465-498, 577-607; XXXVIII, pp. 14-39, 168-182.

1895

95a *Les Règles de la méthode sociologique* (Paris: Alcan). (The above articles, with slight modifications, and a preface).

95b "L'Enseignement Philosophique et L'agrégation de Philosophie," R P, XXXIX, pp. 121-147.

95c "Crime et Santé Sociale," R P, XXXIX, pp. 518-523.

95d "L'origine du mariage dans l'Espèce Humaine, D'après Westermarck," R P, XL, pp. 606-623. (Review of Westermarck's *History of Human Marriage*).

95e "Lo Stato attuale degli Studi Sociologici in Francia," R S, III, pp. 607-622, 691-707.

1897

97a *Le Suicide: Etude de Sociologie* (Paris: Alcan).

97b "Il Suicidio dal Punto di vista sociologico," Ri It S, I, pp. 17-27 (a translation, with very slight modifications of *Le Suicide*; pp. 1-15).

97c "Il Suicidio e l'Instabila' Economica," R S, VII, pp. 529-547. (A translation of *Le Suicide*; pp. 264-288.)

97d "Richard, G., *Le Socialisme et la science sociale*," R P, XLIV, pp. 200-205 (Review).

97e "Labriola, Antonio, *Essais sur la conception matérialiste de l'histoire*," R P, XLIV, pp. 645-651 (Review).

1898

98a *L'Année Sociologique*, Vol. I.
  1. Préface, pp. i-vii.
  2. "La Prohibition de l'inceste et ses origines," pp. 1-70.
  3. Reviews of works on family, marriage, punishment, social organization, socio-geography, etc.

98b "Représentations individuelles et représentations collectives," R M M, VI, pp. 273-302. (Reproduced in *Sociologie et Philosophie*).

98c "L'Individualisme et les intellectuels," R B, 4e Série, X, pp. 7-13.

98d "Letter to the Editor of the *American Journal of Sociology*," A J S, III, pp. 848-849.

1899

99a *L'Année Sociologique*, Vol. II.
    1. Préface, pp. i-vi.
    2. "De la définition des phénomènes religieux," pp. 1-28.
    3. "Note sur la morphologie sociale," pp. 520-21.
    4. Reviews of works on cults, mores, family, marriage, property rights, penal law, social morphology, etc.

99b Contribution to : "Enquête sur la guerre et le militarisme," *L'Humanité Nouvelle*, May, 1899, pp. 50-52.

99c Contribution to: "Enquête sur l'introduction de la sociologie dans l'enseignement secondaire," R I S, VII, p. 679.

1900

00a *L'Année Sociologique*, Vol. III.
    1. Reviews of works on political and social organization, family, marriage, contracts, social morphology, etc.

00b "La Sociologie en France au XIXe siècle," R B, 4e série, XIII, pp. 609-613, 647-652.

00c "La Sociologia ed il suo dominio scientifico," Ri It S, Anno IV, pp. 127-148.

1901

01a *L'Année Sociologique*, Vol. IV.
    1. "Deux lois de l'évolution pénale," pp. 65-95.
    2. "Introduction à la section de sociologie criminelle et statistique morale," pp. 433-436.
    3. Reviews of works on mentality of groups, social, political and domestic organization, law of property, statistics of domestic and conjugal life, social morphology, etc.

01b "De la Méthode objective en sociologie," R S H, II, pp. 3-17. (The Preface to the Second Edition of *Les Règles*.)

01c *Les Règles de la méthode sociologique, revue et augmentée d'une préface nouvelle* (2nd ed.; Paris: Alcan).

01d "Lettre au directeur de la *Revue Philosophique*," R P, LII, p. 704.

1902

02a *L'Année Sociologique*, Vol. V.
    1. "Sur le totémisme," pp. 82-123.
    2. Reviews of works on object and method of sociology, social philosophy, juridical and moral sociology, social and domestic organization, statistics of domestic life, social morphology, etc.

02b *De la Division du travail social*, avec une nouvelle préface intitulée "Quelques remarques sur les groupements professionels," (2nd ed.; Paris: Alcan).

02c "Palante, G., *Précis de sociologie*," R S H, IV, pp. 114-115 (Review).

1903

03a *L'Année Sociologique*, Vol. VI.

    1. "De quelques formes primitives de classification: Contribution à l'étude des représentations collectives," pp. 1-72 (With M. Mauss).

    2. Reviews of works on object and method of sociology, mentality of groups and collective ethology, social, domestic, and political organization, statistics of domestic and conjugal life, social morphology, etc.

03b "Pédagogie et Sociologie," R M M, XI, pp. 37-54. (Reproduced in *Education et Sociologie*).

03c "Sociologie et sciences sociales," R P, LV, pp. 465-497 (with P. Fauconnet).

1904

04a *L'Année Sociologique*, Vol. VII.

    1. Reviews of works on social, domestic and political organization, general theories of law and ethics, crime and the criminal in general, social morphology, education, etc.

04b "La Sociologie et les sciences sociales," R I S, XII, pp. 83-84 (*Résumé d'une conférence*; followed by discussion, pp. 86-87).

1905

05a *L'Année Sociologique*, Vol. VIII.

    1. "Sur l'organisation matrimoniale des sociétés australiennes," pp. 118-147.

    2. Reviews of works on juridical systems, domestic and political organization, penal law, social morphology, etc.

05b Contribution to: "La Morale Sans Dieu: Essai de solution collective," *La Revue*, LIX, pp. 306-308.

05c "On the Relation of Sociology to the Social Sciences and to Philosophy," S P, I, Macmillan, London. (Abstract of a paper laid before the Sociological Society of the School of Economics and Political Science [University of London], pp. 197-200, and Reply to Criticisms, p. 257).

05d "Sociology and the Social Sciences," S P, I, London, pp. 258-280 (with P. Fauconnet). (An abridged translation of "Sociologie et sciences sociales," 1903.)

05e Discussion of: "Sur la séparation des Eglises et de l'Etat," in *Libres Entretiens* (première série; Paris: Bureaux des "Libres Entretiens"), pp. 317-377, 453-508.

1906

06a *L'Année Sociologique*, Vol. IX.

    1. Reviews of works on methodology, social philosophy, psychology of groups in general, social, political and domestic organization, law of property, functioning of domestic and matrimonial institutions, etc.

06b " La Détermination du fait moral," B S F P, VI, Séances du 11 février et du 22 mars, 1906. (Reproduced in *Sociologie et Philosophie*.)

06c " L'Evolution et le rôle de l'enseignement secondaire en France," R B, 5e série, V, pp. 70-77. (Reproduced in *Education et Sociologie*.)

06d " Le Divorce par consentement mutuel," R B, 5e série, V, pp. 549-554.

1907

07a *L'Année Sociologique*, Vol. X.

    1. Reviews of works on general conception of sociology, law and ethics in general, social, political, and domestic organization, juridical and moral systems, etc.

07b Lettres au Directeur de la *Revue Néo-scolastique*, R N S, XIV, pp. 606-607, 612-614.

07c Contribution to: *La Question religieuse: enquête internationale*, M F, LXVII, p. 51. (Reprinted in volume of same title edited by Fr. Charpin, 1908, pp. 95-97.)

1908

08a Discussions of:

    1. " Pacifisme et Patriotisme," séance du 30 décembre 1907.

    2. " La Morale positive: Examen de quelques difficultés," séance du 26 Mars, 1908.

    3. " L'Inconnu et l'inconscient en histoire," séance du 28 mai, 1908.

    in B S F P, VIII.

08b "Aux lecteurs de *l'Année Sociologique* " in Bouglé, C., *Essais sur le régime des castes* (Paris: Alcan), pp. v-viii.

08c Discussion of:

    " De la Position de l'économie politique dans l'ensemble des sciences sociales " in *Bulletin de la Société d'Economie Politique*, séance du 4 avril, 1908, pp. 61-73.

1909

09a Discussions of:

    1. " Science et Religion," séance du 19 Novembre, 1908.

    2. " L'Efficacité des doctrines morales," séance du 20 mai, 1909.

    in B S F P, IX.

09b " Note sur la spécialisation des Facultés des Lettres et l'agrégation de philosophie," R I E, LVII, pp. 159-161.

09c " Examen critique des systèmes classiques sur les origines de la pensée religieuse," R P, LXVII, pp. 1-28, 142-162. (Corresponding to Chaps. II and III of *Les Formes élémentaires de la vie religieuse*.)

09d "Sociologie religieuse et théorie de la connaissance," R M M, XVII,
pp. 733-758. (The Introduction to *Les Formes élémentaires*. As
incorporated in the volume, section III, of this article [pp. 754-
758], is omitted).

09e "Sociologie et sciences sociales" in *De la Méthode dans les sciences*
(1ère série; Paris: Alcan), pp. 259-285.

1910

10a *L'Année Sociologique*, Vol. XI.
1. Préface, pp. i-iii.
2. "Note sur les systèmes religieux des sociétés inférieures," pp.
75-76.
3. "Note sur les systèmes juridiques et moraux," pp. 286-288.
4. Reviews of works on social philosophy, sociological conditions
of knowledge, totemic system, domestic and matrimonial
organization, suicide, etc.

10b Discussion of:
"La Notion d'égalité sociale," séance du 30 décembre, 1909, in
B S F P, X.

1911

11a Discussion of:
"L'Education sexuelle," séance du 28 février, 1911, B S F P, XI.

11b "Jugements de valeur et jugements de réalité," in *Atti del IV Con-
gresso Internazionale di Filosofia* (Bologna: 1911), Vol. I, pp.
99-114 (Published also in R M M, XIX, pp. 437-453. Reproduced
in *Sociologie et Philosophie*).

11c Articles:
1. "Education," pp. 529-536.
2. "Enfance," pp. 552-553 (with F. Buisson).
3. "Pédagogie," pp. 1538-1543
in *Nouveau dictionnaire de pédagogie et d'instruction primaire
publié sous la direction de F. Buisson* (Paris: Hachette). (1 and 3
reproduced in *Education et Sociologie*.)

11d "Préface" in Hamelin, O., *Le Système de Descartes, publié par
L. Robin* (Paris: Alcan), pp. v-xi.

1912

12a *Les Formes élémentaires de la vie religieuse: Le système totémique
en Australie* (Paris: Alcan).

12b Discussion of "Sur la culture générale et la reforme de l'enseignement," in *Libres Entretiens* (8e série; Paris: Union pour la
vérité), pp. 309-348.

1913

13a *L'Année Sociologique*, Vol. XII.
1. "Note sur la notion de civilisation," pp. 46-50 (with M. Mauss).
2. "Note sur les systèmes religieux des sociétés inférieures,"
pp. 90-91.

3. "Note sur les systèmes juridiques," pp. 365-366.

4. Reviews of works on methodology, collective psychology, sociological conditions of knowledge, ethics, juridical systems, domestic and matrimonial organization, geographic bases of social life, etc.

13b "Le Problème religieux et la dualité de la nature humaine," B S F P, XIII, séance du 4 février, 1913.

1914

14a "Le Dualisme de la nature humaine et ses conditions sociales," *Scientia*, XV, pp. 206-221.

14b Discussion of: "Une Nouvelle position du problème moral," séance du 2 janvier, 1914, B S F P, XIV.

1915

15a "La Sociologie," in *La Science francaise* (Paris: Ministère de l'Instruction publique et des Beaux- arts), Vol. I, pp. 39-49. (Reprinted separately, Paris: Larousse).

15b *Qui a voulu la guerre?: Les origines de la guerre d'après les documents diplomatiques* (Paris: Colin). (With E. Denis.)

15c *L'Allemagne au-dessus de tout: la Mentalité allemande et la guerre* (Paris: Colin).

1916

16a *Lettres à tous les Francais* (Paris: Comité de publication). (With others. 1st, 5th, 10th (in part) and 11th letters signed by Durkheim.)

1917

*17a "Notice sur André Durkheim," *L'Annuaire de l'association des anciens élèves de l'Ecole Normale Supérieure*.[1]

PUBLISHED POSTHUMOUSLY

17b Discussion of: "Vocabulaire technique et critique de la philosophie," B S F P, XV, pp. 1-2 (sacré), p. 57 (société).

1918

18a *La Vie universitaire à Paris* (Paris: Colin). (With others). (Préface; Première partie, chapitres I et II; Deuxieme partie, introduction signed by Durkheim).

18b "Le Contrat Social de Rousseau," R M M, XXV, pp. 1-23, 129-161.

1919

19a "La Pédagogie de Rousseau," R M M, XXVI, pp. 153-180.

*19b Contribution to: Abauzit, F., *Le Sentiment religieux à l'heure actuelle*, (Paris: J. Vrin).[2]

1 Item referred to by Worms, R., R I S, XXV (1917), 568.

2 Item referred to by Benrubi, J., *Les Sources et les courants de la philosophie contemporaine en France* (Paris: Alcan, 1933), Vol. II, p. 963, footnote 2.

1920

20a "Introduction à la morale," R P, LXXXIX, pp. 79-97.

1921

21a "La Famille conjugale: conclusion du cours sur la famille," R P, XC,
     pp. 1-14.

21b "Définition du Socialisme," R M M, XXVIII, pp. 479-495, 591-614.
     (Reproduced in *Le Socialisme*.)

1922

22a *Education et Sociologie* (Paris: Alcan). (Reproduces 11c1, 11c3, 03b,
     06c.)

1923

23a "Histoire du socialisme: Le socialisme au XVIIIe siècle," R M M,
     XXX, pp. 389-413. (Reproduced in *Le Socialisme*.)

1924

24a *Sociologie et Philosophie* (Paris, Alcan). (Reproduces 98b, 06b, 11b.)

1925

25a *L'Education Morale* (Paris: Alcan).

25b "Saint-Simon, Fondateur du positivisme et de la sociologie," R P,
     XCIX, pp. 321-341. (Reproduced in *Le Socialisme*.)

1926

26a "Critiques de Saint-Simon et du Saint-Simonisme," R M M, XXXIII,
     pp. 433-454). (Reproduced in *Le Socialisme*.)

1928

28a *Le Socialisme, édité par M. Mauss* (Paris: Alcan).

1933

33a "La Sociologie" in *La Science Francaise* (Nouvelle edition entière-
     ment refondue; Paris: Larousse), Vol. I, pp. 27-35 (Reprint of
     article of 1915, followed by a note on "La Sociologie en France
     Depuis 1914," by Marcel Mauss, pp. 36-47.)

1937

37a "Morale professionelle" (avec une introduction par Marcel Mauss)
     R M M, XLIV, pp. 527-544, 711-738.

37b "Montesquieu: Sa part dans la fondation des sciences politiques
     et de la science des sociétés," translated from the Latin by F.
     Alengry, *Revue d'Histoire Politique et Constitutionelle*, I, pp.
     405-463. (A translation of 92a.)

1938

38a *L'Evolution Pédagogique en France* (Paris: Alcan). Volume I: *Des
     Origines à la Renaissance*; Volume II: *De la Renaissance à
     Nos Jours*.

IN PREPARATION

La Morale, edited by Marcel Mauss.

APPENDIX B

A SELECTED BIBLIOGRAPHY OF WORKS ON DURKHEIM AND HIS SOCIOLOGY [1]

(Consult, *passim*, *L'Année Sociologique* and *Les Annales Sociologiques*.)

Alpert, H., "France's First University Course in Sociology," A S R, II (1937), 311-317.

Apchié, M., "Quelques remarques critiques sur la sociologie d'Emile Durkheim," A P D S J, VI (1936), 182-195.

Aron, R., Demangeon, A., Meuvret, J., Polin, R., *et al.*, *Les Sciences Sociales en France: Enseignement et Recherche* (Paris: Hartmann, 1937).

Barnes, H. E., "Durkheim's Contribution to the Reconstruction of Political Theory," P S Q, XXXV (1920), 236-254.

——, and Becker, H., *Social Thought From Lore To Science* (N. Y.: Heath, 1938), Vol. II, Chap. XXII.

Barth, P., *Die Philosophie der Geschichte Als Soziologie* (4th ed., Leipzig: Reisland, 1922), Vol. I, pp. 628-642.

Bayet, A., *La Science des faits moraux* (Paris: Alcan, 1925).

Belot, G., "L'Utilitarisme et ses nouveaux critiques," R M M, II (1894), 404-464.

Bentley, A. F., "Simmel, Durkheim, and Ratzenhofer," A J S, XXXII (1926), 250-256.

Blondel, Ch., *Introduction à la psychologie collective* (Paris: Colin, 1928).

Bouglé, C., *Bilan de la sociologie française contemporaine* (Paris: Alcan, 1935).

——, *Qu'est-ce que la sociologie?* (6th ed.; Paris: Alcan, 1932).

——, *Leçons de sociologie sur l'évolution des valeurs* (Paris: Colin, 1922). Translated as *The Evolution of Values* (N. Y., Holt, 1926).

——, "Le Spiritualisme d'Emile Durkheim," R B, LXII (1924), 550-553. (Reproduced as Introduction to Durkheim, 24a.)

——, "Emile Durkheim," E S S, V, pp. 291-292.

*——, and Déat, M., *Le Guide de l'Etudiant en Sociologie* (3rd ed.; Paris: Rivière, 1931).

——, Davy, G., Granet, M., Lenoir, R., Maublanc, R., "L'Oeuvre sociologique d'Emile Durkheim," *Europe*, XXII (1930), 281-304.

Branford, V., "Durkheim: A Brief Memoir," S R, X (1918), 77-82.

Brunschwicg, L. and Halévy, E., "L'Année Philosophique, 1893," R M M, II, (1894), 564-590.

Bureau, P., *Introduction à la méthode sociologique* (Paris: Bloud et Gay, 1923).

---

1 Works that are chiefly bibliographical in nature are preceded by an asterisk.

Catlin, G. E. G., "Introduction to the Translation," *The Rules of Sociological Method* (Chicago: Univ. of Chicago Press, 1938), pp. x-xl.

*Conze, E., "Zur Bibliographie der Durkheim-Schule," K V S, VI (1927), 279-283.

Davy, G., *Emile Durkheim: Choix de Textes avec étude du système sociologique* (Paris: Rasmussen).

——, "La Sociologie de M. Durkheim," R P, LXXII (1911), 42-71, 160-185.

——, "Emile Durkheim," R M M, XXVI (1919), 181-198; XXVII (1920), 71-112.

——, *Sociologues d'hier et d'aujourd-hui* (Paris: Alcan, 1931).

Deploige, S., *Le Conflit de la Morale et de la Sociologie* (3rd ed.; Paris: Nouvelle Librairie Nationale, 1923).

Duprat, G. L., "Auguste Comte et Emile Durkheim," in *Gründer der Soziologie*, "Sozialwissenschaftliche Bausteine," Vol. IV, (Jena: Fischer, 1932).

*Essertier, D., *Psychologie et Sociologie* (Paris: Alcan, 1927).

*——, *La Sociologie, Extraits et Notices*, "Philosophes et Savants Français du XXe siècle" (Paris, Alcan, 1930).

——, and Bouglé, C., "Sociologie et Psychologie: Remarques Générales," An S, Série A, fasc. 1 (1934), 121-148.

*Fauconnet, P., "The Durkheim School in France," S R, XIX (1927), 15-20.

——, "The Pedagogical Work of Emile Durkheim," A J S, XXVIII (1923), 529-553, Appears in French in R P, XCIII (1922), 185-209 and as Introduction to Durkheim, 22a.

——, and Mauss, M., "Sociologie," G E, XXX, pp. 165-176.

Febvre, L., Tonnelat, E., Mauss, M., Niceforo, A., Weber, L., *Civilisation: Le Mot et l'Idée* (Paris: Renaissance du Livre, 1930).

Fouillée, A., Charmont, J., Duguit, L., Demogue, R., *Modern French Legal Philosophy* (Boston: Boston Book Co., 1916).

Gehlke, C. E., *Emile Durkheim's Contributions to Sociological Theory* (N. Y.: Columbia Univ., 1915).

Ginsberg, M., "The Place of Sociology," in *The Social Sciences: Their Relations In Theory and In Teaching* (London: Le Play House, 1936), pp. 190-207.

Goldenweiser, A., "Religion and Society: A Critique of Emile Durkheim's Theory of the Origin and Nature of Religion," in *History, Psychology, and Culture* (N. Y.; Knopf, 1933), Part IV, Chap. I.

Günzel, K., *Die Gesellschaftliche Wirklichkeit: Eine Studie der Emile Durkheim's Soziologie* (Ohlau i Schl.; Eschenhagen, 1934).

Gurvitch, G., "La Science des faits moraux et la morale théorique chez E. Durkheim," A P D S J, VII (1937), 18-44.

Halbwachs, M., "La Doctrine d'Emile Durkheim, R P, LXXXV (1918), 353-411.

——, *Les Origines du sentiment religieux d'après Durkheim* (Paris: Stock, 1925).

——, *Les Causes du Suicide* (Paris: Alcan, 1930).

——, *Morphologie Sociale* (Paris: Colin, 1938).

Hermansen, R., "El Sociologó francés Emilio Durkheim," *Atenea*, Ano IV, May, 1927, pp. 205-214.

Høffding, H., "Les Formes élémentaires de la vie religieuse," R M M, XXII (1914), 828-848.

Jacovella, O., "Sociologia e pedagogia in Emilio Durkheim," Ri P, XVIII (1925), 280-309, 445-473, 536-586.

Jyan, Choy, *Etude Comparative sur les doctrines pédagogiques de Durkheim et de Dewey* (Lyon: Bosc Frères et Riou, 1926).

Lacombe, R., *La Méthode sociologique de Durkheim* (Paris: Alcan, 1926).

La Fontaine, A. P., *La Philosophie d'E. Durkheim* (4th ed.; Paris: J. Vrin, 1926).

Lapie, P., "La Definition du Socialisme," R M M, II (1894), 199-204.

Leguay, P., "M. Emile Durkheim," in *Universitaires d'aujourd'hui* (Paris: Grasset, 1912).

Lenoir, R., "Emile Durkheim et la conscience moderne," M F, CXXVII (1918), 577-595.

Leuba, J. H., "Sociology and Psychology: The Conception of Religion and Magic and the Place of Psychology in Sociological Studies," A J S (1913), 323-342.

Lévy-Bruhl, H., "Rapports du Droit et de la Sociologie," A P D S J, VII (1937), 21-25.

Lévy-Bruhl, L., *La Morale et la science des moeurs* (4th ed.; Paris: Alcan, 1904). Translated as *Ethics and Moral Science* (London: Constable, 1905).

——, *La Mentalité Primitive* (4th ed.; Paris: Alcan, 1925).

Lowie, R. H., *The History of Ethnological Theory* (N. Y.: Farrar and Rinehart, 1937), Chap. XII.

Lupu, I., *Die Grundlagen der Gesellschaft, das Recht und die Religion in der Durkheimschule: Ihr besonderer Widerhall in der Jenenser Jerusalemschen Soziologie* (Iasi: Viata Românească, 1931).

Marica, G. E., *Emile Durkheim: Seine Ideentwicklung und Seine Stellung in der Sociologie* (Jena: Fischer, 1932). Reproduced as Volume VI of *Sozialwissenschaftlichen Bausteine* under title of *Emile Durkheim: Soziologie und Soziologismus*.

Marjolin, R., "French Sociology: Comte and Durkheim," A J S, XLII (1937), 693-704, as corrected by the author, *ibid.*, pp. 901-902.

Mauss, M., "In Memoriam, L'Oeuvre inédite de Durkheim et de ses collaborateurs," A S, n. s., I, pp. 7-29.

——, "Division et proportions des divisions de la sociologie," A S, n. s., II, pp. 98-176.

——, "Rapports réels et pratiques de la psychologie et de la sociologie," J P, XXI (1924), 892-922.

Merton, R., "Durkheim's Division of Labor in Society," A J S, XL (1934), 319-328.

Mitchell, M. M., "Emile Durkheim and the Philosophy of Nationalism," P S Q, XLVI (1931), 87-106.

Parodi, D., *La Philosophie contemporaine en France* (2nd ed.; Paris: Alcan, 1920), Chap. V.

Parsons, T., *The Structure of Social Action* (N. Y.: McGraw-Hill, 1937). esp. Chaps. VIII-XII.

Pécaut, F., "Emile Durkheim," R Pe, n. s., LXXII (1918), 1-20.

——, "Auguste Comte et Durkheim," R M M, XXVIII (1921), 639-655.

Perry, R. B., "Des Formes de L'Unité Sociale," in *Congrès des Sociétés Philosophiques américaine, anglaises, belge, italienne, et française, Communications et Discussions* (Paris: Colin, 1921), pp. 445-470. (Followed by Discussion by Lenoir, Fauconnet, Pécaut, and Perry, pp. 470-473).

——, *General Theory of Value* (N. Y.: Longmans, Green, 1926), esp. Chaps. XIV-XVII.

Piaget, J., "Logique genétique et sociologie," R P, CV (1928), 167-205.

Radcliffe-Brown, A. R., "On the Concept of Function in Social Science," A A, n. s., XXXVII (1935), 394-402.

Richard, G., *L'Athéisme dogmatique en sociologie religieuse* (7e cahier de la *Revue d'histoire et de philosophie religieuses*; Strasbourg: Istra, 1923).

——, "La Pathologie sociale d'E. Durkheim," R I S, XXXVIII (1930), 113-126.

Simiand, F., *Le Salaire, l'évolution sociale et la monnaie* (Paris: Alcan, 1932), Vol. I, Methodological Introduction.

Simpson, G., "Emile Durkheim's Social Realism," S S R, XVIII (1933), 3-11.

——, "An Estimate of Durkheim's Work," in *Emile Durkheim on the Division of Labor in Society* (N. Y.: MacMillan, 1933), pp. xxv-xliv.

Sorel, G., "Les Théories de M. Durkheim," D S, I (1895), 1-26, 148-180.

Sorokin, P., *Contemporary Sociological Theories* (N. Y.: Harper's, 1928), pp. 463-480.

Starcke, C. N., *Laws of Social Evolution and Social Ideals* (Copenhagen: Levin and Munksgaard, 1932), esp. pp. 294-315.

Tarde, G., *Les Lois sociales* (Paris: Alcan, 1898).

Telezhnikov, F., "E. Durkheim o predmete i metode sociologii," *Vestnik Kommunisticheskoi Akademii*, XXX (1928), 159-188.

Tosti, G., "Suicide in the Light of Recent Studies," A J S, III (1898), 464-478.

Tourtoulon, P. de, *Philosophy in the Development of Law* (N. Y.: Macmillan, 1922), Book II, Chap. V.

Tufts, J. H., "Recent Sociological Tendencies in France," A J S, I (1896), 446-457.

Webb, C. C. J., *Group Theories of Religion and the Individual* (London: Allen and Unwin), 1916.

Worms, R., "Emile Durkheim," R I S, XXV (1917), 561-568.

INDEX